MORE ADVANCE PRAISE FOR
A WATCHMAN IN THE NIGHT

"Reporting for the Associated Press in New York City in 1976, I started praying for journalists to apply the Bible to daily news coverage. Cal Thomas became a big answer to those prayers in 1984, as the Lord opened a door for him to write a syndicated column. He has been a watchman on the wall, giving readers wisdom, understanding, and prudence in the news of the day and week."

—Russ Pulliam, *Indianapolis Star*

"If journalism is the first draft of history, Cal Thomas gives us his second draft with all the wit and trenchant commentary that he has made famous. He has been faithful as America's watchman."

—Os Guinness, bestselling author

"His columns are always timely and thought-provoking. Cal makes me think."

—Tracy Clark, Cal Thomas's longtime syndicated editor

"I guarantee you won't be disappointed as you join Cal on this journey through the decades. You will learn, you will reflect, and you will get some much-needed clarity on the swirling events of today."

—Connie Pollock, former editor at Los Angeles Times Syndicate

"Cal Thomas expertly weaves personal experiences, past historical events, and present conditions to produce a fascinating, engaging read. The Founding Fathers would heartily approve."

—Cheryl Chumley, bestselling author of
Socialists Don't Sleep and *Lockdown*

A WATCHMAN IN THE NIGHT

A WATCHMAN IN THE NIGHT

What I've Seen Over 50 Years Reporting on America

CAL THOMAS

Humanix Books

www.humanixbooks.com

Humanix Books

A WATCHMAN IN THE NIGHT
Copyright © 2023 by Cal Thomas
All rights reserved

Humanix Books, P.O. Box 20989, West Palm Beach, FL 33416, USA
www.humanixbooks.com | info@humanixbooks.com

Humanix Books is a division of Humanix Publishing, LLC. Its trademark, consisting
of the words "Humanix Books," is registered in the United States Patent and
Trademark Office and in other countries.

ISBN: 9-781-63006-237-8 (Hardcover)
ISBN: 9-781-63006-238-5 (E-book)

Printed in the United States of America

10 9 8 7 6 5 4 3 2 1

To the memory of my daughter,
Caray Lee Thomas (1965–2018).

Contents

Introduction

During my active media years, a complaint that I often heard was that mainstream media is not fair to Republicans, conservatives, and evangelicals.

As with many media leaders, my response most often was defensive. I discounted criticism.

However, my views changed over time. I saw there was merit to the criticism that we frequently were more liberal—especially on our editorial and op-ed pages.

I observed the decision by *New York Times* publisher Punch Sulzberger to recruit conservative writer William Safire as a regular columnist. That was a bold and very wise decision.

As I rose from a reporter on the *Macon Georgia Telegraph* to executive vice president of Texas Broadcasting in Austin, to executive editor and then publisher of the *Dallas Times Herald*, and then to president and publisher of the *Los Angeles Times*, and finally to CEO of CNN, I had firsthand experience overseeing the news and editorial content of what I considered five of the most outstanding American news organizations.

When I became president of the *Los Angeles Times* in 1977, I oversaw the Los Angeles Times Syndicate. I felt that we needed to secure and to distribute a very highly regarded conservative balance. For four years, Cal Thomas had been the chief spokesman and writer for Reverend Jerry Falwell. It was his first and only departure from a journalism career that has spanned six decades. NBC's John Chancellor once said that everyone in journalism should be allowed one trip to the "other side" and then choose on which side to remain. In 1984, Cal chose to return to and remain in journalism.

Willard Colston, president of that syndicate, asked me to "take a look" at several articles that Thomas had written. I did. Thomas wrote clearly and expressed his opinions intelligently. His views infuriated some of my more liberal members of the *Los Angeles Times* editorial page.

Colston and I decided to take a chance. We were very disappointed when Anthony Day, editor of the *Los Angeles Times* editorial page, refused to agree to run Thomas's column. When Day left, the *Times* picked up Cal's column to the delight of conservative readers and the horror of liberal ones. Rarely has the letters section had so many responses to a columnist.

Sales of Thomas's columns began to soar. Newspapers in the United States and abroad purchased it. Over time, he became the most well-distributed columnist of all. He eclipsed such esteemed names as Art Buchwald and Bill Safire.

I was very proud to have been a strong supporter of him. While our political views are very different, we became friends. His column added a much-needed conservative voice to newspapers, talk shows, and bookshelves.

A WATCHMAN IN THE NIGHT captures so much of Cal's life and times. I recommend it with enthusiasm, even to those of us who are more on the left-hand side than Cal.

Tom Johnson
Former president/publisher, *Los Angeles Times*
Former president, CNN
Atlanta, Georgia

Preface

"Ask me a question, and I will give you my answer.
This is what I have done—and am continuing to do—
as I seek to serve God first and then my country."

When many people hear "1984," it brings to mind the novel by George Orwell, in which he predicted a future dominated by "Big Brother." Was he ever prescient! Government has now invaded virtually every area of our lives, from the light bulbs we buy to our toilets and cars, to cameras watching us on virtually every street corner in major cities.

To me, 1984 means something different. It was the start of my syndicated newspaper column, which rapidly grew to appear in more than half the nation's newspapers.

People often ask me how a conservative and a Christian could succeed in an industry that is seemingly hostile to values and beliefs that come from such an ideological and religious perspective. It's a good question and not one that is easily answered. It helped that I was a radio and TV reporter for many years before becoming a columnist. That role helped me to see which programs and ideas worked and which did not.

It also helped that I joined organizations with fellow journalists and personally visited many editors as I traveled across the country. And it helped mightily that Tom Johnson, then the publisher of the *Los Angeles Times*, opened the door for me at the newspaper's syndicate.

Instead of re-arguing the same positions in my column and sounding like the few other conservatives writing at the time, I began to focus not only on what works (the title of a previous book), but what fulfills the goals of what our Founders wrote in the Preamble to the Constitution: "We the people of the United States in order to form a more perfect union, establish justice, insure domestic tranquility, provide for the common defense, promote the general welfare, and secure the blessings of liberty to ourselves and our posterity . . ."

These words cannot be read often enough—along with the Constitution itself—because they assume certain "self-evident truths," as Thomas Jefferson wrote in freedom's companion document, the Declaration of Independence.

Today, truth has become relative and subjective, not objective. Everyone claims to have his or her own "truth." And don't dare to use gender-specific pronouns without asking another person which ones they prefer. You might be condemned by the ever-watchful speech police. As long as your "truth" makes you feel good, that is all that matters. If someone else has a contrary "truth," that's OK, as long as they are happy. This leads to a culture that self-destructs over confusion as to what it is and should be. A people must have a purpose, and a nation must have the goal of being able to define itself and what it stands for ("to the Republic for which [the flag] stands") has been America's.

The goal of my columns is to remind people that immutable truths exist and to ask them to consider even recent history in which certain programs and policies—such as tax cuts, less government spending, fewer regulations, and moral boundaries—contribute to the preservation of our liberties. Football fields and basketball courts are defined by boundaries. If a nation loses its boundaries, it will eventually cease to be.

In ancient Israel, a watchman looked out for any threats that might come during the night when the city gates were closed. These might have included invading armies, or just someone out to rob, or cause harm to people or their property.

America has been invaded by a worldview contrary to our founding, and it is suffering mightily as a result. I have sought to play the role of a "watchman," warning readers what will happen if we refuse to embrace objective truth and apply it to ourselves, as well as our country. These principles have been the driving force behind my columns.

The late Roman Catholic Bishop Fulton J. Sheen was on the mark when he said decades ago, "Truth must be sought at all costs, but separate isolated truths will not do. Truth is like life; it has to be taken on its entirety or not at all. . . . We must welcome truth even if it reproaches and inconveniences us—even if it appears in the place where we thought it could not be found."

The problem in our day is that too many people don't know where to find truth—if they bother to search for it at all—or recognize it when they see it. Ours is a relativistic age that regards truth the way the Roman provincial governor Pontius Pilate did. "What is Truth?" he asked rhetorically and sarcastically before One who had said he was and is "the truth."

Former *ABC News* anchor Ted Koppel once said, "Truth is not a polite tap on the shoulder; truth is a howling reproach." I like that.

Truth is not what the late Supreme Court Justice Oliver Wendell Holmes said about it: ". . . the majority vote of that nation which can best all the rest."

That notion leads to cynicism and dictatorship.

In the pages that follow, you can walk with me through a social, spiritual, and political "diary," in which I recall passing events and what I wrote about some of them.

Those old enough will recall this history because they lived through it. Younger people will see this as a modern lesson and be exposed to economic and moral truths that worked before and can again if they are embraced. Social media, mainstream broadcasters, and many newspapers have distorted our past and thus are corrupting the present and possibly the future.

History doesn't have to repeat itself, though it often does because too many refuse to learn from it. We are not the first generation to have lived. We don't want to live in the past, but we should learn from it.

The best part of the journalism business in which I have spent virtually all of my professional life is the people I have been privileged to meet and observe up close. From political leaders—starting with John F. Kennedy and including every president since—to international leaders, like Margaret Thatcher, Israeli prime ministers, and people in show business including Julie Andrews, Carol Channing, Marvin Hamlisch, Barbara Cook, Stephen Sondheim, Stephen Spielberg,

Glen Campbell, Johnny Cash, and Elvis Presley (only saw him perform twice, but sadly, we never met)—my journey has been a blessing and a privilege.

My hope is that readers will learn from these column excerpts and personal remembrances from the years in which they were written so we might repeat successes and not repeat failures.

We should not be like the lyric in the Don McLean song "Vincent": "They didn't listen, they're not listening still. Perhaps they never will."

My fellow columnist, George Will, who owns something I don't and never will—the Pulitzer Prize—once called me "a moral environmentalist." I always took that as a compliment. Will is a self-described atheist. To paraphrase what C. S. Lewis wrote in his classic *Mere Christianity*, one can't deny God and then claim a standard by which morality and right and wrong can be judged.

Still, it proves a point Paul makes in Romans: "For (God's) invisible attributes, namely, his eternal power and divine nature, have been clearly perceived, ever since the creation of the world, in the things that have been made. So they are without excuse." (Romans 1:20 ESV)

Moral law exists, not because it was Man's creation, but because it was created by God for our protection and benefit and to reflect His holiness.

I do not claim to be more "moral" than George or anyone else. Judgments about such things are above my "pay grade." We are all "sinners"—a word that has long ago fallen out of fashion, but accurately describes our human nature. It is a major reason why government cannot repair or cure this disease that takes a Divine intervention. What I do claim is a standard by which all people must ultimately be measured. I remember during an appearance in the 1980s on the *Phil Donahue Show* when Phil questioned my sense of right and wrong: "I didn't make the rules, Phil. If you have a problem with them, take it up with the author."

It is what Thomas Jefferson—clearly not what some would call a "deeply religious" man—was getting at when he wrote in the Declaration of Independence about how our rights are "endowed by our Creator," which makes them out of the reach of government authorities. That philosophy continues to be debated today. Does government grant us rights, or does it merely, again as Jefferson wrote, exist to "preserve" rights which pre-exist government?

What rights am I talking about? Why, those that God endowed and must be "secured" by government. Why is that necessary? Because, as James Madison noted, "If men were angels," government would be unnecessary.

Men and women are not angels. That is why our lower nature must be controlled, either from inside by spiritual power, or from outside by governments which acknowledge they are ultimately responsible to an authority higher than themselves and their institutions.

These presuppositions about morals, who gets to set "the rules"—moral, economic, and political—and our ultimate accountability to God, are what have guided me in my personal life and in the columns I have written and continue to write.

Not only do I believe these things "preserve, protect, and defend" a nation; they also preserve and protect its citizens from succumbing to self-interest, which is a problem that increasingly besets and challenges us in the early years of the twenty-first century. But then this has been a challenge throughout history, because again, human nature never changes. If you understand that, you will not be fooled by politicians making promises they either can't keep, or that don't work.

Now that you know who I am and whose I am, let's get started on our "road trip."

Cal Thomas
Coral Gables, Florida

"The Lord said to me: 'Put a watchman on the city wall. Let him shout out what he sees.'"
—Isaiah 21:6 New Living Translation

1984

The Year of a Landslide for Ronald Reagan

Ronald Reagan clinches a second term, winning 49 states. He calls the Soviet Union "the evil empire," shocking the media and the Washington establishment.

The Soviet Union boycotts the Summer Olympics.

The Senate Juvenile Justice Committee investigates the shocking rise in sexual abuse of children.

The Democratic National Convention is held in San Francisco and the Republic National Convention in Dallas.

Black leaders decry the discrimination that made it difficult for black men to succeed.

AIDS ravages the country.

The British and Chinese sign an agreement to return Hong Kong to China in 1997.

CAL'S TAKE

"No power on earth is greater than a mind and soul reawakened. Our Constitution begins 'We the people,' not 'Us the government.'"

April 17, 1984. The first column I wrote for syndication appeared in fewer than ten newspapers. It dealt with an incident I saw on an airplane. A little girl, sitting across the aisle from me, was clutching a Cabbage Patch doll and crying softly.

I asked the flight attendant if she knew what was wrong.

She responded, "Oh, we get these kinds all the time. The children of divorce being shuttled back and forth between parents."

It was my turn to cry.

I asked, what are we doing to our children? Most marriages can be strengthened if people will honor their vows. Unfortunately, too many parents put temporal happiness ahead of everything, and the human and societal wreckage is there for all to see.

Ronald Reagan clinched a second term, winning 49 states. The exception was his Democratic opponent Walter Mondale's home state. That prompted Reagan to quip, "Well, Minnesota would have been nice."

Reagan delivered a speech to the National Association of Evangelicals in which he labeled the Soviet Union an "evil empire." The media and Washington establishment were shocked. Reports were that the State Department kept deleting the phrase from Reagan's speeches, and he kept re-inserting it.

The Soviet Union, perhaps in part because of Reagan's labeling, boycotted the Summer Olympics that year.

In a column titled "Ask the Experts," I said there was no better source of Soviet intentions than people who had escaped the country to warn the West the "peace and cooperation" promised by Moscow was propaganda. Arkady

Shevchenko, the highest-ranking Soviet official to defect, said the most effective way to avoid nuclear war was for the United States to be "extremely strong. That is what they understand . . . their goal, their global strategy, is to reach their objectives without nuclear war."

Could that apply to China today? Reagan's "peace through strength" policy was a success, although the media and many Democrats derided it, preferring "negotiations" and "diplomacy." This is a common mistake when dealing with evil dictators—believing that if we do nice things for them, they will reciprocate. Such attitudes guarantee war, not prevent war.

During a Senate Juvenile Justice Committee hearing in the summer of 1984, I wrote that children as young as nine testified they had been sexually abused by babysitters, family "friends," and acquaintances. "The National Association of Social Workers estimates that one in eight American females will be the victim of sexual abuse before the age of 18. Incidents of sexual abuse against young boys by men is increasing rapidly." In the internet age, these figures exploded due to the easy availability of pornographic films and imagery.

Worldview is key to just about everything. In a column titled "How Others See Us," written while I attended the Democratic National Convention in San Francisco, I quoted remarks by Reverend Jesse Jackson, who had recently returned from a visit with Fidel Castro in Cuba. Jackson sought to "explain" Castro and seemed to ignore his multiple human rights violations, saying, "He's in the Third World, and I have a Third World experience growing up in America . . . a lot of experience in suffering and exploitation."

Shortly after Jackson's return from Cuba, I wrote about fifty-three Olympic athletes from such Third World nations as Mozambique, Zimbabwe, Uganda, Panama, Tanzania, and Somalia. They had come to the United States to complete their training for the Olympic Games.

One athlete, Chris Madzokere of Zimbabwe, was interviewed by *ABC News*: "We never thought we'd be able to have a chance to use (these facilities) in preparation for the Olympic Games." His voice trembled with emotion. Madzokere had come to praise America, not to bury her.

The issue of race remained at the center of American politics. In August 1984, I wrote about an Urban League report on the American black male that contained "a lot of truth." "There was a 'steady attrition' on the number of black men capable of supporting a wife and children," said the study. "The black male is damaged by discrimination, which shows up in the form of self-destructive behavior such as drug abuse and alcoholism that black men are particularly heir to."

I quoted Reverend E. V. Hill, pastor of Mt. Zion Missionary Baptist Church in the Watts area of Los Angeles. Hill said he believed the problems for black American men can be traced to the end of World War II. "The black man found it almost impossible to find a job. The federal government instituted a number of 'in the meantime' programs to overcome the jobs disparity . . . ."

Here's a story Hill told me: "At our church, we had a class just graduate in bus driving. We took twelve unemployed school dropouts. Four were convicted felons. They came in with curlers in their hair and marijuana sticks in their mouths. We kept them for six months. We spent several weeks exposing them to lectures from successful people who used to be where they were. Out of the twelve, six stayed with the program. I took them to a company where I tried to persuade the boss to give these men job training. He liked them so much they were hired outright and are being paid between ten and twelve dollars an hour. The six dropouts are on the corner." There is a lesson here that can be applied today, but too many politicians prefer to re-fight the same battles, making the same accusations about racism while little changes.

AIDS was ravaging the country. Health and Human Services Secretary Margaret Heckler announced that the National Cancer Institute's Dr. Robert Gallo and his colleagues found the cause of AIDS: a retrovirus they labeled HIV (human immunodeficiency virus). *U.S. News and World Report* magazine ran a cover story that said, "AIDS: It's now everyone's disease." In response, I wrote that it is not everyone's disease as long as the blood supply was protected. It was the result of human behavior, mostly men having sex with other men. This brought the first of many waves of hate mail and demands that my newspaper syndicate censor or fire me. I learned that if you stand up to bullies, they will eventually back down.

I also wrote about a letter I had received from a Virginia woman who was concerned about what her 13-year-old daughter was being taught in her public school. The sex education classes were mixed, she said, and parents were not notified about them. "The film that was shown gave the impression that getting a venereal disease is nothing to be ashamed of—it's just a disease and even good people get it. A toll-free number was given for students to call and receive treatment without their parents ever having to know about it!" She was angry because the class presumed that all teens were having sex at such a young age and that abstinence was not even a consideration.

I wrote the woman and suggested she enroll her daughter in a private or home school. This issue would explode in 2021, beginning with a revolt by parents in Loudon County, Virginia.

On the international scene, Hong Kong returned to China. I went there and wrote that, while the communist regime in Beijing promised a special "50-year" protection of this unique city, it likely would not last. Communists lie, I reminded readers. Not exactly breaking news. Unfortunately, that prediction came true as Beijing cracked down on the former British colony, limiting freedoms and arresting dissidents.

Public schools and what is being taught in them, especially history, were also subjects I addressed this year, along with the ACLU and Christmas, teen suicide, whether Reagan had a mandate after his 49-state election blowout, censorship by the Left, arms control negotiations, the lack of black Republicans, the stereotyping of corporations as uncaring, attempts to ban manger scenes from public property, the lack of media credibility (and why they don't change), and Afghanistan (before 9/11).

Senator Paul Tsongas (D-MA) captured my attention when he made public his struggle with terminal cancer. He never attended Washington social functions, preferring to have dinner with his wife Niki and their daughters. One night after putting the girls to bed, he turned to Niki and said, "After all these years spent in Washington, all I'll be remembered for is that I loved my wife." Niki responded, "And what's wrong with that?" Indeed.

1985

The Year of Politics, Religion, and Education

L et's look at what things cost in 1985.

The average cost of a new house was $89,330 (in 2021, it was $340,000).

A new car averaged $9,005. Today, it's around $40,000.

A gallon of gasoline cost $1.09. It 2022, it fluctuated between $3 and $4 per gallon for regular—$6 or more in California.

A first-class letter was priced at 22 cents. Thirty-seven years later, it is 55 cents.

The Coca-Cola Company introduced "New Coke." It became the Edsel of soft drinks. Few liked it, and the concoction was soon eliminated.

CAL'S TAKE

"In business, poor performance leads to bankruptcy or, at a minimum, a restructuring of the company. In American education, failure entitles the bankrupt system to even more taxpayer dollars."

Highlight of the year for me was lunch with Ronald Reagan. He told me, "Some people think this job is all-powerful, but I will frequently give an order only to see it frustrated several levels down in the bureaucracy." The "swamp" was deep even then.

Senator Ted Kennedy debated Reverend Jerry Falwell at a National Religious Broadcasters convention in Washington. The subject was religion and politics. Kennedy conceded that religious conservatives have a right to be involved in the political life of the country, but he raised the issue of their "proper role." Who gets to define "proper"? There was predictable disagreement over how to handle the apartheid regime in South Africa (both men said apartheid was evil). Falwell called abortion "the national sin of America," but said churches needed to do more to help pregnant women in distress—which he did.

The real breakthrough, as I saw it, came when Kennedy acknowledged that, because he and Falwell had come to know each other in person rather than through the media and what others said about each man, "a new civility" existed between the two. Falwell responded, "I hope all of us are forever in the process of learning and growing and that nothing is accomplished until we move out of the screaming stage into civil discussion." However, civility should not replace convictions on things that matter.

In 1985, the advertising of beer and wine on TV—especially during heavily watched sports contests—caught the attention of Congress and, for a brief time, the media. I say brief time because the networks made a lot of money from beer and wine advertising and apparently felt less coverage of efforts to control it would be better for their profit margins.

It was inconsistent for the media to ban ads for cigarettes—when smoking had been linked to lung and other forms of cancer—and continue to carry ads promoting alcoholic beverages. In 2022, ads for casinos and sports betting would reach new highs, adding to addictive behavior.

The pro-life movement received a major boost when Dr. Bernard Nathanson, who had been the top abortionist in New York, was "converted" to the pro-life view. Nathanson showed the film *The Silent Scream* at the White House and was quickly ignored by the media, which had viewed him favorably in his previous pro-choice life. The black-and-white and somewhat grainy film showed an abortion, during which the baby appears to be screaming in pain.

The power of the film was undeniable, so much so that the Left condemned Nathanson and accused him of undermining the rights of women. Since that film, technology advanced considerably and now four-dimensional color sonograms of babies can be seen, which is the main reason Planned Parenthood and other abortion providers do not show pictures to pregnant women prior to an abortion. Statistics have shown that an overwhelming number of abortion-minded women choose to deliver their babies once they have seen a picture of their child in the womb.

I wrote about the "moral erosion" in America and compared it to vanishing sand on the seashore. Noting the horrible 1973 *Roe v. Wade* decision that struck down abortion laws in all fifty states and how it led to abortion on demand at any stage of pregnancy and for any reason, I referenced how two dozen "severely handicapped" infants were allowed to die without surgery at the Oklahoma City Children's Memorial Hospital because they flunked a test printed in the

American Academy of Pediatrics's magazine. The "formula" established a "quality of life" standard by multiplying the child's physical and mental condition by the anticipated "contribution from home and family and the contribution of society." If you think this sounds like the eugenics favored by the founder of Planned Parenthood, Margaret Sanger, and Adolf Hitler, you would be right.

What went into the minds of public school and university students was a big issue, as it became in subsequent years. Secretary of Education William J. Bennett had the temerity to quote Thomas Jefferson at a news conference. He said Jefferson believed one of the aims of education should be the "improvement of one's morals and faculties." Bennett, a strong supporter of school choice for elementary and secondary schools, also said that if young people want to go to super expensive universities the federal government does not have an obligation to pay for it.

At a series of Department of Education hearings held in various cities, parents testified to what was being taught in some of their schools. A woman in Palm Beach, Florida, testified, "When my daughter was 12 years old, she was given a questionnaire by her seventh-grade health teacher without my knowledge or consent. She was asked: 'What reasons would motivate you to commit suicide?' Five reasons were listed from which she was to choose one."

A grandmother from Orlando testified that in one of her county's school programs, "first graders made their own coffins out of shoe boxes."

A woman from Tucson, Arizona, testified about a high school health class that taught it was normal to hate your parents.

There was plenty more, and it has gotten worse since then. The question then becomes why would we willingly send our children into these "re-education camps"? We don't send our military members to Russia, China, or Iran for training.

Crime is always a big issue for politicians and this year was no different. I wrote about President Reagan receiving nominees for the United States Sentencing Commission, an outgrowth of a 1984 law that established guidelines to reduce sentence disparity in federal cases where two people who commit the same crime receive different prison terms. I suspect many people who know I am a conservative favor a "lock 'em up and throw away the key" approach to crime. I do not, because it hasn't worked.

For nonviolent, non-dangerous offenders, I prefer the biblical restitution approach. You rob me or steal something of value from my home, and you must pay me back ten times its value. Violent crimes are another matter, and the public must be protected. Even in some of these instances, the goal ought to be a changed life more than punishment. It's why prison ministries, like Prison Fellowship, have a much better success rate than secular programs—because they address changes in the heart and soul where all motivation, both criminal and charitable, begin.

The debate about taxes and government programs was as heated then as it is now. Here's a quote you will love given our current debt and the Biden administration's determination to grow big government even bigger and put us under the burden of record debt. In 1985, Senator Edward Kennedy (D-MA) said, "We cannot and should not depend on higher tax revenues to roll in and redeem every costly program. Those of us who care about domestic progress must do more with less."

No Republican or conservative could have said it better, but alas, government has become a drug to many, and the notion of personal responsibility and accountability for one's decisions has nearly evaporated in an era of envy, greed, and a sense of entitlement.

Pornography captured the attention of the Reagan administration, but not in the way that sounds. A Presidential Commission on Pornography was created to "control its production and distribution, if appropriate." Like other efforts over many years, the commission failed, mostly because as the prophet Jeremiah observed thousands of years ago, "The human heart is the most deceitful of all things, and desperately wicked. Who really knows how bad it is?" (Jeremiah 17:9 NLT). With Internet access, pornography is more available than ever and addicting more men and women.

A "sign of the times" this year was the Hallmark card company's printing of divorce cards. Hallmark had the reputation of being the most traditional card company in the country, but in 1985 it began issuing cards that "celebrated" a divorce. I asked the company to send me some copies, which they did. One showed a cartoon figure cutting a ball and chain from his leg and expressing himself: "AAAaaaa!" Inside the card it said, "Free at last. Congratulations." There were no cards to comfort the children wounded by divorcing parents.

British Prime Minister Margaret Thatcher, a woman of convictions and tenacity, transformed Britain's welfare state, taxation and so much more. She was eventually turned out of office (like Winston Churchill before her) because some men cannot put up with strong conservative women. Thatcher made them look weak, which they were.

This story was probably told as a joke, but still, it says something about Thatcher.

After her first election in 1979, Thatcher took her all-male cabinet to dinner. The waiter approached and took her order.

Thatcher: "I'll have the beef."

Waiter: "What about the vegetables?"

Thatcher: "They'll have the same."

I had the honor of meeting Thatcher on several occasions and will always admire what she did along with Ronald Reagan and Pope John Paul II. Their policies and faith led to the collapse of the Berlin Wall and communism in the Soviet Union. She was a brick, as the English say.

Shortly before political correctness had tightened its grip on America came an editorial in the respected *Journal of the American Medical Association*. It took note of the sexual promiscuity, abortion, anti-celibacy, AIDS, and reckless behavior leading to severe consequences: "This is a great time to practice sexual monogamy."

Sometimes one finds truth in the least likely places.

Other issues the world confronted in 1985 were apartheid, the growing drug crisis among youth, poverty, and a contentious relationship between church and state.

1986

The Year of Historic and Tragic Events

The first black governor of Virginia since Reconstruction, Douglas Wilder, is sworn in.

The space shuttle Challenger explodes 73 seconds after it lifts off from Cape Canaveral. All seven crew members are killed, including Christa McAuliffe, who was going to be the first teacher in space.

The Martin Luther King Jr. national holiday begins.

The Rock and Roll Hall of Fame inducts its first group of singers and musicians, including Elvis Presley, James Brown, Little Richard, Fats Domino, Chuck Berry, Ray Charles, Sam Cooke, the Everly Brothers, Buddy Holly, and Jerry Lee Lewis. In my first job as a disc jockey on WINX in Rockville, Maryland, I had played records by each of them, so it was personally thrilling to see them honored.

After years of pressure, the Soviet Union finally releases from prison Anatoly (now Natan) Scharansky, who promptly moves to Israel with his wife, Avital. She tirelessly lobbied for many years for his release.

The first anti-smoking ad appears on TV, featuring actor Yul Brynner, who died of lung cancer on October 10. He says it is his smoking habit that is about to kill him, and the ad is designed to persuade people to quit.

New York City passes its first gay rights legislation.

Halley's Comet makes its closest approach to Earth at 39 million miles.

Desmond Tutu is elected Archbishop of Cape Town, South Africa.

Michael Jordan sets an NBA playoff record, scoring 63 points in a single game.

After much hype, Geraldo Rivera opens Al Capone's safe and finds it empty.

The Chernobyl nuclear power plant mishap occurs in the Soviet Union.

Barry Bonds makes his major league debut with the Pittsburgh Pirates. Years later, he would be at the center of a controversy surrounding many players accused of using performance-enhancing drugs.

Remains of the *Titanic* are at last discovered, and a video grabs the world's attention.

Oprah Winfrey's show is televised nationally for the first time. And the rest, they say, is history (or *her*story).

Auschwitz survivor Elie Wiesel is awarded the Nobel Peace Prize for his efforts to ensure the Holocaust is remembered.

Reagan signs a historic immigration bill that lacks an identification provision, which leads to a flow of illegal migrants who break the law to enter the country that would reach a tidal wave years later.

CAL'S TAKE

"If life is not a continuum from conception to natural death, then all of us are potential victims if we fall out of favor with a ruling elite."

An early column addressed "bogeymen" in politics. One must always have an enemy to raise money. I recalled a conversation with a leading conservative who said he once responded to complaints that too many of his fundraising letters were negative. So, he said, he sent out a positive letter one month "and no one sent any money." That's pretty cynical, but it's true.

The Baltimore public school system instituted a "sex survey" of students in grades seven to twelve. Officials explained the survey was necessary because there were 97 live births to girls between ten and fourteen in the previous year and over three thousand births statewide. Baltimore had the dubious distinction of having the highest teen pregnancy rate in the country, despite it having provided sex education courses from Planned Parenthood since 1967. Maybe someone should have suggested and supported abstinence.

President Reagan abandoned his State of the Union address scheduled for the evening of the Challenger disaster and delivered an address to the nation—written by the talented Peggy Noonan—that included this memorable tribute to the astronauts: "The crew of the space shuttle Challenger honored us by the manner in which they lived their lives. We will never forget them, nor the last time we saw them, this morning, as they prepared for their journey and waved goodbye and slipped the surly bonds of earth to touch the face of God." Like many Americans, I watched the tragedy on live television.

I spent an hour with evangelist Billy Graham talking about how he had demanded removal of barriers between black and white attendees at his Crusades beginning in 1951. He said his life was often threatened by racists and that he didn't feel his mission was to participate in demonstrations, despite his strong stand against discrimination.

Graham said King told him, "That's OK. You take the stadiums, and I'll take the streets."

Bill Moyers, the former Lyndon B. Johnson spokesman and a commentator for *CBS News*, did a remarkable documentary for *CBS Reports*, countering a National Urban League statement that blamed President Reagan for much of the economic disparity between blacks and whites.

Though a liberal, Moyers noted the reason why 60 percent of all black children are born out of wedlock and why half of all teenage girls at the time became pregnant had nothing to do with Reagan. Instead, it was caused by a breakdown in the black family. It is an obvious conclusion that most on the Left refuse to acknowledge.

In years following, it would be learned that black women abort more of their babies than any other racial or ethnic group.

The major media was almost universally critical of Reagan's Strategic Defense Initiative proposal, which he unveiled during a nationally televised address from the Oval Office. It was derisively dubbed "Star Wars," but was later believed to have been a contributing factor to the collapse of the Soviet Union, which did not have the resources to keep up.

In a column for *USA Today*, I noted that contributing to the decline of the public school system was a booklet handed out at a PTA meeting. Except the title had changed. It was no longer PTA, but PTSA, the "S" standing for students. The handbook was a list of "student rights."

I wrote: "The only right I had in school was the right to remain silent. If I gave up the right to remain silent, anything I said could, and probably would, be used against me in a meeting with the vice principal."

Why is it that when we hear about Women's History Week (or month as the occasion was established this year), the value of mothers who have made the choice to stay at home with young children is never considered a positive contribution to the nation? Feminists, who are pro-choice when it comes to abortion, are inconsistently anti-choice when it comes to women who choose to not work and instead homeschool their children. For this, the word "hypocrisy" was invented.

Madalyn Murray O'Hair, perhaps the country's most famous atheist, resigned as head of her organization, American Atheists. On one of my CNN *Crossfire* co-host assignments, I interviewed O'Hair's successor around Christmas time. He was arguing against religious displays, such as manger scenes and even Christmas trees, on public property. I remember saying to him, "Why are you messing with my holidays? I don't mess with yours on April 1."

My wife, Charlotte Ray Thomas, graduated from college this year. It prompted a column about the roles of men and women. She supported me when I went back to college, and now it was my turn to support her by handling kitchen and childcare duties. I was proud of her and what she had accomplished. She would go on to earn a master's degree and head the counseling office at Fourth Presbyterian Church in Bethesda, Maryland.

Proving that history so often repeats itself was the opening line to a column I wrote in May: "As the nation prepares to officially observe the 100th anniversary of the newly refurbished Statue of Liberty, it is important to consider the difference between the immigrants who came to these shores around the turn of the century and those who are now illegally entering the country from Central America, egged on by something called the 'Sanctuary Movement.'"

TV host Pat Robertson announced he was running for president after resigning from his ordination vows. I noted the hypocrisy of the media and Democrats who were perfectly fine with Reverend Jesse Jackson's presidential candidacies, but recoiled at Robertson for allegedly violating "church-state separation."

Speaking of hypocrisy, the Supreme Court ruled against the Reagan administration's effort to require hospitals to provide life-prolonging treatment to babies who survived an abortion. Justice John Paul Stevens criticized the administration for unjustified "intrusion on state autonomy." Yet, the court felt no reluctance to intrude on state autonomy in its 1973 *Roe v. Wade* decision, striking down laws outlawing or regulating abortions in every state.

Antonin Scalia was nominated and confirmed to the Supreme Court and became one of the greatest defenders of the Constitution ever to sit on that bench. I remember telling him at a social function to "stay healthy." He had a marvelous sense of humor, but his seriousness about the Constitution and the role of judges and legislatures was what had the most impact.

One of his more memorable statements (there were many) was this: "A system of government that makes the people subordinate to a committee of nine unelected lawyers does not deserve to be called a democracy."

The Court ruled 5-4 in favor of striking down Georgia's anti-sodomy law that made criminal homosexual sex acts. The Court would later overturn all such laws and legitimize same-sex marriage.

Planned Parenthood outdid itself (which I didn't think possible) by paying for an ad campaign on Baltimore city buses, in newspapers, and on local TV stations that asked a question: "What's an orgy?" Supposedly it was to encourage conversations between teens about sex because the city had the highest teen pregnancy rate in the country for a city its size. I don't recall any evidence that the ads achieved their stated goal, but when one is a liberal, results don't matter—only intentions.

Four hundred people demonstrated outside the *Washington Post* after its Sunday magazine did a story on black criminals. The demonstrators rightly claimed the media mostly portrays black people, in the words of Reverend Walter Fauntroy, as "thieves and robbers and drug addicts." As a native Washingtonian, I have always complained that the media rarely focuses on successful black Americans. This is a subtle form of racism.

The *Washington Post*'s executive editor, Benjamin Bradlee, wrote a column apologizing to the city's black citizens. I noted that Christian conservatives also suffer from stereotyping by the secular media, but that doesn't produce an apology, much less different treatment of that group.

An ad in the *New York Times* urged women who may have lost "the man of your dreams" because of divorce to buy "the fur of your dreams." I questioned the ad's insensitivity to marriage. Later, groups would question the value of wearing furs at all.

A preview of things to come occurred in Fresno, California, where the city attorney ordered the Salvation Army's public service ad removed from city buses after he received just two complaints from people who did not like the ad. It said, "Sharing is Caring . . . God Bless You." The atheist complainers were offended by the reference to God. The ads were restored the following year after a public outcry, but the city banned the display of a Menorah in a public park after complaints from the ACLU.

I wrote several columns about the Iran–Contra affair of exchanging arms for hostages but noted that Congress kept changing its mind on the legality of aid to anti-communist forces in Nicaragua. President Reagan turned out to be right about the Sandinistas. They were supported by Cuba and other communist nations in their effort to take over that Central American country and use it as a base for a possible attack against America.

I was invited to speak at Harvard's 350th anniversary. NBC's John Chancellor introduced me. I was in the company of elites, including Justice Harry Blackmun, author of the horrible *Roe v. Wade* decision.

Harvard appeared to dislike what some of its former presidents said and stood for. I quoted Nathan Pusey, who said that the graduate should be able to pronounce the name of God without embarrassment. I noted that for many among the Harvard faculty, God *was* an embarrassment.

The year ended with a column about several racial incidents in which white men beat up black men. Unfortunately, some things don't change because of the tainted human heart.

1987

The Year of Better Late than Never

Terry Waite, the Church of England envoy to Lebanon, is kidnapped and held hostage.

TV evangelist Jim Bakker resigns as head of the PTL Club due to a brewing sex scandal.

Los Angeles Dodgers executive Al Campanis resigns amid controversy over his racially charged remarks about the alleged inability of black people to manage baseball teams.

"The Simpsons" appears as a short cartoon on the Tracey Ullman Show.

At the Brandenburg Gate, President Ronald Reagan publicly challenges Mikhail Gorbachev to tear down the Berlin Wall.

Britain and France sign an agreement to build a tunnel under the English Channel, later dubbed "The Chunnel."

The Federal Communications Commission rescinds the Fairness Doctrine, paving the way for cable TV opinion networks and talk radio.

In the Middle East, the First Intifada begins in the Gaza Strip and West Bank.

CAL'S TAKE

"Sometimes people need a kick in the pants to get them
to do what they would be doing if government weren't
there as a perpetual parent."

The "at-home" drug RU 486 was introduced. First developed in France, the drug either prevents implantation of a
fertilized egg or dislodges the embryo from the wall of the
uterus after implantation.

In a claim that brought much derision on the Christian
church and individual believers, Oral Roberts said God told
him to build a 777-bed hospital that remained half-empty
and claimed to have seen a nine-hundred-foot-tall Jesus. He
announced that if he didn't raise $5 million by March, God
would strike him dead. He then said God had granted him a
"stay of execution" until 1988 to raise the money. The claims
got Roberts's TV program canceled on many stations across
the country.

In the liberal *New Republic* magazine, Mickey Kaus made
a rare admission. Responding to the spread of AIDS, Kaus
wrote, "To be blunt about it, what's more important—casual
sex, or avoiding a biological holocaust?" He added, "Today,
none of us wants to admit we made a mistake, that this wonderful experiment (the sexual liberation movement of the
1960s) was an epic social blunder."

Better late than never, I suppose.

This was the bicentennial year of the writing of the United
States Constitution, one of the greatest documents ever
penned by human hands. I wrote about a Hearst survey that
discovered only a bare majority understand the document

and what it means when it comes to restraining government and guaranteeing our liberties.

The survey found fifty-nine percent were unaware that the Bill of Rights is the first ten amendments and nearly half believed the Constitution contains the Marxist declaration, "From each according to his ability, to each according to his need."

Given what is taught in many of our public schools and universities, this should come as no surprise. As I have repeatedly written and argued, what is surprising is why so many parents send their kids to these "mind control camps" that undermine the history of the country and their faith.

This year seemed to produce, if not a spiritual revival, then at least a greater interest in matters of the soul.

The class with the largest enrollment—more than nine hundred students—was called "Jesus and the Moral Life." It was taught in a converted church building by the liberal professor Harvey Cox, whom I had come to know. Cox, who became famous for his book *The Secular City*, which some claimed ushered in the "God is Dead" movement, presided over a class which apparently believed God was very much alive and they wanted to find out more about Him.

Among the selections of music played as students entered the classroom was a country song, the lyrics of which included, "You've got to walk, talk, and live like Jesus every day." There may be hope, even for Harvard.

In Virginia, Governor Douglas Wilder—the first black American to win that office in the capital of the Confederacy—did something remarkable for a Democrat. In a speech at his alma mater, Howard University in Washington, DC, Wilder said it is time for "a revolution against indolence and sloth." How refreshing, especially today when indolence and sloth are increasingly supported with government checks for the indolent and slothful. The words sound like they might have been the satirical name of a law firm in a Three Stooges film.

The Vatican issued a statement calling on governments to strictly limit medical interference in human procreation by imposing "moral norms." They are a little late since "immoral norms" are now "normal."

A New York Daily News editorial responded to the Vatican statement by questioning whether any such thing as moral norms exists. It also dismissed the Vatican document by embracing the default position liberals use to avoid any discussion of a moral issue. That would be "church-state separation."

A black man who went by the name "Reverend Ike" was a guest on CNN's *Crossfire*, which I cohosted on this particular evening. Ike's philosophy could be boiled down to two credos: The *lack* of money is the root of all evil; and God doesn't want you to wait for pie in the sky by and by when you die, He wants you to have your pie now—with whipped cream on it.

This "prosperity gospel" has infected too many churches and denominations. It never ends well for those who preach it (other than to benefit themselves) and those who believe in it.

The subject before the Washington, DC, Board of Education was sex education. People were invited to testify about what was being taught—and what was proposed—in the city's public schools. Antonio Booth, a fourth grader, gave his opinion: "I don't know much about sex, but I prefer to wait until I am much older to learn. You should wait until you're married to have sex. . . . I'm having serious enough problems with what is written in my books now."

"Out of the mouths of babes," as the saying goes.

Gary Hart, a Democratic senator from Colorado, was forced to withdraw from his presidential run after an extramarital affair with Donna Rice. Hart denied any wrongdoing and challenged the media to follow him around, which it did. The question I raised in my column was how and why should the public trust his political promises if he couldn't keep a promise to his wife to "forsake all others"?

"Campaign '88 and the Adultery Issue" was the title of one column. It was about the shift from holding people accountable to their marriage vows and those who would excuse adultery, blaming not the people who commit it, but journalists and others who expose it.

I debated a senior political reporter for a weekly news magazine. This man had been married for just three years. He accused me of being too "rigid" in my views on marriage and unfaithfulness. He said there are extenuating circumstances over the course of a marriage and that people can fall out of love.

"Did you include those circumstances in the vow you made to your wife at the wedding?" I asked.

"Of course not," he replied rather indignantly.

"Then, my friend, what we are dealing with is your ability to keep a promise and whether you might someday be considered a liar."

There have been efforts made over many years—decades, even centuries—to curb the spread of vulgar and pornographic materials.

This year, the Federal Communications Commission (FCC) adopted "sweeping restrictions" on broadcast media in response to complaints about radio shows hosted by Howard Stern and a guy appropriately calling himself "The Greaseman." Like water running downhill, these and other "shock jocks" found new ways to disseminate their trash. They went to satellite radio when it became available. The FCC has no jurisdiction over satellite stations.

AIDS was a growing problem this year. ABC held a four-hour "town meeting" on the subject. On the program, then Representative (and later Senator) Dianne Feinstein said something remarkable for a liberal Democrat: "We can no longer be a promiscuous society." She is from San Francisco where promiscuity is a way of life, but she was right.

Evolution and Creation lost in the Supreme Court when the Justices ruled 7–2 that a Louisiana law mandating the teaching of both views of our origins was unconstitutional, because it gave equal consideration to both.

No matter that many scientists consider the Creation view to have scientific credibility. The Court appears to think that tolerating, much less teaching, anything that can be considered "religious" is a violation of the First Amendment's Establishment Clause. It appears they didn't read—or ignored—the rest of it about the "free exercise" of religion, which that document says cannot be restricted by government.

Robert Bork's nomination to the Supreme Court failed for two reasons: the Left defined Bork and the Reagan administration was not ready for the onslaught against him. Bork was portrayed by Senator Ted Kennedy (D-MA) as a man who would force women seeking abortions to use rusty coat hangers on themselves in back alleys. The adjective "borked" has been used since then to describe lies told about Republican nominees to the Court.

William Sloan Coffin died this year. He was "pastor" of the ultra-liberal Riverside Church in New York. During the Vietnam War, Coffin frequently was part of anti-war demonstrations and participated in draft card burnings. Coffin had long abandoned any preaching about a kingdom other than the one on Earth. He was so radical that members of his own church accused him of bringing "infamy, disrepute, and near destruction" to the church.

Why should right-wingers get all the discredit?

The New York State Board of Regents mandated "AIDS education" in the state's public schools. The problem, as Representative Jack Kemp (R-NY) noted, was that there was "no moral or ethical framework for teaching children about ethical behavior. . . . It focuses solely on ideas of 'safe sex' and puts AIDS and the common cold in the same category of communicable diseases."

Not many people know that I am named after the two sons of Calvin Coolidge, John (my first name) and Calvin (my middle name). My grandfather and Grace Coolidge, the former First Lady, were first cousins.

Young Calvin died at age seventeen from an infection, but John lived a long life. I met him and his wife Florence at their home in Plymouth Notch, Vermont. It is the site where President Coolidge took the oath of office by candlelight following the death of Warren Harding. My mother had attended John and Florence's wedding and kept a piece of the wedding cake in our freezer for years until it became petrified.

John told me his father was the first president to establish regular meetings with the press, seeing them twice weekly.

They were always background conferences, with reporters not allowed to quote the president directly, unlike today's televised events.

In 1926, President Coolidge stated why he met regularly with the press: "I regard it as necessary to the carrying on of our republican institutions, that the people should have a fairly accurate report of what the president is trying to do."

I interviewed Secretary of Education William Bennett who told me he believed it would take another ten years to undo the damage caused to public school students because of political meddling and social experimentation that resulted in declining test scores and underqualified teachers.

Unfortunately, things have only gotten worse with even more social experimentation (now known as critical race theory and wokeness). I will repeat myself: we should stop giving them the "raw material" to create new generations of secular progressives and start sending them to private schools (I favor vouchers which are now allowed in several states) and to universities that do not undermine our history, traditions, values, and faith.

Pope John Paul II visited the United States. Speaking in Columbia, South Carolina, the Pope warned against the continued breakdown of the family. He blamed it on "a false notion of individual freedom" and warned us to use our freedoms wisely.

"America," he said, "you cannot insist on the right to choose, without also insisting on the right to choose well—the duty to choose the truth."

If only we knew what truth looks like in our day.

In what would soon signal a growing trend, a Louisiana high school student was censored when she sought to use a four-letter word and language related to that word in her valedictory speech to fellow graduates. The four-letter word was L-O-R-D.

The Moral Majority officially died this year as its founder, Jerry Falwell, announced its demise.

I wrote that Falwell's presence on the national scene produced positives and negatives for the country and for the image of the Christian church. One of the positives was encouraging more Christians to become involved in the political life of the nation. Among the negatives included too close an association with this fallen and corrupt world which gave the church a tainted image as if it were an arm of the Republican Party.

A District of Columbia appeals court ruled that Georgetown University, a Catholic institution, must grant campus homosexuals the same access to its facilities and services as every other student group. The court said the government's "compelling interest" to end discrimination based on "sexual preferences" superseded Georgetown's freedom of religion defense.

It would be one of many subsequent rulings that undermined religious freedom and speech in years to come.

1988

The Year of Ethics and Morality

An election year: Democrats hold their national convention in Atlanta, nominating Michael Dukakis, the Massachusetts governor, and Texas Senator Lloyd Bentsen as his running mate.

Republicans hold their convention in New Orleans. George H. W. Bush picked Indiana Senator Dan Quayle as his running mate.

The eight-year-old war, killing 1.5 million, between Iran and Iraq finally ends. Nothing positive results.

Pan Am Flight 103 from London to New York explodes in midair over Lockerbie, Scotland, killing 243 passengers and sixteen crew members onboard.

CAL'S TAKE

"People, like water, will run downhill, seeking their lowest level unless something interdicts them."

The *Los Angeles Times* took a poll (where would we be without polls and focus groups?) and found, not to my surprise, that parents would like better labeling on movies.

Jack Valenti, a former aide to Lydon B. Johnson and head of the Motion Picture Association of America, opposed changing the rating system from G, PG, PG-13, R, and NC-17 to "S" for sex, "V" for violence, or "L" for bad language. Valenti claimed such changes would only add to confusion. But that was the point in asking that the system be changed, wasn't it—to lessen confusion?

Films have only gotten worse since then. Most now contain more blasphemies, bad language, sexual situations, and nudity than ever before.

In a rare moment of candor for politicians, six members of the United States Senate were quoted in a front-page *Washington Post* story in which they bemoaned the drudgery of life on Capitol Hill. "There's a sense in which the whole system is breaking down," lamented Senator Daniel Evans (R-Wash.), who along with the others, announced they were not seeking reelection.

I noted the reason for their frustration was that the entire government had exceeded the boundaries set for it in the Constitution. When reelection becomes paramount and lobbyists rule with their campaign contributions, the result can only be frustration because it was not meant to function this way. Perhaps "DC" should stand for "Dysfunction City."

In what still serves as a remarkable statement given the condition of what passes for education these days, the president of Princeton University, Harold T. Shapiro, appealed to American higher education to be more mindful of the moral and spiritual needs of college students: "We are better at research than at the public discourse required to transmit ideas and values. Science and learning do not by themselves satisfy our need to provide meaning to our lives."

Sometimes a gift for the obvious can resonate in a culture headed in the other direction. Shapiro's comments had roots in the founding principles of Princeton and other Ivy League colleges, which early on, dedicated themselves to training ministers and missionaries and believed that a knowledge of Scripture was part of a solid education. My, how times have changed (but that Truth has not).

At a Poynter Institute for Media Studies conference in St. Petersburg, Florida, the subject was how the media covered—and should cover—AIDS.

I concluded from the conference that the scientific, medical, and media establishments had virtually abandoned the ethical and moral dimensions surrounding AIDS and were more intent on "managing" the disease that is largely caused by behavior.

In a classic statement of relativism, Dr. Stephen Joseph, the health commissioner for New York City, asked, "Whose code of ethics and whose standard of behavior will we use?"

I responded, "The opposite of morality is not neutrality; it is immorality. The standard that ought to be used is the one that worked before the relativists began to unravel the social fabric."

In another debate, I was accused of wishing to return the country "to the days of Ozzie and Harriet." I responded, "I'll defend Ozzie and Harriet if you defend Beavis and Butthead." (You have to remember both in order for that to be funny.)

This year marked the twentieth anniversary of the Kerner Commission Report on racial divisions in America. Little has changed, at least in the political sphere. Democrats sought to blame Ronald Reagan for continuing problems in the black community. I noted that the facts proved otherwise.

I wrote that black family instability was and remains the major problem. Twice as many black Americans divorce than white Americans. Welfare had accomplished little in lifting poor black families out of poverty. In fact, they were and remain part of what some have called a "poverty industry."

I interviewed an old friend and colleague, James Adams, who at the time was an anchor for a local Washington, DC, TV station. Adams, who is black, said, "It bothers me to see so many young kids wasting the opportunities my father and mother gave me. My father used to tell me, 'There's nothing in the streets after midnight but trouble.' Now kids are in discos until three o'clock in the morning."

He was fortunate to have a stable, two-parent home. That is the key for any child growing up, no matter their race.

This marked the end of my two-year "career" as the only conservative commentator on NPR's *All Things Considered* program. The reason given to me by the program's new executive producer, Neal Conan, was that I had become "too predictable." Conan told the public broadcasting newspaper *Current*, "I found him stylistically anachronistic—very 1940s stentorian."

They talk like that at NPR. I laughed when I heard myself described as "predictable," as if the liberal worldview that dominates NPR is not.

In San Diego, I met with some members of the crew of the *Pueblo*, the ship that was captured by North Korea in 1968 and whose men were tortured in prison camps. Commander Lloyd Bucher told me, "I am totally amazed at the inability of Congress to apply various lessons that have been learned throughout history. To imagine that any communist regime is not going to follow in the steps of its progenitors is a sad mistake."

He was speaking about Nicaragua, but his insight might also apply to China, Iran, and terrorists.

The *Pueblo*'s intelligence officer, Stephen Harris, told me that he had no firm convictions about communism prior to his capture, but "when I was able to observe how it affected not only us, but the people who lived under it, everything changed."

In one of my early trips to Israel (I have now visited the Middle East twenty-seven times), I interviewed a twenty-year-old Israeli soldier. Lt. Vital Lavon told me of his frustration that network TV reporters never show Muslim Friday prayers during which Imams frequently incite believers to violence against Israelis.

"They also don't tell you that (Palestinian) adults encourage young children, aged eleven to thirteen, to throw rocks and bottles at the (Israeli) soldiers. They do this for two reasons. First, it is more dramatic on television. Second, the adults know that the children can get away with more than they can."

Bias against Israel and the Jewish people remains an ongoing problem, and not only in the United States media and among certain politicians.

Rolling Stone magazine commissioned a survey of Baby Boomers, and it revealed some shocking results: 40 percent of those surveyed could not think of a single circumstance under which they would fight to defend America. The reason, according to the survey, was that the Boomers were pre-occupied with themselves.

I noted "the generation that rejected materialism and condemned their parents for contributing to poverty, by embracing capitalism rather than socialism, now says money is its top concern . . ."

Prosperity and never having to invest in your country can have a serious downside.

Oliver North was the commencement speaker at Liberty University. In an interview with me, North likened Vietnam to Nicaragua as two wars that the United States did not have the desire to finish (Afghanistan would be number three).

North told me, "Those who sent a generation of young men off to war lost faith in themselves. The sons of this nation were maimed, crippled; they died for naught because the political leadership of this country lost its will . . . they lost faith in the ideals of freedom and democracy. They betrayed millions of people to death and tyranny. And that cannot happen again." Unfortunately, it did (again, see Afghanistan).

A debate broke out when William F. Buckley Jr., announced he favored decriminalizing drug use as a means of solving the crime problem. His rationale was that if drugs were made legal and subject only to minimal controls, the cartels would evaporate because the profits from drug sales would dry-up.

It was an interesting proposition, but I wondered about the government's responsibility to attempt to curtail certain behavior and protect especially the young from starting down a path that leads to ruin for many. Laws deter certain behavior, probably for a majority of people.

It is always amusing when a doctrinaire liberal, like *Washington Post* columnist Carl Rowan, gets a dose of reality. Rowan, who was an advocate for more gun laws, confronted a group of young people who trespassed on his backyard (which had a pool and Jacuzzi). It was two o'clock in the morning, and Rowan used his gun to shoot one of them in the hand. Rowan said the youths had been drinking beer and smoking marijuana and "lunged at me."

Adding to his hypocrisy (do as I say, not as I do), DC Police said Rowan's gun was not registered. I wrote, "The penalty for possessing an unregistered firearm in Washington can be up to $1,000 and one year in jail. The penalty for unlawful entry is only $100 and six months in jail."

Rowan suffered no consequences, probably because he was a liberal Democrat.

If you are following markers that reveal the decline in culture, look no further than a statement issued this year by the ACLU: "It is our position that teaching monogamous, heterosexual intercourse within marriage is a traditional American value (and) an unconstitutional establishment of a religious doctrine in public schools."

How's that "anything goes" worldview working out in practice, ACLU?

"Tough on crime" rhetoric was again heard from Republican presidential candidates. I noted that since the recidivism rate is so high for ex-convicts (FBI statistics revealed 74 percent of ex-cons are re-arrested), perhaps the tough part wasn't working. I recall a great line from the film *The Shawshank Redemption*, in which Andy says to Red: "The funny thing is—on the outside, I was an honest man, straight as an arrow. I had to come to prison to be a crook."

The United States has more people in prison per capita (though in 2021, California began letting out even violent offenders because of COVID-19 and overcrowding) than any nation except the Soviet Union and South Africa (at this time).

The Department of Justice says 36 percent of inmates are in prison for nonviolent offenses. As mentioned, I support restitution, meaning paying back people who have been financially harmed by a criminal. Then there's the cost. It costs between $60,000 and $80,000 per bed to build a new prison. It takes $11,600 annually to house and feed an inmate, totaling a staggering $6 trillion per year (all figures are in 1988 money). That money could be better spent, or greatly reduced, if politicians focused on real solutions and not posturing during their campaigns.

NBC announced elimination of its broadcast standards department, prompting me to ask: "They have standards?"

In a column about a panel of doctors trying to separate moral questions surrounding abortion from research involving the tissue of aborted babies, I wrote: "Inhumanities are often perpetrated in the name of the highest humanitarian and social principles. That is what makes them so dangerous, because it is easy to be blinded by the light of good intentions and ignore the darkness that will surely follow."

Cokie Roberts said on ABC's *This Week* program that we don't know when life begins anymore because our country has become "more pluralistic." How's that for a standard? Would she also apply that to, say, views about race and gender?

I'm not a prophet, but what I wrote just before the 1988 election seems nearly prophetic: "Recent history shows conservatives have learned how to win elections—but they have not yet demonstrated they know how to use power."

Many credited the Willie Horton ad campaign for contributing to the November election victory of the Bush–Quayle ticket. Horton was a convicted murderer serving a life sentence who was let out under a Massachusetts weekend furlough program. He did not return and ultimately committed assault, armed robbery, and rape before being captured and re-sentenced.

The campaign ad was used against Dukakis who was accused of being "soft on crime."

The country observed the twenty-fifth anniversary of John F. Kennedy's assassination. The media ignored the death of a far more influential man who passed away the same day. I didn't. C.S. Lewis wrote three dozen books, which have been translated into many languages and continue to sell about two million copies every year. The media always have their favorites, and their greatest power is the power to ignore.

In a final Christmas press gathering at the White House, I was able to exchange brief farewells and thanks to the president and Mrs. Reagan. I wrote at the end of a column: "Washington won't be the same without him." And it hasn't. His policies worked.

1989

The Year of Freedom to Do Good and Evil

Iran's Ayatollah Khomeini dies.

Freedom demonstrations occur in Beijing's Tiananmen Square, which the Chinese communists brutally suppress.

The Soviet Union pulls out of Afghanistan.

The collapse of the East German government and the destruction of the Berlin Wall ends the seventy-year ideological conflict known as the Cold War.

President George H. W. Bush begins his term.

CAL'S TAKE

"We tolerate, even promote, many things we once regarded as evil, wrong, or immoral. And then we seek 'explanations' for an act that seems beyond comprehension. Remove societal restraints on some evils and one can expect the demons to be freed to conduct other evil acts."

President Ronald Reagan asked Surgeon General C. Everett Koop to conduct a study of the effects abortion has had on women. Koop said such a study would cost $100 million and have to include "sixty different categories of pregnancy."

Appearing on ABC's *Good Morning America*, Koop was asked about his pro-life views. His response: "I've always been able to separate my personal beliefs from my responsibilities as surgeon general."

How many people who are "pro-choice" in government have ever separated their personal beliefs from public policy?

Koop and philosopher-theologian Dr. Francis Schaeffer had earlier written a book together titled *Whatever Happened to the Human Race?* In that book, the two men said: "Abortion does not solve all problems; often it just exchanges one set for another . . . (abortion insures) that many women will turn into the kind of hard people they may not want to be. For others, it is a bewildering nightmare to be overwhelmed with longings for the baby to be back in them and to be able to complete that which had begun."

It didn't take a $100 million study to reach that logical and provable conclusion.

Bob Woodward of the *Washington Post* discovered a series of 1972 memos between Supreme Court Justices Harry Blackmun and Potter Stewart that revealed the forthcoming decision striking down all abortion laws in the country was "arbitrary," lacked legislative—even constitutional—justification, and was related to a previously unknown "right to privacy" that is not written in the Constitution.

That the decision was also based on fraudulent testimony in the case of "Jane Doe," who, as Norma McCorvey, later became fiercely pro-life, didn't matter. The evil deed would be done and millions of lives have been lost ever since, not to mention the physical, emotional, and spiritual damage caused to many women.

Psychologist Judith Wallerstein published a book titled *Second Chances: Men, Women, and Children a Decade after Divorce.*

She wrote: "It would be hard to find any other group of children—except perhaps the victims of a natural disaster—who suffered such a rate of sudden serious psychological problems."

Wallerstein tracked for ten years, beginning in 1970, a group of children of divorced parents. She found "41 percent of those children doing poorly; they were entering adulthood as worried, underachieving, self-deprecating, and sometimes angry young men and women. The rest were strikingly uneven in how they adjusted to the world . . ."

Parents suffered, too, she said, and their divorce often added additional stress to their children.

Senator Edward Kennedy delivered a speech at Yale University, in which he criticized the newly inaugurated president, George H. W. Bush, for what Kennedy said was his "coming to Washington without larger goals and purposes."

In a kind of left-handed compliment (pun intended), Kennedy said of Bush's predecessor: "Ronald Reagan was a successful candidate and effective president above all else because he stood for a set of ideas. He stated them in 1980—and it turned out that he meant them—and he wrote most of them not only into public law, but into the national consciousness."

Never mind that Kennedy opposed most of Reagan's ideas and sought to undermine some of them, especially his back-channel talks with the Soviet Union. Kennedy's point was correct and his remarks would be good for contemporary Republicans to emulate.

Traveling to Beijing, I met Fang Lizhi, an astrophysicist and university professor, who had become a thorn in the side of the communist government and an inspiration to students and others gathering for a freedom demonstration in Tiananmen Square. The communist government eventually sent in troops who killed thousands of citizens in an action that shocked the world.

As the demonstrators had started to gather, Fang told me the worst course for the United States would be to buckle under to Chinese government demands for human rights to be treated as an internal matter. He also said he believes Marxism is "outdated," and one-fourth of his students have no interest in Marxist doctrine. "All they want to do is go abroad and make money."

Back in Washington, "press ethics" comes up at a gathering of the American Society of Newspaper Editors convention. The *Washington Post* ran a story about reporters who received large speaking fees. ABC's Sam Donaldson refused to divulge his fees, but defended being paid to speak, saying, "I don't hold any public office, nor do I seek one. I essentially believe that what I do falls in the category of private business, just like dentists, doctors, lawyers, and people who run cattle."

Not exactly. People in those professions don't get to decide what is news and how it's covered every night, reporting it to millions of viewers.

Sex education in public schools came up in political debate. Virginia mandated every county to have a "Family Life" curriculum. The chairman of the committee that forced the Planned Parenthood agenda down the throats of students and parents said, "It isn't easy being an adolescent. We're trying to give them the tools." Does it have to be a chainsaw?

I wrote about a seventh-grade class science project in Gatlinburg, Tennessee. Twelve-year-old Carrie Walker decided she would produce a project about the development of human life. She brought ten jars to school containing babies that her father—a pathologist who said they were from miscarriages—had provided. They ranged from six weeks of gestation to five months.

The principal ordered them removed, but not before some children had seen them. Some second graders asked: "Why was the baby in the bottle? Is that baby going to come out and be alive? Do you kill the baby to put it in a jar?" An eighth-grade girl said, "That was a real little person in there. I never want to get an abortion."

A comment by the county curriculum director, Jim Wade, was particularly instructive: "To an untrained eye, the five-months-along ('fetus') was definitely a child." I responded, "Apparently it takes a considerable amount of 'training' for people to deny the obvious."

Although the principal had said young children were "too sensitive" to view the project, it sounded to me like some adults were the problem. Children can see through adult disingenuousness.

Hollywood used to love to do religious movies because they appealed to large audiences. Today, if it does any at all, the goal is to ridicule people who believe in a power outside themselves. They would never think of demeaning Muslims, but with Christians it is always open season.

Example. Universal released a picture titled *The Last Temptation of Christ*. The studio issued a statement that the film will not "defame" the One who many worship as Savior.

An excerpt from a working script revealed the lie: "Jesus and Mary Magdalene make love on blankets spread over straw. He kisses her breasts, her lips.

"Magdalene: 'I feel like I've just been born. That this is the first day of my life.'

"The Jesus character: 'I never knew the world was so beautiful. I was blind. I didn't know that the body was so holy. . . .'"

It goes on, but you get the idea. No wonder film attendance and Academy Award TV ratings have declined.

A story published by the *Washington Post* (back when it practiced real journalism) disclosed between 1972 and the middle of 1974, DC General Hospital's Obstetrics and Gynecology Department sold the bodies and organs of aborted babies for $75 each to a laboratory in suburban Maryland. The money they received from the lab went to such things as department equipment, a TV set, and soft drinks and cookies for visiting professors.

In a column about polls showing Bush would roundly defeat Dukakis in the forthcoming election, I questioned whether Bush would use the power of the presidency to advance a conservative agenda and what that agenda would look like.

I quote then-British Prime Minister Margaret Thatcher, who said after her third election victory: "Just why did we win? I think it is because we knew what we stood for, we said what we stood for. And we stuck by what we stood for."

Republicans and conservatives, take note.

George H. W. Bush won the election by a landslide, garnering more than four hundred electoral votes and most states.

Many—especially conservatives—believed it should look like a third Reagan term. As usual, the major media, which supported Michael Dukakis, tried to downplay Bush's victory. A *USA Today* editorial noted: "Bush must pursue a realistic agenda." They never say that when a Democrat wins.

Bush named New York Congressman Jack Kemp as Department of Housing and Urban Development (HUD) secretary. Kemp had more credibility in minority communities, not only because of his professional football history when he played with and against many black players, but because he seemed to genuinely care for poor people. He often said that Democrats measure success by how many people are on welfare, while Republicans measure success by how many people are freed from welfare.

Back in Hong Kong, I wrote about all the promises the communist Chinese government made to maintain this unique city's freedom of speech and press. Hong Kong had been a British territory for decades. The British acted as if they could trust Beijing's promises, probably because they wanted to. Self-deception is nothing new.

If they believed history and even contemporary examples, they would have known that communists lie.

The Bush administration announced a "war on drugs." Acknowledging the obvious, Attorney General Richard Thornburgh said only the restoration of "values" in America will break the siege of American cities. So why is the government launching a war on drugs? Better a "war" to restore values.

Actually, it's the old supply-and-demand theory. As long as there is a demand for drugs, there will always be a supply.

One of numerous columns about Israel and its Middle East neighbors repeated an often-made point that at the center of the conflict between Israel and the Palestinians is a theological worldview. Israel believes it has a religious as well as a natural right to its ancient land. Islamists believe Allah wants them to take over all the land and kill Jews in the process. Not understanding this religious motivation, especially by Islamists, since Israelis simply want to live at peace with their neighbors, means the pressure will always be on Israel to "do more" than it has done.

The Islamists ought to be doing less—less terrorism, less killing generally, and less killing of Jews specifically. This moral equivalency has infected American policy for decades and is a major reason why the conflict continues.

Flag burning as a form of protest became a big issue. The Left argued that conservatives have raised the American flag to a level of idolatry, while conservatives argued that the Left disrespected the flag and what it stands for.

The Supreme Court would later side with the Left.

That the media are heavily weighted with liberals is beyond dispute. Robert Lichter, who headed the Center for Media and Public Affairs in Washington, conducted a survey of graduate students at the prestigious Columbia University Journalism School. Asked their preferences in the 1972 election, 91 percent preferred Democrat George McGovern while only 9 percent favored Richard Nixon. Most of their heroes were liberals and some even communists.

Ninety-six percent of them favored abortion and only 18 percent said homosexual practice is wrong.

ABC News broadcast a program called *Black in White America*. It is amazing how often the same arguments are repeatedly made.

This time, the network had someone on who said something reasonable and true. Kristine Bailey, who ran her public relations firm in Los Angeles, wanted a reformation in black churches and a return to the roots from which sprang the power they once had.

"You can only go on blaming other people for your lot, then you've got to take some responsibility yourself," said Bailey. "The number of gang members is nowhere near the number of churchgoers."

That is wisdom that needs to be heard in contemporary America.

I laughed at a comment made by Justice Thurgood Marshall. At a meeting of federal judges, Marshall said his colleagues on the Supreme Court had gone beyond the boundaries of legal disputes to reach "broad and wholly unnecessary" conclusions.

Robert Bork got some revenge for the way he was treated during his Senate confirmation hearings by writing a book titled *The Tempting of America: The Political Seduction of the Law*. Bork laid blame for the decline of the legal establishment at the feet of politically influenced jurists.

The biggest news of the year was the fall of the Berlin Wall on November 9, as regimes allied with the Soviet Union collapsed like dominoes. I was in Berlin shortly after the crumbling had started, and I carved a piece of the wall and put it in a plastic box to save as a historic memento.

In a Christmas column, I noted that God, having seen our desperation and inability to achieve our highest aspirations, directly intervened by sending the "Prince of Peace," and that through Him, we might have peace with God and—only then—peace with each other.

1990

The Year of Heading into Peace and Prosperity

The Soviet Union falls—or was pushed or collapsed under its own weight. The eighty-year Cold War is over.

Sadly, it is not the end of communism, or the inexplicable devotion to the failed system and its evil twin socialism by so many, especially on the American left.

The rise of the Internet ushers in a new era of communication, business, and entertainment.

Nelson Mandela is released from prison, and the world celebrates.

President Bush nominates David Souter for the Supreme Court after being assured by his chief of staff, John Sununu, that he would be OK on the abortion question. After his confirmation, Souter ran to the Left and was anything but OK on the issue.

Mikhail Gorbachev "wins" the Nobel Peace Prize for presiding over the collapse of the Soviet Union. Like the Pulitzer Prize, the Nobel has lost all meaning. They once gave it to Palestinian terrorist leader Yasser Arafat.

Margaret Thatcher steps down as prime minister of Great Britain, forced out by low-testosterone men in her party who apparently felt she made them look weak—which she did, because they are. Thatcher was the most consequential prime minister since Winston Churchill.

CAL'S TAKE

"Government has a legitimate function, but the private sector has one too, and it is superior. In other words, people are better than institutions."

A debate raged over whether military women should be assigned to combat roles. Eventually they were. The debate continues over whether they should also be subject to the draft if that practice is ever declared necessary.

When Washington, DC, Mayor Marion Barry was caught in an FBI sting smoking crack cocaine with a woman in a hotel, NAACP leader Benjamin Hooks blamed racism and claimed it was part of a conspiracy to drive black politicians from office. Given the large number of black Americans now serving with distinction in public office all over the country, that claim rang hollow. Still does.

Barry's wife, Effi, seemed to rationalize her husband's extramarital affairs and those of certain other politicians when she said, "This kind of involvement is a necessary nuisance that the wife of a power figure has to deal with." I recall *Tonight Show* host Jay Leno saying that if he behaved as Barry and Bill Clinton did, "I would be out on the sidewalk with my suitcase."

Black leaders, including some black clergymen, defended the behavior of the corrupt Barry, who was set to go on trial on charges of drug use and perjury. His defense was that "many others are doing what he did, so why pick on him?" Yes, but "many others" are not the mayor of America's capital city, who should be expected to set a good example.

Andy Rooney, the popular commentator for CBS's long-running *60 Minutes* program, was suspended for ninety days because of alleged remarks he made (which he denied) to a young interviewer, who he claimed didn't take notes. The remarks were allegedly about blacks and homosexuals, two "classes" protected by the media. But when ratings for the show declined, Rooney was hastily brought back on the air, saying he had "learned a lot." So did I. Ratings and corporate profits trump just about everything else.

Individual artists and music groups campaigned to wrap themselves in the First Amendment and defended taxpayer funding of their work, even though many called it salacious and, in some cases, smutty and pornographic. One of them was a band called 2 Live Crew whose "lyrics" would have gotten their mouths washed out with soap by my—and probably their—grandmothers.

There was considerable lobbying in state capitals and in Washington that opposed placing warning labels on albums containing anti-social and explicit language. The "artists" claimed it could lead to censorship of all artistic expression.

It was a silly argument, akin to saying that placing limits on how fast cars can go means the government might someday forbid us from driving at all. What happened to "the right to know"?

I wrote of China's crackdown on protests following the 1989 uprising in Tiananmen Square, in which untold thousands were killed at the hands of their government. Fang

Lizhi, the brilliant astrophysicist I had interviewed the previous year in Beijing (he was popular among the young demonstrators), was holed up with his wife at the United States embassy. Diplomacy by President Bush eventually led to his release and a teaching position in the United States.

Richard Harwood, the ombudsman for the *Washington Post*, admitted the obvious when he said his newspaper is "pro-choice" in its editorials and news coverage. But then the paper and other media claim not to be "biased." They say it with a straight face.

I visited the Berlin Wall and noted that communists don't make many things well, but they were craftsmen when it came to walls to keep people in bondage. What a thrill it was to see workers tear away at this symbol of oppression: "Where guards once paced, ready to shoot anyone who tried to escape from East to West, strollers now push baby carriages and walk arm-in-arm as if this were a park in any city. On the Eastern side, vendors hawk bratwurst and drinks with all the practiced expertise of a veteran hot dog man at the ballpark."

Those who died trying to escape would have rejoiced to see this day and the many that followed.

President Bush ordered the Department of Justice to conduct a study on "hate crimes" committed in the United States. He said his goal was to eliminate prejudice. He might as well have tried to eradicate original sin. Why does government always assign such powers to itself? Putting too much faith in government is a false religion that cannot deliver on its promises.

The governor of Michigan, James Blanchard, announced that the state will not build any more prisons after 1992 when a current $900 million, twenty-seven-prison construction project was to be completed. The reason? No room and too costly. So, nonviolent, non-dangerous offenders will be treated in local punishment programs. Good idea.

In a rare victory for religious freedom, the Supreme Court, by an 8–1 vote, upheld the 1984 Federal Equal Access Act. Justices said a public school cannot bar voluntary prayer groups from meeting on school property when virtually every other group that holds secular gatherings is free to do so.

President Bush broke his promise to "read my lips, no new taxes" by agreeing with House Democrats on a tax hike. It doomed his reelection prospects as the Democrats failed to live up to their promise to cut spending. Surprise! That promise was as good as Dracula pledging not to drink more blood.

On a visit to Bermuda, I interviewed Premier John Swan. I called him "a leader who happens to be black" and recorded his distaste for American black leaders like Jesse Jackson and Al Sharpton, who talk about helping their fellow blacks but do little for them. Swan was doing much to help the entire population of his island nation, black and white. Swan's message? Hard work, self-reliance, and taking personal responsibility for one's actions. Why does he get it, and the so-called "black leadership" in America doesn't?

A media survey by *Times Mirror* (then owner of the *Los Angeles Times*) asked why readers and viewers have declined, especially among those eighteen to twenty-nine years old? The 151-page document was titled *The American Media: Who Reads, Who Watches, Who Listens, Who Cares?* What interested me about the survey was that these media institutions never blame themselves for their mostly one-sided (that is, liberal) coverage; they blame the consumers, or in this case, non-consumers. This attitude has contributed not only to the decline of the consumption of mainstream media but also in the public's trust. It is the only business that doesn't care what people think, and so it is paying a price in diminished circulation, fewer ads, and lower TV ratings.

As language became coarser on broadcast television, I wrote that I had "filed for divorce" after forty years of "marriage" to what was mostly decent entertainment. Only a few examples: In a CBS program called *Uncle Buck*, a six-year-old girl said to an adult, "You suck." On ABC, a woman in the show *Married People* told her husband, "You're a son of a bitch, but I love you." Jeff Sagansky, who headed the entertainment division for CBS, believed kids talk like this "all over America" and he wanted to do shows based on "that reality." He billed *Uncle Buck* as a "family show." What kind of family would allow and does he allow his own young kids to watch this stuff?

An NBC program featured a beautiful teacher and young male students who express their sexual attraction to her. It was called *Hull High*. Executive producer Gil Grant said of the sexual innuendo between students and the teacher: "It's a kind of kid's fantasy, a boy's fantasy."

If people want to find a cause-and-effect relationship between entertainment and the consequences of unmarried and extramarital sex, they need look no further than programs like this.

The Centers for Disease Control and Prevention would become highly controversial twenty years later, but this year it spent more than $600,000 to underwrite a program for homosexuals called "Black and White Men Together." The Washington, DC-based *Blade*, a gay newspaper, called the program "hot, horny, and healthy" workshops that feature "condom races" in which participants see how quickly they can fit a condom over a dildo. The stated purpose was to prevent the spread of AIDS among minority men. Your tax dollars at work.

Lee Atwater, chairman of the Republican National Committee and one of the toughest fighters in politics, shocked Washington and the entire political world when he announced: "I have found Jesus Christ. It's that simple . . . and I'm glad I found him while there's still time." Atwater had been diagnosed with terminal brain cancer and would die several months later. He demonstrated the difference faith had made in his life by writing to old political enemies to apologize for his behavior toward them. How often people wait for a tragedy to occur before they consider what truly matters, but better late than never.

Shades of things to come: The NFL Commissioner, Paul Tagliabue, threatened to move the 1993 Super Bowl from Arizona if the state failed to pass a measure declaring a holiday in memory of Martin Luther King Jr., even though the national holiday remains in force. I called his statement "unsportsmanlike conduct." In subsequent years other professional sports would begin reflecting political points of view to their detriment that predictably resulted in a diminished number of fans attending games and low TV ratings.

President Bush issued a list of "Thirteen Points" in an attempt to convince voters he was not "going wobbly," as Thatcher once warned him not to do. Among them was his explanation as to why American forces were in the Persian Gulf to topple Saddam Hussein over his occupation of Kuwait: "We are (there) because the world must not and cannot

reward aggression." His son would make a similar decision following September 11, 2001, after sending troops to
Afghanistan—a war that ended with far different results.

Violent deaths in major cities were setting records. They
still are. All politicians can do is call for more "gun control,"
but lack of self-control is the problem. As the Proverb says,
"When people do not accept divine guidance, they run wild.
But whoever obeys the law is joyful" (Proverbs 29:18 NLT).

The *Philadelphia Inquirer* ended the year with an editorial
saying a good way to fight poverty would be to pay black
welfare recipients to try a new contraceptive device. The goal
presumably would be, as Ebenezer Scrooge might have put
it, to reduce the surplus welfare population. After an outcry
from its black employees, The *Inquirer* published another editorial apologizing for the earlier one. Honestly, if you can't
trust liberal newspapers, who can you trust?

1991

The Year of the Gulf War and Rodney King

The USSR officially dissolves, though not the threats posed by the subsequent president and former KGB agent, Vladimir Putin.

President Bush orders Operation Desert Storm to rid Kuwait of occupying Saddam Hussein troops.

Rodney King is beaten by Los Angeles police officers, sparking riots and ushering in an era of cell phone video recording of police behavior.

More than two hundred thousand people attend a parade in Washington to celebrate the return of eighty-eight hundred soldiers from the Persian Gulf War.

Disney releases *Beauty and the Beast*, the first animated film nominated for Best Picture.

The Big Bang Theory is debunked by the Infrared Astronomical Satellite, which found the universe is full of superstructures and companion super voids that appear far too vast to have formed since the Big Bang. They might have consulted Genesis 1, saving time and trouble.

Vice President Dan Quayle, one of the most unfairly mocked and reviled VPs in American history, is assured of a spot on the 1992 Republican ticket.

The New York State Department of Health issues guidelines that say health care workers infected with AIDS do not have to tell their patients. Another instance in which politics trumps sound medical practice.

The term "political correctness" gains cache to describe censorship from the Left and the imposition of speech codes and historical revisionism.

CAL'S TAKE

"The brutality of communism was quickly swept under history's rug, in large part because so many on the left had embraced it as the solution to humankind's problems."

The "peace movement" returned with retreads like Ramsey Clark and Daniel Ellsberg leading opposition to the Persian Gulf War. Polls showed overwhelming support for President Bush's actions.

ABC's *Good Morning America* asked viewers: "Is the news media doing a responsible and fair job of covering the Gulf War?" To their surprise—but not mine—83 percent of the 62,180 who responded said no. But they never change because most people in media don't care what the public thinks.

What were the "lessons" that should be learned from the Persian Gulf War? First, the necessity of having a president who clearly articulates goals and sets about sharing them with the American people. Second is the value of having international support. Third is having a battle plan. Fourth is handling the media, which during a Republican administration can be counted on to oppose just about everything the president wants to do. Bush did all four of these well and had the overwhelming support of the public as a result.

I wrote that Bush should take advantage of his high popularity from the war victory and immediately focus on domestic issues, starting with government spending. He didn't. With the exception of his nomination of Clarence Thomas to the Supreme Court, his domestic record was thin. It is mostly his broken promise not to raise taxes, along with the media's hysterical opposition, that sank his presidency.

Liberal churches continued to embrace the "spirit of the age" and raced to keep up with secular progressives by ordaining and marrying homosexuals.

Lee Atwater died and the obituary writers could not grasp his conversion story. I wrote that the media can handle the "conversion" of someone from one party to the other, but not the conversion to One not of this world. They should spend more time in church.

President Bush announced he favored "school choice," but it went nowhere in Congress—though now it has caught fire in many states—mostly because of teachers' unions and the money they give to Democrats.

A Minnesota law prohibited "cross-racial adoptions" and so a county judge ordered a white couple to give up a twenty-one-month-old black girl because the adoption violated the state's Minority Preservation Act. The judge justified her ruling—and the law—by saying it was meant to correct "substantial problems arising out of the realities that Minnesota is more than 90 percent white in its racial makeup." As Forrest Gump's mama said, "Stupid is as stupid does."

Mikhail Gorbachev made the ridiculous claim that, without American economic aid, Russia might return to the repression of the Stalin era. I had to hand it to him for his chutzpah, though he might have considered capitalism.

Thurgood Marshall retired from the Supreme Court, setting off what has become the modern battle to dominate the institution that the Founders believed would be the least powerful branch of government. Were they ever wrong. I interviewed Reagan's attorney general, Edwin Meese, who told me: "We are moving forward into a period of stability and predictability, not wide sweeps based on what a few think the law should be." If only.

Bush nominated Clarence Thomas for the Supreme Court, setting off another period of instability and unpredictability as the Left went insane trying to stop him. In the most memorable line during his confirmation hearing, Thomas accused the all-white Senate Judiciary Committee (including Chairman Joe Biden) of conducting "a high-tech lynching."

Writing about the premiere of the film *Boyz n the Hood*, I noted it was one in a series of black exploitation films, full of sex, drugs, violence, and profanity. The opening "was accompanied in a dozen cities by gunfire and violence that left one man dead and more than twenty wounded."

A group of liberal Republicans claimed being pro-life harmed the party's electoral prospects. Just the opposite.

There was a debate about "family values" on ABC's *Good Morning America*. One guest said marriage should be reserved for people of "different sexes." The other guest said such a definition would unfairly exclude people. I wrote that the

debate illustrates what is wrong with America: "the aban-
donment of an objective standard for truth and the process
by which it might be discovered." Predictably, things have
only gotten worse.

The issues of taxing and spending continued to be debated. New York Governor Mario Cuomo claimed the state
was "broke" despite taxes and fees on everything from income to hotel rooms, newspapers, and restaurants. As usual,
Democrats in Congress wanted to raise federal taxes, but not
cut spending, wanting to placate interest groups in a kind
of vote-buying scheme. Nothing has changed, and the debt
grows and grows with interest exceeding the GDP of many
countries.

As the Soviet Union began its decline to "the ash heap of
history" (as Ronald Reagan predicted), I wrote that communism should not be allowed to slip into history without being
held accountable for its murderous record. I called it "one of
the most wretched plagues ever visited on the planet." Untold millions—perhaps tens of millions—died under the Soviet regime.

Singapore banned the latest album from Guns N' Roses
for its profanities and vulgarities. Responding to the sale of
four million copies in the United States and other countries,
record label president David Geffen gave us a quote for the
ages: "When you give the people what they want they'll show
up in droves." I called it a fine epitaph for a generation that
places no limits on anything.

Margaret Thatcher, the former British prime minister,
spoke at a Heritage Foundation dinner in Washington that
I attended. She called for a rebirth of conservatism and said,
"The practical case for democracy and capitalism is proven

almost beyond dispute." One of my favorite quotes from her: "The problem with Socialism is that you soon run out of other people's money."

The House of Representatives bank was closed after major revelations about members who bounced checks and failed to pay for their meals at the House restaurant. The restaurant bill alone was $300,000. When asked whether he had bounced any checks, Rep. Dan Rostenkowski (D-Ill), who chaired the House's tax-writing committee, responded: "None of your damned business." It is precisely our business because they are supposed to be working for us, not themselves, but his response is indicative of the attitude of too many in Congress.

Western state Republicans met in Hawaii and predicted a White House win next year, along with the strong possibility of regaining majorities in the Senate and the House. Optimism doesn't always triumph over reality as we were about to see.

Senator Edward Kennedy (D-MA) delivered a remarkable speech at the Harvard school named after his brother, Jack. In a rare transparent moment he said, "I am painfully aware that the criticism directed at me in recent months involves far more than honest disagreements with my positions, or the usual criticism from the far right. It also involves the disappointment of friends and many others who rely on me to fight the good fight." Kennedy said he recognized "the faults in my private life. I realize I alone am responsible for them, and I am the one who must confront them." My column was about the difference between sorrow and true repentance. I came to love and pray for him.

Chris Wallace, then with ABC News and later with Fox and later still with CNN streaming service, did a propaganda hit on pregnancy help centers, challenging their credibility and the work of their mostly volunteer and meagerly funded facilities, which are dwarfed by independent abortion clinics that rake in gobs of money because they charge for their grisly "services." Wallace claimed the help centers used "psychological manipulation" and "scare tactics" to persuade women not to abort their children. It is a lie, but being in the major media means never having to admit that you are lying.

Former basketball great Wilt Chamberlain claimed he had slept with twenty thousand women. Not long after, Earvin "Magic" Johnson disclosed he had contracted AIDS, presumably from engaging in behavior similar to that of Chamberlain. There is a lesson there.

The following is not a joke: Los Angeles City Councilman Zev Yaroslavsky called for an investigation into whether the conservative Christian beliefs of Assistant Police Chief Robert L. Vernon interfered with his ability "to perform official duties fairly and without bias." No one asks such a question of atheists.

Department of Housing and Urban Development Secretary Jack Kemp testified before a congressional committee to say that the war on poverty is being lost because "the old ways simply don't work" and still cost plenty of money but help fewer people emerge from dependency.

I ended the year with a column about the death of journalist Harry Reasoner and a surprising commentary he wrote about Christmas and God becoming a man. It was amazing for someone at his level of journalism to write with such honesty on the subject.

1992

The Year of the Election and Bible Misquotes

An election year during which George H. W. Bush and the Republicans blow an opportunity to extend their political winning streak. Voters traded a decent, faithful-to-his-wife man (Bush) for a philandering and lying politician and his wife (Bill and Hillary Clinton). More on that in a moment.

New Hollywood releases, such as *Beauty and the Beast*, draw record crowds and profits, yet the film industry also pollutes culture with more R-rated and NC-17 movies with fewer in the audience.

The first reports about Bill Clinton's alleged affairs with women begin to surface in the national media. I initially give him the benefit of the doubt, but subsequent evidence shows he did not deserve it.

CAL'S TAKE

"One of the reasons people hate politics is that truth is rarely a politician's objective. Election and power are."

Bill and Hillary appeared on *60 Minutes* to deny charges of his extramarital affairs. They lied, as we would later learn. This defender of "women's rights" and his enabling wife had no problem, along with the likes of political operative James Carville, smearing his female accusers. Carville famously said: "Drag a hundred-dollar bill through a trailer park, you never know what you'll find."

Bill Clinton tried to explain that he did not "avoid" the military draft in the 1960s, but did "make himself available" for the draft after writing a letter to his draft board in opposition to the Vietnam War. It would be a familiar pattern of deception and disingenuousness for the future president.

Pat Buchanan won the New Hampshire presidential primary, defeating by a slim margin the ultimate nominee, Bob Dole. Buchanan's victory caused panic within the Bush White House and among establishment Republicans.

The chairman of the National Endowment for the Arts, John Frohnmayer, was fired after the NEA was criticized for funding homoerotic "art" that included depictions of Jesus as gay and a $637,000 grant to the makers of a film titled *"Jesus Christ Condom."*

President Bush tried to blunt Pat Buchanan's candidacy by apologizing three times in fewer than twelve hours for breaking his "read my lips, no new taxes" pledge. He said, "I wish I had it to do over." Unfortunately for him, the damage was done. Bill Clinton and congressional Democrats would subsequently raise taxes, and Clinton would tell a Houston audience he may have raised taxes "too much."

In a debate over taxpayer funding of PBS, Senator John McCain (R-AZ) charged the Corporation for Public Broadcasting (PBS's parent) for "blatant efforts" to air clearly biased programming in violation of its charter. Democrats countered that McCain was trying to kill Big Bird. McCain cited plenty of evidence to little avail. As Reagan used to say, the only proof of eternal life in Washington is a government program.

Strobe Talbott, editor of *Time* magazine, as reported by the *Wall Street Journal*, lobbied his journalistic colleagues about Clinton's "passionate opposition to the Vietnam War," and that's why he sought to evade the draft, if in fact he did evade the draft. Talbott would later work in the Clinton administration. I wrote about the "revolving door" between government and journalism that helped diminish the credibility of journalism. It is difficult to lower any further the credibility of government.

The president "took my advice" and started hammering congressional Democrats for their ethics scandals and passing a tax increase bill. Even the *New York Times* editorial page took note, rejecting the Democrats' claim that their bill would grant tax relief to middle class families. We hear this every four years and people still believe it.

I wrote a column called "Anti-Semitism: The Disease That Will Not Die." It referenced the presidential candidacy of David Duke and the increasing anti-Jewish rhetoric in the culture. One example was the rock music industry and its increased level of anti-Semitic lyrics. In a "song," rapper Ice Cube advised his former group, N.W.A., to put a bullet in the temple of its Jewish manager because you just can't achieve your goals "with a white Jew telling you what to do." Unfortunately, this was not an isolated incident. So much for the slander that Jews control all media.

Hillary Clinton said if we elect Bill, we also get her. A two-for-one deal. The two are the definition of the word "co-dependent" and have used each other to gain political power and influence.

Texas billionaire Ross Perot announced he was running for president and wound up splitting the Republican vote, electing Bill Clinton in the fall.

I argued that if pro-choicers were honest (which they are not), they would agree to fully disclose abortion alternatives to pregnant women, including sonograms. We have truth-in-labeling and truth-in-lending laws. Why not have "truth" about what's in the womb?

On the seventh day of jury deliberations, a Los Angeles jury acquitted four police officers of assault and three of the four of using excessive force on Rodney King. Five days of rioting followed. President Bush appeared on television to say the violence is "not about civil rights" or "the great issues of equality," but "the brutality of the mob, pure and simple." King was no saint. In March 1991, King—who was on parole for robbery—led police on a high-speed chase through Los Angeles. He was charged with driving under the influence. Reverend E. V. Hill, pastor of Mt. Zion Church in South Central Los Angeles, told me he doesn't believe the rioters were reacting to the jury verdict so much as they were "filling their pantries and living rooms and replacing old furniture. Every drugstore was targeted professionally because drugs are there. Jewelry stores, too." Hill, who is black, disapproved of the jury verdict, but said the law-abiding protested in church by praying, singing, and speaking.

Bill Clinton—probably after polling—stood up to Jesse Jackson and soul singer Sister Soulja, who said in an interview that black people should take a week off from killing other black people and start killing whites. She later predictably claimed her remarks "were taken out of context" and slammed Clinton for lacking integrity. She was right about Clinton, but what is the context for favoring the killing of white people?

A unanimous Supreme Court struck down "hate crime" laws in many states and cities. The laws had imposed special penalties on people who engaged in speech or activities offensive to certain racial, gender, ethnic, or "sexual orientation" groups.

I bemoaned the creation of the Lesbian and Gay Journalists Association, not because of their "orientation," but because it is just one more in a series of associations of journalists whose members are limited by race, ethnicity, and now sexual behavior. Why, I wondered, can't people just be journalists and practice traditional journalism, starting with the conveying of unadulterated truth to the public?

The Democrat Party convention met in New York City and nominated Bill Clinton and Al Gore for president and vice president. The media consistently labeled Clinton and Gore "moderates," without defining the term.

Democrats tried to win some religious voters from the Republican Party by quoting (often misquoting) Scripture and spinning it to justify government spending and programs. I commented: "Democrats have found God! From Jesse Jackson, who called the Virgin Mary a 'single mother' (perhaps because Jackson is not acquainted with the Father), to Bill Clinton and Al Gore, Democrats are wrapping themselves in the Bible and religious themes." Gore quoted the Bible as saying: "Our eyes have not seen, nor our ears heard, nor our minds imagined, what we can build." The only verse that comes close to that is 1 Corinthians 1:29: "But as it is written, eye has not seen, nor ear heard, neither have entered into the heart of man, the things which God has prepared for those that love Him." Big difference. Gore took it one step further when he said: "In the words of the Bible, 'Do not lose heart.

This nation will be renewed.'" No such verse exists. Perhaps Gore had come down with a case of "global warming." I think I was the only person in the mostly secular media to point out these misquotations and abuses of Scripture.

Republicans held their national convention in Houston. Barbara Bush, long suspected of being "pro-choice," came out four days before the convention and said such matters as abortion, along with homosexuality, should be private concerns and government should stay out of them. Her statement did not help her husband's campaign. Dan Quayle and his wife delivered excellent speeches containing issues that Republicans and conservatives cared about. Marilyn Quayle even noted that men and women are "different." Imagine that! She said women make "different sacrifices and we get different rewards."

I coined a new term for politicians who invoke the name of God but on whom He seems to have little to no influence. Instead of "godless," I suggested calling them "less-God." A Gallup Poll found only 10 percent of Americans have "transforming faith," meaning it makes a discernible difference in their lives. That finding is a major reason so many have such difficulty advancing laws that reflect their beliefs.

The Federal Communications Commission said ads by pro-life groups depicting aborted babies do not fall under the agency's definition of "indecent." I wrote that pictures carry a powerful message for good or evil, and that seeing what the killing of an unborn child looks like can cause many abortion-minded women to re-think their position.

The DC public school system, one of the worst in the country, approved the distribution of free condoms to any student who wanted them. It also decided parents neither have to give permission nor need to be notified. They should have focused more on what goes into kids' brains, as test scores are among the lowest in the nation.

Lyndon Johnson used to say his grandfather died at the Alamo. He later told author Doris Kearns Goodwin that his grandfather really died at the Battle of San Jacinto during the fight for Texas Independence from Mexico, but he called it the Alamo because more people had heard of it. The truth was that Johnson's grandfather died in neither battle. He died in bed. Shades to come with a similar habit of lies told by Joe Biden.

Christopher Columbus was convicted as a marauding invader at a mock trial in a San Francisco high school. Yes, they were just as crazy then as they are now. In a sense, the kids won because years later Columbus Day would be replaced with Indigenous Peoples' Day.

An October presidential debate produced no surprise as ABC's Carole Simpson displayed her bias in questioning President Bush, while demonstrating cordiality to Bill Clinton. Typical.

In the final debate before the election, Bush came out swinging. I wonder where this Bush had been and why hadn't he emerged sooner?

In its endorsement of Clinton for president, a *New York Times* editorial seemed contradictory: "(Clinton) has, when pressed, shown a discomfiting tendency to blur truthful clarity." I said this was a discomfiting way of saying he doesn't tell the truth. It didn't matter to the newspaper when the choice was between a Republican and Democrat. They would endorse Satan if he had a "D" after his name.

Clinton won the election, and I wrote that the Reagan revolution was over.

The media suddenly discovered a healthy economy, which they had rejected before the election. Such hypocrisy.

Michael Kinsley wrote a column for the *New Republic*, in which he admitted the press was mostly liberal (who knew?), but added, "So what?" He then condescendingly said if conservatives were intelligent (like he was, presumably) they, too, would be liberals.

Following a Supreme Court ruling, which banned references to God at public school commencements, the superintendent of public schools in Frederick County, Virginia, issued a memorandum instructing teachers to no longer refer to "Christmas," but instead call the season "winter holiday." I noted how the Soviet Union had also used a similar term to replace "Christmas."

Bill Clinton's true beliefs were revealed in his naming of Dr. Johnnetta B. Cole to head one of his "cluster groups" responsible for recommending Cabinet appointments. Cole, I noted, was a radical activist with strong ties to revolutionary groups, the Cuban government and assorted domestic and international communists working to spread revolutionary principles throughout the world.

My Christmas column for the year recalled my first Christmas in December 1942, when I was three weeks old. I found an ad in *Life* magazine that was directed at the sons of fathers away in World War II. That included my Dad and four of his brothers. The ad said my father had been "loaned to America. The war has taken him away from us, but his love warms our family hearth."

Beautiful!

1993

The Year of Bill Clinton, the Branch Davidians, and Black Hawk Down

Bill Clinton is sworn in as the forty-second president of the United States.

General Motors Corporation sues NBC, after *Dateline NBC* allegedly rigged two crashes showing that some GM pickups can easily catch fire if hit in certain places. NBC settles the lawsuit the following day.

In New York City, a van bomb parked below the North Tower of the World Trade Center explodes, killing six and injuring more than one thousand.

A fifty-one-day stand-off at the Branch Davidian compound near Waco, Texas, ends with a fire that kills seventy-six people, including David Koresh. Attorney General Janet Reno comes under heavy criticism for ordering an assault on the compound and not "waiting out" Koresh and his followers.

An executive order requires the United States Air Force to allow women to fly war planes.

Bill Clinton announces his "Don't ask, don't tell" policy regarding homosexuals serving in the American military.

Deputy White House Counsel Vince Foster dies by suicide in Virginia. Conspiracy nuts go wild.

A federal judge sentences LAPD officers Stacey Koon and Laurence Powell to thirty months in prison for violating motorist Rodney King's civil rights.

Ruth Bader Ginsburg is sworn in as an associate justice on the Supreme Court.

Palestine Liberation Organization (PLO) leader Yasser Arafat and Israeli Prime Minister Yitzhak Rabin shake hands in Washington, DC, after signing a peace accord. I am there and say it wouldn't last.

The North American Free Trade Agreement (NAFTA) passes the legislative houses in the United States, Canada and Mexico.

President Clinton signs the Brady Handgun Violence Prevention Act into law, requiring purchasers of handguns to pass a background check.

CAL'S TAKE

"One mark of a deteriorating society is when people cannot discern between truth and lies. Another is that they don't care and will believe whatever their itching ears want to hear."

A group of forty pro-life leaders wrote Billy Graham, asking him not to pray at the Clinton–Gore inauguration for fear of seeming to endorse their pro-abortion policies. I disagreed and Graham went ahead.

Early on, Clinton said he wanted to be known as "the ethics president." That would not last long, as his governorship in Arkansas proved.

Clinton promised to eliminate one hundred thousand federal jobs as one way to reduce the size of the budget. Like many promises by politicians, it never happened, and government continued to grow unrestrained.

In one of the most bigoted and stereotypical assaults on Christians, *Washington Post* writer Michael Weisskopf called them "largely poor, uneducated, and easy to command." After being inundated with complaints, the *Post* ran a "correction," saying there was no "factual basis" for Weisskopf's claim. Later, *Post* ombudsman (person?) Joanne Byrd tried to explain Weisskopf's comment, saying the media don't know many of "these people." I reacted by saying some were probably living in her neighborhood, running down property values! Imagine if she had said something similar about virtually any other group. Such a view contributes to the belief that most of the media are biased against conservatives and Christians.

The Dutch government approved a measure allowing doctors to kill their patients if they wanted help dying. Supposedly the law contained strict conditions, but a line had been crossed. I note that once one category of human life is devalued (as in abortion), it is a short step to threatening other categories (such as euthanasia).

President Clinton promised to increase taxes on "the rich," a familiar Democrat position that continues to resonate. Notice how Democrats never talk about cutting spending. Clinton did propose some spending cuts, but wanted to increase spending elsewhere. I compare this to reducing one's credit card bill by not spending $200 on a favorite item, then dining out at a fancy restaurant and putting $200 on the same card. That used to be called "flim-flam."

In a forerunner to what would become Obamacare a decade later, Bill Clinton turned over his health care policy to Hillary. It went nowhere. Even the press was skeptical and surprisingly critical, denouncing numerous secret meetings on the plan.

An unnamed Republican senator met with President Clinton and afterward said one word described him: "slick." He has long been known as "Slick Willie," and nothing has changed.

Former Secretary of Education William Bennett released a study called "Index of Leading Cultural Indicators." In it, Bennett looked at America's cultural decline, allowing the evidence to speak for itself. He argued real cultural change will not come through Washington, but with a change of attitudes among the people.

Byron White, one of two Supreme Court justices who voted against *Roe v. Wade* in 1973, retired. Clinton, who promised no "litmus test" for a nominee, used one but called it a "right to privacy" test. Same thing when it came to abortion.

I wondered whether a march on Washington by homosexuals and bisexuals in support of same-sex marriage would end it if they got their way, or would there be new demands for tolerance of other forms of behavior and relationships? Future events that included transgenderism, sex change operations paid for with tax dollars for those in the military, and gender identity claims would answer that question.

A female attorney in Milwaukee contributed to "Take Our Daughters to Work Day" (orchestrated by the Ms.

Foundation), telling thirty-six seventh graders that they should not bother to get married because marriage can interfere with their careers (and marriages, she said, usually end anyway). The girls would be better off, she claimed, to remain single and "sleep around all you want."

President Clinton said his ten-point drop in approval ratings (USA Today poll) was because he had to make "tough decisions." No, it was his policies, which were different from his campaign promises. Sound familiar?

The administration reversed the Mexico City Policy, which prohibited federal funding of international organizations that offered abortions as part of their "family planning" programs. Republican presidents would reinstate the policy and Democrats would again eliminate it.

A debate erupted over university speech codes designed to protect especially minority students from "harmful words." This would later expand to "safe zones" at many universities where students could go to avoid listening to speech they disliked, no matter the content. This included "trigger words" that make the snowflakes uncomfortable. So much for free expression.

Judge Robert Bork, who should have been on the Supreme Court, called Ruth Bader Ginsburg, who would soon become a justice, "nutty" because of her view that the Constitution was a "living document" and changes with the times.

Pat Nixon died. I said calling her "Plastic Pat," as her critics sometimes did, was unfair. She lived a life of dignity and grace and dutifully supported her husband, even though she disliked politics. They were married for fifty-three years. Richard Nixon wrote me a nice letter thanking me for the column about Pat. He also attacked the media! At least he was consistent.

In her confirmation hearings to become surgeon general, Dr. Jocelyn Elders said pro-lifers "need to get over their love affair with the fetus." Following her confirmation, Elders condoned the idea of teaching schoolchildren to masturbate as a way of avoiding the spread of the AIDS virus. She also supported free condoms for children. Under enormous pressure, especially from Republicans, Clinton was forced to eventually remove her from office.

ABC launched the first R-rated TV series called *NYPD Blue*. Others would follow with even worse programming.

I interviewed Senator Ted Kennedy about his declared change of direction in life following a remarkably honest speech at the Kennedy School of Government at Harvard. Kennedy gave credit to his wife, Vicki, who he said, "has so immeasurably enhanced my life and has brought joy and happiness and emotional security and stability." He invited me to dine with them at their home in McLean, Virginia, and we became friends, proving that politics does not have to make enemies of fellow Americans. He even attended a party celebrating the twenty-fifth anniversary of my column. Heads snapped.

On a visit to Kennebunkport, Maine, I saw a T-shirt with the likeness of IRS form 1040 stamped on it. It was during the time Clinton campaigned for tax increases. On the shirt it said: "Clinton's simplified 1040 Form—Part 1, Income: How much money did you make last year? Part 2: Send it in." The proprietor told me she had sold so many that she'd lost count.

I attended a gathering in Washington of successful black Americans called Black Expo USA. I wrote a lament that the media coverage so often focused on young black criminals

and black victims of crime. It appeared I was the only journalist who showed up. There was nothing on the evening
news. This, I said, was its own type of racism.

George Tiller, an abortionist in Wichita, was shot and
wounded by a supposedly pro-life fanatic. The incident followed the murder of Florida abortionist David Gunn. I condemned both as violations of pro-life beliefs.

In a "back to what kind of school" column, I noted the average cost of a public education had risen to $5,920 per pu-
pil. Yet, that has not resulted—and still hasn't—in improved
performance and higher test scores. If the amount of money
spent on education were related to achievement, America
would have the best educated kids in the world.

A government study revealed half of adult Americans were
such poor readers and writers that they couldn't perform
such relatively simple tasks as calculating the price difference between two items, or filling out a Social Security form.
I saw a bumper sticker that said, "If you can read this, thank
a teacher," and asked, "Whom do you thank (or blame) if you
can't read it?"

Vice President Al Gore pledged to reduce "waste, fraud,
and abuse" in government, saving taxpayers $108 billion.
It didn't happen and never does because politicians protect
their turf, and to them, spending is fertilizer for that turf.

A USA Today-CNN-Gallup poll revealed the feminist
movement had less effect on American women than the Left
had hoped. More women than men, noted the poll, think
wives should stay home while their husbands work. That
would change, but the poll shocked the Left. I wrote, "For
thirty years, feminists have asserted that women cannot
achieve complete liberation or satisfaction without a career,

an abortion, a divorce and an attitude." The poll revealed otherwise.

Hillary Clinton testified before five congressional committees and appeared on *Larry King Live* to promote her health care ideas. I called it socialism, pure and simple. Fortunately, not even congressional Democrats bought it and it died, to be resurrected later under a new name: Obamacare.

Somali terrorists paraded dead American bodies and a live prisoner before TV cameras following their helicopter crash in Mogadishu. The incident exposed President Clinton's inexperience in foreign policy and a weakness that would come back to haunt us. A film of the affair is titled *Black Hawk Down*.

Following my speech at the University of Michigan, Ann Arbor, a female student told me she disagreed with my view that a society had to be based on certain fixed absolutes if it was to avoid dysfunction and moral chaos. I asked her what she would replace my value system with? She said she was unsure. That prompted the following exchange.

Me: What year are you in and what's your major?

Student: I'm a senior and my major is ethics.

Me: On what do you base your ethics?

Student: I don't know. I'm still trying to figure that out.

If her parents were paying for this type of "education," they should have demanded a refund.

In an ironic turn, President Clinton blamed the press for not giving him the credit he thought he deserved. In an interview with *Rolling Stone*, Clinton said, "I'm sorry if I'm not very good at communicating, but I have not gotten a hell of a lot of help since I've been here." That was demonstrably false, but Clinton was good at playing the victim card.

In a remarkable address for any liberal, TV producer Norman Lear told a National Press Club audience, "At no time in my life (he was seventy-one then) has our culture been so estranged from spiritual values . . . our problems lie beyond the reach of politics alone." I liked Lear and interviewed him for one of my previous books, *Blinded by Might: Why the Religious Right Can't Save America.*

A judge in Wayne County, Michigan, declared that the state law prohibiting assisted suicide was unconstitutional. Judge Richard Kaufman drew a distinction between people who wished to kill themselves because they have what he termed a "low quality of life" and those who have a "higher quality of life." This amounted to the government determining who was fit to live and who was not. Shades of Adolf Hitler and Margaret Sanger.

In a Christmas column I noted that the hope of a Pax Americana—a new American age of peace—following the fall of the Berlin Wall and the liberation of Eastern Europe four years earlier, seemed increasingly remote. Even a *Washington Post* editorial lamented street shootings, drug use, and other signs of cultural collapse: "While the severity of actions ranges from simple cheating at school to pushing drugs, to cold blooded murder . . . the depth of the problem has reached a point where common decency can no longer be described as common. Somewhere, somehow . . . the traditional value system got disconnected for a disturbing number of America's next generation." Even a stopped clock is right twice a day.

1994

The Year of Clinton Scandals and the Contract with America

S kater Nancy Kerrigan is clubbed on the right leg by an assailant, under orders from figure skating rival Tonya Harding's ex-husband. He accepts a plea bargain, admitting to charges of racketeering in exchange for testimony against Harding. She is fined $100,000 and banned from the sport.

The Superhighway Summit held at UCLA is the first conference to discuss the growing World Wide Web. Vice President Al Gore presides (having laid claim to inventing the Internet).

President Bill Clinton and Russian President Boris Yeltsin sign an agreement to stop the preprogrammed aiming of nuclear missiles toward each other's countries and also provide for the dismantling of the nuclear arsenal in Ukraine.

A 6.5–6.7 earthquake rattles Los Angeles, killing fifty-seven people and injuring more than eighty-seven hundred.

Steven Spielberg's Holocaust drama, *Schindler's List*, wins seven Oscars out of twelve nominations, including Best Picture and Best Director.

Kurt Cobain is found dead at his home; the cause is suicide.

Former President Richard Nixon dies in New York. He was eighty-one.

Serial killer John Wayne Gacy is executed for the murder of thirty-three young men and boys.

Jacqueline Kennedy Onassis dies from cancer. She was sixty-four.

Nicole Brown Simpson and her friend Ronald Goldman are murdered outside her condo in Los Angeles. O. J. Simpson flees in a white Ford Bronco, chased by police. In a "trial of the century" broadcast live on TV, O. J. is acquitted.

The Lion King is released. Critics love it and the film earns Walt Disney Pictures $422,783,777 in the United States and $951,583,777 worldwide. It is the highest-grossing film of the year and the highest-grossing animated film of all time.

Jeff Bezos founds Amazon.

Stephen Breyer is sworn in as an associate justice on the Supreme Court.

NBC airs the pilot episode of *Friends*, which becomes a major hit.

The movie production company DreamWorks is founded by Steven Spielberg, Jeffrey Katzenberg, and David Geffen.

Republicans gain control of Congress, and Newt Gingrich becomes Speaker. It is the first time in forty years the Republicans enjoy a majority in both the House and the Senate.

George W. Bush is elected Texas governor.

Ronald Reagan announces he has Alzheimer's disease in a poignant letter to the American people.

CAL'S TAKE

"The high-minded definition of politics is: 'the art or science of government; the art or science concerned with guiding or influencing governmental policy.' It is only when you keep reading in Webster's Ninth New Collegiate Dictionary that you get closer to the truth: 'political activities characterized by artful and often dishonest practices.'"

I interviewed the spokesman for the Egyptian Foreign Ministry in Cairo, Nagil El Ghatrifi, who predicted that talks between Israel and the PLO will succeed in the near future. They did between Israel and Egypt, but not with the PLO—or officially any other Arab-Muslim nation surrounding Israel. Until later when Donald Trump scored a miracle.

Bill Clinton succumbed to pressure and named a special prosecutor to look into his and Hillary's dealings with the defunct Whitewater Development Corporation. I wrote that integrity was the most valuable asset for any president—or any other person for that matter—and that because Clinton had waited so long to name one, denying any wrongdoing along the way, he contributed to a further decline in his integrity quotient.

Mother Teresa delivered one of the finest messages I have ever heard at the National Prayer Breakfast in Washington. With the pro-choice President Clinton and Vice President Al Gore looking mostly at their water glasses, she tied abortion to the growing violence in America's streets. "If we accept that a mother can kill her own child, how can we tell other people not to kill each other? Any country that accepts abortion is not teaching its people to love, but to use any violence to get what they want."

Mother Teresa then appealed directly to abortion-minded women: "I am willing to accept any child who would be aborted and give that child to a married couple who will love the child." She received a standing ovation, but not from the dais.

Assistant Health and Human Services Director Phillip Lee said people who have contracted HIV–AIDS suffer from a "disability" and so should be allowed into the United States from other countries to attend the Gay Games in New York. Public health regulations prohibited anyone with a "communicable disease of public health significance" from entering the country. But when you change the name from disease—spread by sexual contact—to disability, then the regulations don't apply. Those who control the language and labels control the conversation and outcome of the debate.

Six White House and three Department of the Treasury officials received subpoenas to tell what they knew about events related to the Whitewater affair. I wrote, "As the subpoenas rolled in, heads started rolling out the White House gate." White House counsel Bernard Nussbaum got the axe. Even the French chef and an usher were fired, though apparently not for anything related to Whitewater. *Time* magazine White House correspondent Margaret Carlson offered this ludicrous defense on CNN: "Democrats haven't known how to behave in the executive branch because they haven't been there in so many years." Apparently, Carlson thought that ethics, like French cuisine, is an acquired taste. She was not alone among many Clinton defenders in the media.

President Clinton was interviewed by *ABC News* about his "faith." I wrote that he talked about faith the way he spoke about Whitewater and health care, taking a thread of fact and creating a tapestry of obfuscation. Asked about gay rights, Clinton said there was nothing about homosexuality in the Ten Commandments. See what I mean?

Justice Harry Blackmun retired. The author of *Roe v. Wade* said of the decision, which he wrote for the majority, "I still think it was a correct decision. We were deciding a constitutional issue, not a moral one." So, sixty million dead babies (and counting) was not both a constitutional and a moral issue? A fundamental role of government is to preserve life, but the court effectively ruled (and subsequent rulings upheld) that life doesn't begin until a born baby starts to breathe.

Billy Graham defended President Clinton during a speech before newspaper editors in Washington. "None of us is perfect," said Graham, who called for "a wall of prayer" around Clinton. I wrote that Graham—a good friend—should have learned from his too-close association with Richard Nixon. I later found out that his wife, Ruth, told her husband that he should listen to me.

Speaking again about his own religious beliefs, President Clinton told *Christianity Today* magazine that moral issues should change as popular opinion changes. He must have forgotten to consult Scripture on that claim. Clinton was once pro-life, like many other prominent Democrats once were, but flipped when it became politically expedient.

Paula Jones accused President Clinton of sexual harassment when he was governor of Arkansas. Clinton defenders began smearing Jones as they did other women who came forward with claims of inappropriate behavior and, in one case, rape. Feminists were strangely silent.

Clinton nominated Stephen Breyer to the Supreme Court. I wrote that Republicans, unlike Democrats, abandoned

their principles in supporting Breyer, who was clearly in
line—and has proved it—with the *Roe v. Wade* decision. Nominees to the court by Democratic presidents are almost never
disappointed by their rulings.

Asked on CBS's *Face the Nation* to define the Clinton foreign policy doctrine, Vice President Gore delivered gibberish,
saying the world is "complicated" and filled with "unusual
turmoil." I called it "Voodoo Foreign Policy" and a display
of weakness.

Oliver North was nominated by the Virginia Republican
Party as its candidate for governor. This prompted numerous
columns, editorials, and "news" stories slamming North's
Christian faith. The familiar labels—extremist, fundamen-
talist, zealot—were tossed like a salad at North. He lost the
election but maintained his faith.

Seattle Police Chief Norm Stamper participated in uniform in a Lesbian-Gay-Bisexual-Transgender Parade. Yet he
denied officers the right to participate in uniform in a March
for Jesus the day before. As radio talk show host Chris Plante
said, "If the left didn't have double standards, they would
have no standards at all."

I asked a question about government-run health care: If
you don't like the way the postal service handles your mail,
why would you think the government can do a good job taking care of your health?

Forrest Gump, starring Tom Hanks, became a smash hit
with audiences who packed theaters. I wrote about the appeal of the film: "Gump reaches the hearts of many precisely
because he represents nothing of what that generation (Baby
Boomers) claim to stand for, but everything it longed for,
then and now."

Speaking of Clinton's declining credibility, I took advantage of a fortune cookie in a Chinese restaurant to make my point. It said, "A liar is not believed even though he tells the truth." I could not have said it better. Sometimes you find wisdom in the most interesting places.

Time magazine advanced the secular belief that we are the product of our genetic makeup and things once considered bad or immoral are not our fault. The cover story was titled "Infidelity: It May Be In Our Genes." I wonder if Bill Clinton bought several copies?

I wrote that Abraham Lincoln's claim that we had a government of, by, and for the people has morphed into a government "in spite of the people." The crime bill, which passed thanks to "moderate" Republicans voting for it, is just another case of throwing money at social programs that largely don't work (remember midnight basketball that was supposed to keep kids off the streets?).

Congress voted entitlements for its members that were more generous by far than what top executives received at Fortune 500 companies. I tried to make the case for term limits, but in order for that to happen, the people who benefit most from careers in politics would have to vote against their own interests. Not going to happen.

In a searing cover story for the *Atlantic Monthly*, Barbara Dafoe Whitehead wrote that the curriculum known as "comprehensive sex education," mandated in seventeen states, had failed children and society. It neither reduced pregnancies nor slowed the spread of venereal diseases. That's because the curriculum lacked a moral foundation and did not encourage kids to do the right thing. And *that* was because schools can no longer teach there is such a thing as right and wrong, or a standard by which these can be measured.

In a column titled "Defining Humanity Down," I wrote about a federal panel of "experts" (God save us from experts) that had recommended the government's fifteen-year-old ban against all research on human embryos be lifted, because they claimed fertilized eggs did not have the "same moral status as infants and children." I wondered if they thought a viable unborn child was more than a fertilized egg? Probably not.

In an exchange with forty publishers, editors, and reporters for moderate and liberal Baptist publications, Bill Clinton claimed the scriptures were "ambiguous" when it came to abortion. I cited several passages that say otherwise. Clinton told them he prays, but I wondered to whom, considering his view about scriptural "ambiguity"? Maybe he prays "to whom it may concern."

Republican members of Congress and candidates signed a historic Contract with America, listing ten things they promised to do if they won a congressional majority. Democrats freaked out when they realized the impact it had on average voters. The card was small enough to fit in a pocket, wallet, or purse, and millions were distributed to voters.

In what appeared to be an attempt to steal votes from religious conservatives, President Clinton supported the two-parent family as the best deterrent to crime. Who knew?

Republicans won an astounding victory, taking back the House and the Senate by substantial margins. I was astonished at how many exit polls revealed the number of voters who self-identified as conservative. Clinton later said, "The era of big government is over." Sadly, it isn't.

Speaker-to-be Newt Gingrich noted the failures of Lyndon B. Johnson's Great Society programs to achieve their stated goals, including the elimination of poverty. He said they created dependency, a model for wealth redistribution, and counter-cultural values—and it ruined the lives of poor people. I called for him to issue a "sub-contract with America," which would include strengthening American families and restoring a moral foundation.

The United States Postal Service offered this Christmas present to America: No more Madonna and Child Christmas stamps as one of many holiday choices. It also declared it would no longer print any stamps that reflected a particular religion. That would change some years later when Muslims got stamps reflecting some of their holidays. The post office wasn't finished. It also decreed no employee could utter the words "Merry Christmas" or "Happy Hanukkah," even in response to people who initiate those greetings. After a deluge of angry calls and letters, a "clarification" was issued that stated no offense had been intended. The Madonna stamp would be returned and employees were free to greet patrons in the spirit of whatever season they celebrate. "Happy Holidays" became the content-less preference for many.

1995

The Year of Domestic Terrorism and the Unabomber

The World Trade Organization (WTO) is established to replace the General Agreement on Tariffs and Trade (GATT).

Bosnian Serb commanders are charged in the United Nations's International Criminal Tribunal with genocide and crimes against humanity during the wars in the Balkans.

Members of the Aum Shinrikyo religious cult release sarin gas on five subway trains in Tokyo, killing thirteen and injuring 5,510.

American singer Selena is murdered by her fan club president, Yolanda Saldívar.

President Clinton announces restoration of United States–Vietnam relations twenty years after the Vietnam War.

Sony enters the video game market with the release of PlayStation.

The *Washington Post* and the *New York Times* publish the "Unabomber Manifesto."

O. J. Simpson is found not guilty of double murder for the deaths of former wife Nicole Brown Simpson and Ronald Goldman.

Operation Desert Storm officially ends.

CAL'S TAKE

"Politicians have limited power. They can't impose morality on themselves. How can they impose it on the country?"

A survey of thirteen college campuses in the Southeast by the conservative Students for America closely split between conservatives and liberals found 56 percent said right and wrong was a matter of personal choice. Only 38 percent believed moral absolutes existed and were absolute. It showed the deep penetration of relativity and secularism even in what used to be the conservative South.

Newly elected Speaker of the House Newt Gingrich announced he was boycotting the network Sunday shows because their only interest was "trying to start fights" and their programs were devoted to "nit-picking arguments" rather than seeking truth. He was right.

Frank Rich wrote in the *New York Times* why he thought few men showed up to watch the film *Little Women*. His conclusion was based on a CinemaScore survey of audiences. Rich said it demonstrated that men don't like "strong women," you know, like Hillary Clinton. I responded that most men love British Prime Minister Margaret Thatcher. It wasn't about gender but ideology.

Republican Governor George Pataki restored capital punishment in New York State. It would later be reversed and affirmed by subsequent Democrat governors, who were OK with aborting the innocent but wanted to preserve the lives of murderers.

Newt Gingrich appeared on Larry King's CNN show to denounce the press for their poor coverage of his Contract with America. Gingrich said it was "despicable demagoguery" for him to be portrayed as someone who wanted to take lunch away from schoolchildren. But it always works for Democrats and their media companions.

Patsy Thomasson, director of the White House Office of Administration, testified before a Senate committee and admitted that eleven staff members had been enrolled in a special random drug-testing program because of concerns about "recent drug use." That explained a lot.

Thousands of files from the Soviet archives were opened, revealing what many suspected during communism's appeal to the American Left: that the Communist Party USA (CPUSA) followed orders from Moscow; that communists were assigned to steal secrets from the Manhattan Project, code name for the American development of the atomic bomb; and proof that Whittaker Chambers was right. Chambers was the *Time* magazine correspondent who first blew the whistle on the network of communist spies in America in 1948 and fingered his accomplice, Alger Hiss, as the Soviet's spy chief in New York.

A bomb set off by Timothy McVeigh in the Alfred P. Murrah Federal Building in Oklahoma City killed 168 people and wounded 680. President Clinton called him and his accomplice "evil cowards." I agreed, but asked why his description of evil is OK with the media, but was not OK with them when Ronald Reagan described the Soviet Union as the "evil empire"? Evil is as evil does.

In a speech at Michigan State University, President Clinton said you cannot pretend to love your country while hating your government. I responded, but you can love your country and hate what your government does when it is in the hands of overzealous and power-hungry leftists.

The administration changed immigration law in order to admit abortion-minded women seeking "asylum" when laws in their countries outlawed the procedure.

The Tenth Court of Appeals assaulted the free exercise clause of the First Amendment when it ruled in favor of a sixteen-year-old high school student and her parents who objected to the school's choir singing two traditional songs that contained the words "Lord" and "God." The court agreed with the plaintiff's claim (the family was Jewish) that the words referred to the Christian God and thus were a prayer outlawed by church-state separation. They must have forgotten to read the Old Testament where both names are used.

I visited Branson, Missouri, the site of a wonderful theme park, where alcohol was not served and families could visit without fear that they or their children will be assaulted by the surrounding cultural rot. The column was titled "A Town That Slime Forgot."

To her credit, Hillary Clinton appeared with Mother Teresa at the dedication of a home for unwed mothers. She asked the Nobel Laureate what could be done to provide more help to women with unplanned pregnancies, a remarkable statement for a pro-choice person. Clinton's press secretary, Lisa Caputo, told me the First Lady assigned two lawyers to the task of cutting red tape so that a home might be established in Washington. Such homes, I noted, were common when abortion was illegal.

New York Governor Mario Cuomo launched a radio show to compete with Rush Limbaugh. It died a quick ratings death because even his fellow liberals did not tune in. I listened to one show. Calling it boring would have been a step up.

In a 5–4 ruling, the Supreme Court said it was not unconstitutional for student activity fees at the University of Virginia to be spent on a Christian publication. Fees were already allowed to go to Jewish and Muslim publications. The petitioners did not argue their case based on the free exercise clause of the First Amendment, but on free speech grounds. The University of Virginia was founded by Thomas Jefferson, who, though a Deist, believed strongly in the freedom of— not from—religion.

In a column titled "Affirming, Not Affirmative Action," I wrote about a man named Murray Riese. He was a restaurateur who died at age seventy-three. Born in Harlem, Riese dropped out of high school and along with his brother, went to work as a dishwasher in 1936 in the middle of the Depression. After four years, the brothers had saved $500, enough to make a down payment on a luncheonette. They parlayed this modest start into an empire that once consisted of more than three hundred restaurants, feeding half a million New Yorkers a day. It's the difference between hard work and seeing oneself as a victim.

California Republican Governor Pete Wilson told me, "Affirmative action is a system of race and gender-based preferences which means that jobs, public contracts, and college admissions are granted not by virtue of individual merit, but instead on the basis of membership defined by race or gender. That's wrong and unconstitutional."

The American Psychological Association (APA) met in New York and considered whether to vote on a resolution by gay activists to "discourage psychologists and other mental health professionals from providing treatment designed to change sexual orientation or from referring to practitioners which claim to do so." I quoted the sex research team of Masters and Johnson who, in their *Homosexuality in Perspective* in 1974, found a 71.6 percent success rate after a six-year follow-up of those wanting to change. As expected, the APA caved to pressure and voted for the resolution. The *Physicians' Desk Reference* also removed all references to homosexual practice being a "disorder."

The House Banking Committee opened hearings on the Clintons' financial dealings in the Whitewater affair. Clinton defenders sought to portray them as "passive investors" in the real estate misadventure on the White River in the Arkansas Ozarks. The Resolution Trust Corporation (RTC) investigator Jean Lewis didn't see it that way. She testified about "concerted efforts" by the RTC, the Department of Justice and the United States Attorney's office in Little Rock to "obstruct, hamper, and manipulate" the inquiry into the bankrupt Madison Guaranty Savings and Loan Association. Madison was owned by James McDougal, a partner with the Clintons. McDougal was convicted and went to prison where he died. As usual, "Slick Willie" and Hillary escaped accountability.

Norma McCorvey, the "Jane Roe" in the *Roe v. Wade* abortion decision, became a Christian and renounced her previous support of abortion on demand. The Left either ignored her or offered worldly excuses for her change of heart. She was used to achieve their ends, so she was tossed aside, like an aborted baby.

Hillary Clinton actually said something I believe in at the United States Women's Conference in Beijing: "Women's rights are human rights." She criticized China's one-child policy and said she opposed China's forced abortions. She was fine with non-forced abortions, of course. Call it selective morality.

O. J. Simpson was acquitted by a Los Angeles jury on two murder charges. I called it "one of the biggest travesties in the history of American jurisprudence." Students at Howard University in Washington celebrated the verdict.

The Million Man March on Washington featured black men "repenting and atoning for sin," as organizers put it. Unfortunately, the sponsor of the event was the anti-Semite Louis Farrakhan, head of the Nation of Islam. Still, seeing so many black men pledging to be better husbands and fathers was worthy of praise.

I wrote about a new show on CBS called *Touched by an Angel*, saying it is a refreshing departure from most of network TV. After meeting the cast and producers, one of the show's stars, Della Reese, told me my column was responsible for boosting the show's ratings and keeping it on the air. It lasted for nine seasons.

The supposed "discovery" of a "gay gene" was trumpeted by the *Washington Post* as a breakthrough akin to discovering a cure for cancer. The reporting was uncritical and the science unscientific, and it was eventually abandoned. It was another example of starting with a premise and then looking for anything that supported the premise. That's not science, but propaganda.

Israeli Prime Minister Yitzhak Rabin was assassinated. His final words at a peace rally in Tel Aviv attested to his belief that peace was possible between Israel and Yasser Arafat's PLO. I wrote, "Carrying wishful thinking to its extreme, former Secretary of State James Baker said on ABC's *This Week* that he no longer believes Arafat wants to eliminate Israel. Asked why Arafat continues to call for Israel's elimination, when he talks to Arabs and his fellow Palestinians, Baker said he shouldn't do that and needs to retract those remarks." Sure.

Just before one of several upcoming government shutdowns over the budget, Treasury Secretary Robert Rubin said, "This is no way to run a country." He was right, but for the wrong reasons. Government shutdowns became one of the extortionist tools used by Democrats to force more and more spending and debt on the country.

Members of the theologically and politically liberal National Council of Churches met for forty-five minutes with President Clinton, and at the end, "laid hands" on him. They prayed he would be "strong for the task." This was the same group that criticized religious conservatives from laying hands on and praying for Republican presidents. Church-state separation, don't you know. It is why the word "hypocrisy" was invented.

1996

The Year of Character and Civility

Hillary Clinton testifies before a grand jury about the Whitewater scandal and says she can't remember a lot. It is the ultimate defense against perjury and telling the truth.

In Los Angeles, Lyle and Erik Menendez are found guilty of first-degree murder for the shotgun killing of their parents. They ask for sympathy because they are now orphans. Really?

Unabomber Theodore Kaczynski is arrested at his Montana cabin.

President Clinton signs the Line Item Veto Act of 1996, granting the American president line item veto power. The Supreme Court of the United States later finds this law unconstitutional. Too bad, even though the Court is constitutionally correct.

The Hoover Institution releases an optimistic report that global warming will probably reduce mortality in the United States and provide Americans with valuable benefits. Is this a joke? Apparently not.

In Philadelphia, a panel of federal judges blocks a law against indecency on the internet. The panel says that the 1996 Communications Decency Act would infringe upon the free speech rights of adults. How's that working out?

The summer Olympics open in Atlanta. A bombing at Centennial Olympic Park kills two and injures 111.

Bob Dole is nominated for president of the United States and Jack Kemp for vice president at the Republican National Convention in San Diego, California.

Osama bin Laden writes *The Declaration of Jihad on the Americans Occupying the Country of the Two Sacred Places* and calls for the removal of American military forces from Saudi Arabia. I thought jihad was about an internal struggle.

Bill Clinton signs welfare reform into law. Hooray!

Tiger Woods makes his professional PGA Tour debut at the Greater Milwaukee Open, four days after winning his third consecutive United States Amateur Championship.

President Bill Clinton and Vice President Al Gore are renominated at the Democratic National Convention in Chicago.

As Iraq continues to refuse inspectors access to a number of sites, the United States fails in its attempt to build support for military action against Iraq in the UN Security Council.

Rapper Tupac Shakur dies after being critically wounded in a drive-by shooting.

Clinton signs the Comprehensive Nuclear Test Ban Treaty at the United Nations.

The Fox News Channel is launched on American cable systems, transforming how news is covered and offering conservatives a vital information source. Liberals predict it can't last. As usual, they are wrong.

A Food and Drug Administration (FDA) panel recommends approval of RU-486, known as "the abortion pill."

The New York Yankees defeat the Atlanta Braves to win their first World Series in eighteen years.

Bill Clinton trounces Republican challenger Bob Dole to win his second term. This election had the lowest voter turnout since 1924.

The General Motors EV1, the first production electric car of the modern era, is launched and becomes available for lease.

Six-year-old beauty queen JonBenét Ramsey is strangled to death and found in the basement of her family's home in Boulder, Colorado. Tabloids and cable networks launch nonstop coverage.

CAL'S TAKE

"Our politics suffers from a shortage of people who put character and country before career and personal gain."

Reports of marital problems between the Prince of Wales and Princess Diana made news. They included tales of infidelity. In a visit to London, I asked a British friend about it. He replied: "It isn't the adultery so much as it is the indiscretion." Why isn't it both? Prince Charles remained quiet while Diana blabbed to the BBC.

The *New York Times* suddenly discovered honesty and criticized the Clintons for lying and obfuscation about Whitewater and so much more. Why did the *Times* just discover the low character of the Clintons, which had been on display for decades? Answer: politics.

In response to a blizzard that hit Washington, President Clinton declared the city "a disaster area." Most, I wrote, would accept a broader interpretation of the word disaster.

Had Bill Clinton not chosen politics as a career, he could have easily become a TV evangelist. In his State of the Union address, he preached virtue while practicing deceit.

I wrote a column about how much I missed Ronald Reagan in Washington. He sent me a handwritten "thank you" on one of his note cards. It is framed in my office, a proud possession.

O. J. Simpson complained that, since his acquittal on double murder charges, he couldn't make money again. Maybe he should have considered being a pitchman for steak knives.

Newt Gingrich called Bill Clinton "the most enthusiastically dishonest politician ever to occupy the White House." There would be more to follow.

Some journalists were outed for contributing to the campaigns of politicians. With the exception of one donation by a local New York anchor, all the rest were campaign gifts from Democrats. All reporters violated their company's policies, but when you're a Democrat, the standards don't matter as much.

Jack Kevorkian was convicted by a Michigan jury for violating a state law banning assisted suicide. It would not be long before several states, beginning with Oregon, made it legal for doctors who once took the Hippocratic Oath never to participate in taking a life to start assisting in "suicides."

The National Association of Scholars released a study, *The Dissolution of General Education 1914–1993*. It found that many institutions of what used to be called "higher learning" had abandoned most of the core academic requirements once considered essential to a liberal arts education. Just one example: there was a debate at Georgetown University in Washington as to whether one should be able to major in English Literature without studying William Shakespeare.

This was a commentary on the sickness of our legal system: A Clinton-appointed judge ruled that eighty pounds of cocaine and heroin seized by police from the trunk of a suspect's car was inadmissible in court. The reason? Judge Harold Baer Jr. of the Southern District of New York said police did not have reasonable suspicion to pull over the driver when they observed four men approach a car at five o'clock in the morning and drop several bags in the trunk. The suspects spotted the police and began to flee, but the judge decided this was not suspicious behavior because the Washington Heights neighborhood was known for corrupt and violent police officers.

A bill passed by the Senate and the House would have restricted "partial-birth abortion." After saying he had "prayed about it," Clinton vetoed the bill, flipping from an earlier position that he wanted abortion to be "safe, legal, and rare."

Jesus made an appearance during the Easter season on all three national magazines: *Time*, *Newsweek*, and *U.S. News and World Report*. Instead of affirming Christian beliefs, though, the stories were full of questions unbelievers had about the Son of God. Can't wait for Christmas to see the next round denying the Virgin Birth.

Justice Antonin Scalia spoke at a prayer breakfast in Jackson, Mississippi, where he shared his faith and even said he believed in miracles. This brought the predictable reaction from secularists in the media who placed him in the category of those who call the Psychic Hotline. *Washington Post* cartoonist Herblock depicted Scalia holding a Bible while his fellow Justices read the Constitution. I wonder if Herblock would have reacted the same way to what Abraham Lincoln said about the Scriptures: "But for this Book, we would not know right from wrong."

People were talking about the "loss of civility" in Washington. I noted this is only mentioned when Republicans are in charge of government, but never when Democrats rule.

The PLO supposedly voted to eliminate from its founding charter a pledge to destroy Israel. Only the gullible and wishful thinkers believed that.

In a column about what Republicans can learn from Ted Kennedy, I wrote he never gave up on his agenda. When his party was in the minority, he sought compromises on his bills in order to move his agenda forward. When his party was in power, he pushed ahead often without compromise.

A dinner was held for Billy Graham after he received the Congressional Gold Medal. President Clinton spoke about his own relationship with God, prompting a Republican senator, who requested anonymity, to tell me: "Bill Clinton is the biggest liar I have ever heard." In Washington, that is quite a distinction.

A jury in Little Rock, Arkansas, convicted Bill Clinton's former cronies and business partners on twenty-four felony counts of fraud and conspiracy. As usual, Bill (and Hillary) escaped accountability.

The Supreme Court, in a 5–4 ruling, outlawed racial gerrymandering in North Carolina and Texas. Justice Sandra Day O'Connor wrote that the law must "acknowledge voters are more than mere racial statistics."

Promised Land, a spinoff of *Touched by an Angel* was slated for broadcast Saturday nights when *Touched by an Angel* moved to Sunday nights. In an interview, CBS Entertainment Division President Les Moonves told me, "What

(*Touched by an Angel*) did for religion, *Promised Land* will do for patriotism."

In Jerusalem, Israeli Prime Minister Benjamin Netanyahu told me what he considered the choice for Palestinians: "They can have peace, or they can have terrorism. They can't have both."

I urged Dole to step aside as the presumptive GOP nominee and throw open the Republican National Convention in San Diego to select a stronger candidate. Dole made a disastrous appearance on *Larry King Live* in which his wife Elizabeth finished his sentences and said what her husband believed, rather than him telling us. Dole refused to withdraw, and the November results were all but determined.

The MSNBC cable channel debuted and demonstrated that it is no different from other cable and network options (Fox News is the lone exception).

Bob Dole picked Jack Kemp as his running mate. I called Kemp's selection a possible game-changer for the GOP.

Bob Dole's acceptance speech at the GOP convention revealed an energized candidate, who lectured Baby Boomers and effectively told them to grow up. It wasn't the type of message designed to win over independents, but he was right about the entitled generation. He stressed character and integrity, qualities missing from President Clinton.

Clinton delivered his renomination acceptance speech at the Democratic National Convention in Chicago. I called it typical of him—all style and no substance. He said he wanted to build a bridge to the twenty-first century. Given his record on taxes and spending, it would likely be a toll bridge.

Presidential pollster Dick Morris resigned after he was discovered cavorting with a $200-per-hour prostitute. Given

Bill Clinton's behavior, I wondered why and said he should be given his job back.

The Senate voted 85–14 to accept the definition of marriage put forth by Senator Dan Coates (R-IN): "The definition of marriage is not created by politicians or judges, and it cannot be changed by them." That would change in subsequent years.

Promised Land was panned by critics, including *USA Today* reviewer Matt Roush, who called the CBS TV show "manipulative and simplistic" because of its appeal to patriotism, family values, and good neighborliness. America could use more of all three.

The Neapolitan saying at the bottom of my Italian restaurant menu seemed to sum up the philosophy about the election: "It matters not who rules us, as long as we eat and drink well."

Clinton beat Dole in the election, though Republicans held on to majorities in the House and the Senate. David Brinkley, always known for his candor, said on election night that President Clinton did not have "a creative bone in his body. Therefore, he's a bore and always will be a bore."

In a speech to the Economic Club of Detroit, independent counsel Kenneth Starr spoke of the importance of civic virtue. Most commentators, myself included, thought he was referring to Bill Clinton's cronies and even the president himself.

A survey by the George Barna Research Group for Lutheran Hour Ministries found that fewer than half of Americans who identify as Christians said the most important part of Christmas is the birth of Jesus.

1997

The Year of Farewell to Princess Diana and Mother Teresa

President Clinton and Vice President Gore begin their second term.

A Santa Monica jury finds former football legend O. J. Simpson liable for the deaths of Nicole Brown and Ron Goldman.

The Dow Jones Industrial Average closes above 7,000 for the first time.

A gunman kills one person and wounds six others before taking his own life on the observation deck of the Empire State Building.

FBI agent Earl Edwin Pitts pleads guilty to selling secrets to the Soviet Union.

In San Diego, thirty-nine Heaven's Gate cultists commit mass suicide at their compound.

For the first time since December 1973, unemployment falls below 5 percent. It would remain below 5 percent until September 2001, prior to the early recession of the 2000s.

Senator Strom Thurmond (R-SC) becomes the longest-serving member in the history of the United States Senate (forty-one years and ten months).

Timothy McVeigh is convicted on fifteen counts of murder and conspiracy for his role in the 1995 Oklahoma City bombing. He is sentenced to death.

In Lacey Township, New Jersey, high school senior Melissa Drexler gives birth in a toilet and leaves the newborn for dead in the trash.

During the Evander Holyfield vs. Mike Tyson II boxing match in Las Vegas, Tyson bites off part of Holyfield's ear.

Andrew Cunanan shoots fashion designer Gianni Versace to death outside Versace's Miami Beach, Florida, residence.

The Dow Jones Industrial Average gains 63.17 to close at 8,038.88. It is the Dow's first close above 8,000. The Dow has doubled its value in thirty months.

The fully restored *USS Constitution* (a.k.a. "Old Ironsides") celebrates her two-hundredth birthday by setting sail for the first time in 116 years.

One million men gather in Washington, DC, for the Promise Keeper's Stand in the Gap event.

Stock markets around the world crash due to a global economic crisis scare. The Dow Jones Industrial Average follows suit and plummets to 7,161.15. The point loss exceeds that of Black Monday. Officials at the New York Stock Exchange invoke the "circuit breaker" rule to stop trading for the first time.

But then the Dow Jones Industrial Average gains a record 337.17 points, closing at 7,498.32. One billion shares are traded on the New York Stock Exchange for the first time.

Ramzi Yousef is convicted of planning the 1993 bombing of the World Trade Center.

The unemployment rate drops to 4.6 percent, the lowest since October 1973.

Mary Kay Letourneau is sentenced to six months in prison after pleading guilty to two counts of second-degree child rape. Letourneau gave birth to her victim's child, and the leniency of her sentence was widely criticized.

James Cameron's *Titanic*, the highest-grossing film of all time until his *Avatar* (2009), premieres in the United States.

Princess Diana dies in a car crash in Paris. The world mourns.

CAL'S TAKE

"Democrats' desperate attempt to focus on campaign finance reform instead of laws that may have been broken by the Clinton–Gore campaign is like Mike Tyson demanding a reform in boxing regulations after biting off a piece of Evander Holyfield's ear."

In his second inaugural address, Bill Clinton called for civility and an end to division. Sound familiar? To Democrats, this meant going along with their proposals and programs.

Fred Wertheimer, former president of the liberal group Common Cause, criticized the administration and the Democratic National Committee for their fundraising tactics (including coffee with the president and even a night in the Lincoln bedroom for high donors).

After saying a year earlier "the era of big government is over," President Clinton proposed spending $51 million more on public schools. Previous spending increases did not result in especially poor children being able to read by the eighth grade. It was another sop to the teachers' unions.

At an NAACP convention in New York, former Rep. Kweisi Mfume, who headed the organization, may have made a major faux pas when he said black Americans "must find a way to do more for (the) self." That went against the usual Democrat line that black people can't do anything without help from Washington.

The Chinese government was accused of illegally attempting to penetrate America's electoral system. It wouldn't be the last time (or for Russia either).

Michael Reagan, the adopted son of Ronald Reagan, (temporarily) left the Republican Party. On his radio talk show, Reagan said he and the party parted ways because he perceived it as "rudderless and in full retreat from the conservative values and beliefs my father championed . . . when the Republicans come back to grassroots America, I'll come back to the Republican Party."

Twenty-two state attorneys general held a news conference to publicly flog tobacco companies for "lying" and "covering-up" their knowledge that tobacco was addictive and can kill people who use it.

Reverend Bill Hybels, one of President Clinton's pastor friends, said our demands for absolute proof about things relating to God, such as the resurrection, were unreasonable. I guessed he didn't trust the witnesses. What kind of comfort was that to his congregation? Or, to put it Paul's way, if Christ is not risen, then we are still dead in our sins.

I praised the twenty-one-year-old Tiger Woods, not a product of affirmative action but a testimony of where hard work and talent can take anyone. He won the Masters Golf Tournament and people of all races cheered.

Ellen DeGeneres announced she was a lesbian. I don't care.

Bill Clinton called for $2.75 billion to be spent to teach children to read by the end of the third grade. How do politicians come up with such figures, and why can't some kids read with what is already being spent? I and a lot of other kids my age were reading by the second grade and didn't need help from the federal government.

It was my first Mother's Day without my mother. I was reminded of what Andrew Jackson said about his mother: "There never was a woman like her. She was as gentle as a dove and brave as a lioness. . . . The memory of my mother and her teachings were, after all, the only capital I had to start life with, and on that capital, I have made my way." The same could be said of my mother, Barbara Elizabeth (Leck) Thomas, and probably could be said of mothers everywhere who had such qualities.

On *60 Minutes*, an unusual story centered on a black man named Steve Berlack addressing an all-black audience. All are unemployed. Among other things, Berlack said, "It's not your skills that are keeping you from succeeding; it is your attitude." It's a far cry from the victimhood usually promoted by the Left, including much of the media.

Lt. Kelly Flinn, the first female B-52 bomber pilot, was discharged from the Air Force because of an adulterous relationship with a married man. She was interviewed by Morley Safer on *60 Minutes*. Safer rolled his eyes at the adultery charge, communicating his view that the idea of punishing adulterous behavior was a leftover relic from the era of Salem witch trials. I predicted that, like so many other curbs on behavior, this "domino" would also soon fall.

NBC sportscaster Marv Albert was charged with sexually mistreating a woman in a Virginia hotel room. I wrote the only difference between Albert and Clinton accuser Paula Jones was that Albert got a trial date.

Psychologists Judith Wallerstein and Julia Lewis released a lengthy twenty-five-year study they conducted on the consequences of divorce, especially on children. They said divorce is a cumulative experience that produced stark emotional scars and shaped attitudes, behavior, and relationships into adulthood.

Bill Clinton announced he's against cloning. He said a law was needed to protect "the miracle of life." Apparently the unborn were not part of that miracle for the pro-abortion president.

I wonder if it was racism—a subject Clinton and Democrats love to focus on—or something else that contributed to an explosion of the illegitimacy rate among blacks—from 23 percent in 1960 to 65.2 percent in 1990?

I was in Hong Kong in observance of ceremonies during which Britain handed Hong Kong back to the Chinese communists. Martin Lee, who chaired Hong Kong's Democratic Party, told me he is prepared to go "all the way" in defense of the freedom the unique city had enjoyed. Beijing promised to uphold that law to maintain Hong Kong's freedom, but communists lie and the reverse would soon enough prove to be the case.

In Guangzhou, China, I interviewed a man who went by the name "Pastor Lamb." He headed the largest "house church" in China with over four hundred attendees, many of whom sat on steps in his multi-story house and listened to his messages on speakers because they couldn't get into the crowded main rooms. Pastor Lamb told me he has spent much of his adult life in prison for preaching outside the Chinese government's approved churches. I asked him if the public security bureau came around much anymore. He said not so much and when I asked why, he replied, "Because every time they put me in jail the church grew." There's a lesson there.

One of the Democratic Party's biggest campaign donors during the last election cycle—Johnny Chien Chuen Chung—told the *Los Angeles Times* he personally handed a $50,000 check to Hillary Clinton's then-chief of staff, Margaret Williams, in response to requests for "help" to defray costs of a Christmas reception that had been billed to the Democratic National Committee. This contradicted administration accounts that "at no time" did anyone solicit donations from Chung. I guess it depended on the meaning of the word "solicit."

Congress and the White House were in rare agreement over the establishment of medical savings accounts into which people could put tax-deductible contributions to take care of themselves for all but major surgeries and illnesses.

I was in the United Kingdom when Princess Diana died. The BBC and other TV networks canceled all programming as the country—and America—went into mourning in ways that equaled or surpassed the John F. Kennedy assassination. Clergy were interviewed on TV, but instead of expressing such things as the transitory nature of beauty, or speaking of the afterlife or the moral lessons that could be learned from her life and death, they instead mentioned her commitment to destroying land mines and hugging people with AIDS. Any secularist could say the same thing, so I asked what good are they? To them, physical beauty covered a multitude of sins.

Mother Teresa died about the same time as Diana, but the media did not devote to her passing a fraction of the airtime they gave to Diana's death.

In a column called "Excuses and Explanations Are for Crooks," I wrote: "Columbus had an easier time discovering America than the Senate Finance Committee is having discovering the truth about the fundraising tactics of the Clinton-Gore reelection campaign."

President Clinton proposed "diversity education" in public schools. Shades of things to come. I said it was long past time for parents to withdraw their kids from what amounts to re-education camps fueled by leftist propaganda.

At a Human Rights Campaign dinner in Washington for the gay, lesbian, bisexual, and transgender organization, President Clinton tried to make a case for an evolving moral law. "We're redefining in practical terms the immutable ideas that have guided us." I wondered how ideas can be immutable if they are evolving?

The Pentagon announced a study about whether putting young men and women together in close quarters during basic military training might lead to sexual activity. I could have saved them the time and expense. It's another reason why people hate Washington.

One of the joys of the business I'm in is the people I get to meet. One of my favorites was the Hollywood and TV actress Loretta Young, who was among the first women to succeed in television and a star of Hollywood's Golden Age. I wrote a tribute to her in advance of her eighty-fifth birthday. She made ninety-eight films (all of which I own), and her popular TV show ran for nine seasons. She introduced me to other Hollywood and Broadway stars. Some of her movie posters (and her Emmy Award) dominate the TV/movie room in my house.

1998

The Year of Monica Lewinsky

The *Lunar Prospector* spacecraft is launched into orbit around the moon and later finds evidence for frozen water in soil in permanently shadowed craters near the moon's poles. Scientists continue to search for intelligent life in the universe. I'm still looking for intelligent life in Washington.

Ramzi Yousef is sentenced to life in prison for planning the 1993 World Trade Center bombing.

The *Drudge Report* breaks the story about President Bill Clinton's affair with Monica Lewinsky, which would lead to his impeachment by the United States House of Representatives.

Titanic becomes the first film to gross $1 billion.

Data sent from the Galileo probe indicates that Jupiter's moon Europa has a liquid ocean under a thick crust of ice.

The Belfast Agreement is signed between the Irish and British governments and most Northern Ireland political parties, with the notable exception of the Democratic Unionist Party. It's nicknamed the Good Friday Agreement.

The Galaxy IV communications satellite fails, leaving 90 percent of the world's pagers without service.

In response to a series of Indian nuclear tests, Pakistan explodes five nuclear devices of its own, prompting the United States, Japan, and other nations to impose economic sanctions.

In St. Petersburg, Nicholas II of Russia and his family are buried in St. Catherine Chapel, eighty years after they were murdered by the Bolsheviks in 1918.

Russell Eugene Weston Jr. enters the United States Capitol Building and opens fire, killing two members of the United States Capitol Police.

Bombings of the United States embassies in Dar es Salaam, Tanzania, and Nairobi, Kenya, kill 224 people and injure over forty-five hundred. They are linked to terrorist Osama bin Laden.

The Omagh bombing is carried out in Northern Ireland by the Real Irish Republican Army. Shortly after, the group calls a ceasefire, signaling an end to the thirty-plus year conflict known as "The Troubles."

Google, Inc. is founded in Menlo Park, California, by Stanford University PhD candidates Larry Page and Sergey Brin.

The government of North Korea adopts a military dictatorship on its fiftieth anniversary.

St. Louis Cardinals first baseman Mark McGwire hits his sixty-second home run of the season, breaking the single season record of 61 which had been held by Roger Maris since 1961.

Matthew Shepard, a gay University of Wyoming student, is beaten and left for dead near Laramie, Wyoming.

A declassified report by Swiss International Olympic Committee (IOC) official Marc Holder reveals that bribes had been used to bring the 2002 Winter Olympics to Salt Lake City during bidding process in 1995. The IOC, the Salt Lake Organizing Committee, the United States Olympic Committee, and the United States Department of Justice immediately launch an investigation into the scandal.

CAL'S TAKE

"When President Clinton starts talking about what is moral, as he did when recommending a national law banning human cloning, it's time for us to lock up our daughters."

The United States House of Representatives forwarded articles of impeachment against President Clinton to the Senate, making him the second president in the nation's history to be impeached.

Three network-affiliated TV stations in Santa Barbara, California, refused to run a political ad that described verbally, but not visually, what occurs during a partial-birth abortion. This censorship is what contributed to the lack of information the public needs to make considered judgment about the procedure.

For the first time in a long time, the government had a surplus. Instead of a refund or tax cuts to those paying the bills, Bill Clinton and the Democrats wanted to spend more.

Many in the media who endorsed, enabled, and excused Clinton's behavior with women now turned on him after the *Drudge Report* leaked a *Newsweek* magazine story that had been suppressed on Clinton's "affair" with intern Monica Lewinsky.

Not to be outdone, Colorado Governor Roy Romer, a Democrat, acknowledged he had a sixteen-year "very affectionate relationship" with a longtime aide, fifty-one-year-old Betty Jane Thornberry. Romer was also chairman of the Democratic National Committee.

During an interview with Barbara Walters on ABC, Monica Lewinsky's father tried to smear Independent Counsel Kenneth Starr, calling him "out of control." That one made me laugh considering Clinton was the real one out of control.

Just four years after Oregon voters narrowly approved physician-assisted suicide, "right to die" advocates said taxpayers had an obligation to subsidize poor people who want to kill themselves. At least they were consistent. They also supported federal funding of abortion.

CNN observed Women's History Month (there is no comparable month, or even day, for men and their history) by airing on four consecutive Sunday nights *A Century of Women: Justice for All*. It was hosted by Hillary Clinton, and the women featured were all hardcore Democrats. There wasn't a single (or married) conservative or Republican woman among them.

Gary Hart, who withdrew from the 1988 presidential race after his affair with Donna Rice, claimed that infidelity should not be a factor in determining one's fitness for public office. I opined that it appeared the nation's moral water table had reached drought level.

Instead of apologizing for his personal behavior and possible law-breaking, President Clinton traveled to Uganda where he apologized for slavery.

Judge Susan Webber Wright dismissed Paula Jones's sexual harassment suit against Bill Clinton. She ruled that Jones had failed to prove she suffered employment or economic reversals after her meeting with then-Governor Clinton where she alleged that he exposed himself and asked her to perform a sex act. Judge Wright said even if her allegations were true, they did "not constitute severe or pervasive abusive conduct for purposes of establishing a hostile work environment claim." It would have been nice to hear from the judge what would constitute a hostile work environment if not this. So much for female solidarity.

CBS decided to carry shock jock Howard Stern on its TV network. I criticized the network for it and Stern asked his listeners to phone in any "dirt" they can find on me. He's still waiting.

I suggested that Republicans should counter the Democrats familiar and perpetual "fair share" argument when it came to taxes with a critique of their out-of-control spending.

Former Associate Attorney General Webster Hubbell, his wife, and two others were indicted on charges for conspiring to avoid paying nearly $900,000 in income taxes, interest, and penalties. What is it about Bill and Hillary Clinton that causes so many people associated with them to suffer so many indignities, personal humiliation and even jail time? Yet, they managed to escape any serious accountability for their own actions.

President Clinton ordered the federal government to start using "plain language" in official documents in order to "send a clear message about what the government is doing." I suggested he might consider applying the same order to himself.

The Children's Scholarship Fund was created by venture capitalist Ted Forstmann and John Walton, heir to the

Walmart fortune. They pledged $200 million to help poor children escape failed inner city public schools. Yes!

What credibility the media had left was further eroded when CNN had to retract a "story" about American soldiers using nerve gas on American defectors in Laos. There was more. A *Boston Globe* columnist was fired for fabricating stories and quotes. The *New Republic* terminated a "hot young writer" for similarly making up parts of twenty-seven articles. The *Cincinnati Enquirer* dismissed a reporter who wrote about the company that sells Chiquita bananas because the reporter practiced "deceitful, unethical, and unlawful conduct." The newspaper agreed to pay the company $10 million and published a front-page apology.

I fulfilled a childhood fantasy when I lunched with Roy Rogers and Dale Evans on the eve of their fiftieth wedding anniversary in Victorville, California. I wrote that I had often had lunch *at* Roy Rogers (fast food), but this was the first time I had lunch *with* Roy. Both were gracious hosts and regaled me with stories about their films.

On a trip to Oxford, England, I stopped at the famous Blackwell's bookstore. Manager Keith Clark told me that C. S. Lewis was one of the few writers whose entire literary output remained in print so many years following his death.

Prime Minister Tony Blair named a woman, Margaret Callaghan, to his Cabinet as his minister for women. I wrote that, given her publicized adulterous and other sexual behavior, she might have been better suited as minister for men.

Clinton apologists were out in force as the House Judiciary Committee considered articles of impeachment of the president. CNN *Crossfire* co-host Michael Kinsley wondered if there would ever have been a stain on Monica Lewinsky's dress if Clinton had had a vasectomy. Lanny Davis went much further when he speculated that the semen on her dress might be someone else's. As they say, you can't make this stuff up.

Ten years after Ronald Reagan spoke to students and faculty at Moscow State University, touting the virtues of capitalism, Bill Clinton returned to the same school and lauded the power of government. That was likely good news to the Soviet leadership.

Senator Joe Lieberman (D-Conn) did something rare. He criticized a president of his own party. Lieberman took to the Senate floor and chastised Clinton for what he called moronic behavior, lying, and dissembling.

President Clinton met with a group of liberal clergies, who "baptized" him with forgiveness. I wrote that Clinton "feels about religion the way he feels about sex. He likes the kind that makes him feel good but requires nothing from him."

The president's "race panel" lamented that black Americans have trouble getting anywhere in life because of "white privilege." Black people who overcame obstacles to succeed are ignored, because the Left wants a permanent underclass on which they can rely for votes.

Vanity Fair magazine published an issue titled *America's Most Influential Women: 200 Legends, Leaders and Trailblazers.* Once again, there was not a conservative woman among them, much less a woman who had chosen to stay home with her young children.

Bill Clinton tried to pressure Israeli Prime Minister Benjamin Netanyahu at a meeting with PLO leader Yasser Arafat at the Wye River farm in Maryland into giving up "land for peace." The formula is and always has been wrong.

Republicans miscalculated, believing the Clinton sex scandal(s) would lead voters to remove him from office. They were wrong. They were also wrong with their prediction that the GOP would add to their majorities in Congress.

The Supreme Court by an 8–1 vote upheld Wisconsin's school choice program, which allowed poor children to escape bad public schools and attend the private school (including religious school) of their choice. The ruling opened the door for school choice programs in other states.

On a post-election cruise sponsored by National Review, economic and social conservatives agreed that Republicans had no message. In cards as well as politics, something beats nothing. The GOP lost five House seats and gained none in the Senate.

The American Society of Newspaper Editors committed itself to ethnic diversity in their member newsrooms. There is no mention of ideological diversity.

Independent Counsel Ken Starr testified before the House Judiciary Committee, laying out a series of offenses and charges against President Bill Clinton, including lying under oath about his affair with Monica Lewinsky. Clinton gave a deposition in which he dissembled, forgot, and lied. His most memorable line: "It depends what the meaning of is, is."

Pornographer Larry Flynt came out as a Democrat. He chose the right party.

A woman was arrested in Gaithersburg, Maryland, on charges of running a house of prostitution out of her condo. Neighbors said nothing about men arriving and leaving at all hours, until some parked in reserved spaces. They then called police. It's nice to know that they had priorities.

1999

The Year of Columbine and Impeachment

The Senate trial begins in the impeachment of President Clinton. He is ultimately acquitted.

A Michigan jury convicts Dr. Jack Kevorkian of second-degree murder for administering a lethal injection to a terminally ill man.

Two Littleton, Colorado, teenagers, Eric Harris and Dylan Klebold, open fire on their teachers and classmates, killing twelve students and one teacher, and then themselves. It would be the deadliest shooting at a high school in American history at the time. The shooting sparks debate in the media on school bullying, gun control, and violence.

The Dow Jones Industrial Average closes above 11,000 for the first time, at 11,014.70.

Star Wars: Episode I—The Phantom Menace is released in theaters. It becomes the highest-grossing film in the series.

Texas Governor George W. Bush announces he will seek the Republican nomination for president.

CAL'S TAKE

"No child is taught to kill, but he has to be taught to love, respect, honor, and value not only his own life, but the lives of his classmates, parents, and teachers. He has to experience love and acceptance. He has to know his life has purpose and meaning. No amount of money can do that."

Political correctness infected musical theater. I saw a revival of *Carousel* in London and noted that the character Mr. Snow was black, his wife white, and their several children of different ethnic groups.

The term "compassionate conservative" was created so Republicans could feel better about themselves. I think the term is redundant, because real compassion seeks to help poor people become self-sustaining and independent of government.

President Clinton was tried in the Senate with Chief Justice William Rehnquist presiding. Not enough senators voted to convict and remove him from office. It was good to be a Democrat.

News emerged of the Taliban in Afghanistan terrorizing millions of women as they forced them to leave jobs and wear burqas. Some things never change.

The NAACP held its ninetieth convention in Washington, DC. Most speakers condemned Republicans. I wrote that they were slaves to the Democratic Party and got nothing for their loyalty and votes.

Juanita Broderick accused Bill Clinton of raping her when he was attorney general of Arkansas. The statute of limitations had expired. Still, feminists said nothing.

Monica Lewinsky did an interview with Barbara Walters for two hours on ABC. It was riveting, as one might be riveted by seeing a train wreck.

President Clinton announced he felt no shame over his impeachment and blamed "Republican partisanship" for his difficulties. At least he didn't blame Monica Lewinsky. He was subsequently disbarred from practicing law. I assume he felt no shame about that either. Whatever became of shame?

School shootings continued in America. I noted that the profiles of many of the young killers were similar—absent or no father, broken homes, a fascination with satanism, Nazism, hate, and violence. Kurt Thompson, a psychiatrist who specialized in helping teenagers, told me that modern teens are suffering from "a horrid sense of disconnection." And they thought social media would bring us closer together, when just the opposite occurred.

Pastor Bruce Porter of the Trinity Christian Center in Littleton, Colorado, delivered the eulogy for seventeen-year-old Rachel Scott, who was one of those killed by the two murderers who took their own lives. His explanation for the escalating violence: "We've removed prayer from our schools, and we've replaced it with violence, hatred, and murder." Just one of many reasons to get kids out of these re-education camps and universities and teach them at home, or send them to schools that support traditional American and religious values.

Florida Republican Governor Jeb Bush won an important victory for school choice as the state legislature passed the nation's first statewide school choice law. The NAACP opposed it, saying it was a threat to public schools. In fact, now black parents overwhelming support school choice to free their kids from failing government schools.

Clinton and Republicans worked together to balance the budget. It likely will never happen again, given the coming debt avalanche.

Vice President Al Gore cast the tie-breaking vote in the Senate on a bill that added new restrictions on gun sales. Gore called the measure "a turning point for our country." It was nothing of the kind because what is needed is self-control and respect for life, not more "gun control." By definition, lawbreakers do not obey the law.

Two conflicting proposals were considered by Congress to address high school shootings. Democrats wanted more restrictions on guns while Republicans wanted no restrictions on the posting of the Ten Commandments. In an increasingly secular culture, guess which side won that battle? Al Gore said his coming presidential campaign would be about "values." We know what "values" he was talking about, don't we?

A visit to my father's hometown in Washington, Indiana, reminded me of the small-town values the coastal elites and many others seem to have forgotten. I noted that when Dad was born in 1908, things were cheap and life was valuable. Now life is cheap and things are valuable.

Clinton visited Hazard, Kentucky, where he promised tax cuts to companies that move there. What's this, a tax cut for businesses to create jobs and stimulate growth? It was the ultimate anti-poverty program. Years later, another Democrat president, Joe Biden, would call for punishing taxes on corporations to fund more government programs. They never learn basic economics.

Conservatives were concerned that Texas Governor George W. Bush, who looked likely to run for president, might not be solid enough when it came to issues that they care about. I asked to speak with him, and he called me from the road. I asked him what signal he would like to send to conservatives who had doubts about his beliefs. He began by talking about his faith in Jesus. I wrote that for the moment I was less interested in how he's getting to Heaven than I was in how he planned to get to the White House.

"The point is," he said, "people need to know where my heart is." He claimed consistency on abortion and said he had tried to reduce them at the state level. Concerned conservatives, he added, "need to focus on my record. I have cut taxes twice: $1 billion the first year, nearly $2 billion the second time. These were the largest tax cuts in state history."

John F. Kennedy Jr. and his wife died in a plane crash. The TV networks went gaga, treating especially his death as the end of Camelot. Camelot never existed. It was a myth created by the media following the assassination of President Kennedy. The myth was created after a casual remark by First Lady Jackie Kennedy that the president loved the Broadway musical by that name.

The New Jersey Supreme Court ruled that the Boy Scouts must admit homosexuals because scouting was a "public entity." This would have disastrous consequences as the Scouts were later the target of lawsuits by former scouts who claimed they had been abused by male Scout leaders. The organization, founded in the nineteenth century, had to declare bankruptcy.

When conservatives think they can use government to change things, they fall into the liberal trap. Government should be a last resort, not a first resource. Conservatives can never out-promise the Left, and when they try, they fail. The

Founders wanted government to be limited so the people could be unlimited. It is the definition of liberty.

George Stephanopoulos goes directly to ABC News from the Clinton White House (without bothering to pass through journalism school or cover anything). He was immediately declared a "journalist," which would be something akin to me declaring myself a professional basketball player. It's a commentary on the sad state of the increasingly biased media.

Calling someone a "bigot" or "racist" makes many people cower in fear. I wrote about the talk show host Dr. Laura Schlessinger, who refused to cower to anyone. Predictably, she was attacked for declaring that homosexual practice was wrong. I wondered what her critics were afraid of since they were winning the culture war. That fall, a record twenty-eight gay, lesbian, and transgender characters were portrayed in network TV shows. Why were gay rights activists afraid of a single voice like "Dr. Laura"? I think it was because truth has a power to counter the spirit of the age. Unfortunately, truth today is subjective, not objective.

I met the wonderful singer Barbara Cook (the original "Marian the Librarian" in the Broadway musical *The Music Man*). It would not be our last time together. I said her singing style "sprinkles grace like Tinkerbell tosses pixie dust, enchanting all within her reach." Cook's musical tribute to Gower Champion harkened back to an era that had been lost, not only on Broadway but throughout culture. Her voice raised the level of style and class in any room she entered.

National Rifle Association president and actor Charlton Heston testified on Capitol Hill that there were currently twenty-two thousand federal, state, and local gun laws on the books, most of which were never enforced. And I would add all of which are not obeyed by criminals.

Los Angeles public school administrators announced that three hundred fifty thousand students, about half of the city's student body, were failing to make the grades necessary for promotion. Most wouldn't be held back because they would clog up the system. Another argument in favor of school choice. If they could only wait twenty years and move to Oregon where the governor had signed legislation that didn't require any learning of the basics in order to graduate from high school.

Asked during the Iowa Republican presidential candidate debate what political philosopher or thinker he most identified with, George W. Bush shocked the journalistic, political, and possibly some in the religious community when he replied: "Christ, because He changed my heart."

2000

The Year of Y2K and a Contested Election

January 1 is going to destroy computers and our way of life. A hyperventilating media predicts Chicken Little "the sky is falling" disasters.

Pope John Paul II makes his first visit to Israel.

President Bill Clinton announces that accurate Global Positioning System or GPS access would no longer be restricted to the United States Armed Forces. Talk about something that has changed the world. Men now have justification for not asking directions!

Vladimir Putin is elected president of Russia.

The first survey of the entire human genome is completed.

The *USS Cole* is badly damaged in Aden, Yemen, by homicide bombers, killing seventeen crew members and wounding at least thirty-nine. A preview of more to come.

Hillary Rodham Clinton is elected to the United States Senate, becoming the first former First Lady of the United States to win public office.

Bush v. Gore is resolved by the Supreme Court, but not until mid-December when Bush is declared the winner.

CAL'S TAKE

"In a free society, government reflects the soul of its people. If people want change at the top, they will have to live in different ways. Our major social problems are not the cause of our decadence. They are a reflection of it."

Bush promised the "most ethical administration in history," and I asked, "Didn't Bill Clinton promise the same thing?" Bush replied, "Yes, but he fell forty-one presidents short." Got to love his sense of humor.

Another year, another survey showed that American public-school students rated miserably in science and math. The Left continued to focus on money because that's what the teachers' unions wanted, but school choice was advancing because that's what many parents and their children wanted and their wishes should come first.

In Texas, the president of a large petroleum firm told me he just bought gas and paid only 68 cents a gallon. I asked him how he managed to get such a great price. "That's the cost before taxes," he responded. The gas pumps once had stickers that told consumers the amount of tax per gallon they were being charged, but that notice suddenly disappeared. I wonder why?

Prior to the Super Tuesday primary elections, Al Gore was asked what kind of Supreme Court justices he might appoint as president. He responded he would select people who believe in "a living, breathing Constitution," which is code for judges making law on their own.

Time Inc. announced it will no longer publish *Life* magazine every week. *Life* had been a staple in American journalism (not to mention doctor's offices) since 1936.

Six-year-old Elian Gonzalez was seized by federal agents, who pointed guns at him and his unarmed father as the Clinton administration bowed to demands and threats from Cuban dictator Fidel Castro. Clinton ordered them to be returned to Cuba, from which they had escaped in a bid for freedom. It was a sad day for a country that has the Statue of Liberty as a symbol. Even sadder were arguments from attorney Greg Craig before the 11th Court of Appeals to reject their claims for political asylum. They should have fled to Mexico and snuck back over the border. That seems to be working in 2022.

Need more evidence of the failure of American public and university education? A new book by Stephen Bertman, professor of languages, literature, and cultures, titled *Cultural Amnesia*, said 60 percent of adult Americans didn't know the name of the president who ordered nuclear bombs be dropped on Japan. If you are in that category, the answer is Harry Truman. Among college seniors, 42 percent were unable to place the Civil War in the correct half-century (it was the second half of the nineteenth century), and 24 percent believed Columbus discovered America in the 1500s (not 1492). The Left's solution, as usual, was to spend more money on education.

As if to underscore my point, the top three finishers in this year's National Spelling Bee were home schooled.

Al Gore, the "inventor of the Internet," conveniently "lost" emails subpoenaed by a House committee and a federal grand jury in their continuing investigations of campaign finance abuses. A White House official blamed a "technical error" for the failure to back up the VP's emails. Uh-huh.

The Supreme Court forbade student-led prayers before public school football games. In his dissenting opinion, Chief Justice William Rehnquist wrote that the majority opinion "bristles with hostility to all things religious in public life." How right he was, and his statement is even more accurate today.

The Court brought more shame on itself when it ruled by a narrow 5–4 majority that a Nebraska law prohibiting partial-birth abortion was unconstitutional. The procedure puts surgical scissors at the back of a baby's head and sucks out its brains as it is partially delivered. Justice Sandra Day O'Connor, who President Reagan said would "not disappoint" on life issues, cast the deciding vote. Why do many Republican nominees to the Court so often disappoint while Democrat nominees rarely do?

George W. Bush addressed the NAACP convention in Baltimore and acknowledged that racism still exists in America. Who knew? Bush shared some good Republican philosophy about prosperity and the growing black middle class. I had hoped he would have reminded the audience of the history of the Democratic Party, which is the party of the Ku Klux Klan, Jim Crow laws, and opposition to civil rights legislation, but alas, he didn't. Still, it was good for a Republican to speak to these loyal Democrat voters and remind them their loyalty to one party has not benefited them much—a point Donald Trump would make in his run for the presidency in 2016. As a result, Trump received more black votes than any modern Republican presidential candidate.

Al Gore was nominated for president and picked Joe Lieberman, an Orthodox Jew, as his running mate. I lauded the selection because of the signal it sent to anti-Semites everywhere.

The broadcast networks selectively covered the Republican National Convention in Philadelphia, choosing what the public would see and hear, and more importantly, what it would not. *Washington Post* TV critic Tom Shales accused the networks of looking "churlish" and displaying "bad citizenship." The establishment media filter ideas through their liberal worldview. Their greatest power is the ability to ignore ideas, stories, and events that don't align with their perspective.

Bush delivered the best speech of his life to that point. In his acceptance of the GOP nomination for president, Bush demonstrated conviction, vision, and class. He even referred to his father—the forty-first president—as "the most decent man I have ever known." That had to resonate with the family-values wing of the party and many other Americans.

Actress Loretta Young, a great friend of mine, passed away. She once threw a birthday party for me at her home in Palm Springs and invited fellow Oscar-winner Jane Wyman to attend. I treasure the picture of them flanking me at the dinner table. I attended her funeral and was listed on the program as an honorary pall bearer—her final gift to me.

A timely book by David P. Schippers, the chief investigative counsel for the House Judiciary Committee, revealed that Al Gore, in collusion with the Immigration and Naturalization Service, allowed one million immigrants to become citizens in 1996. Gore apparently hoped they would vote for him out of gratitude in 2000. Schippers wrote that his examination

of the immigrants' files found 20 percent of those with records of violence in their native countries had also committed crimes after they became American citizens. There would
be much more of this in the Biden years.

Students and parents in Batesville-Leesville, South Carolina, circumvented a court ruling prohibiting prayer prior to
football games. They bring radios to the games and someone
at a radio station offered a prayer that was sent over the sta-
dium loudspeakers. I love innovation!

The key phrase in Independent Counsel Robert Ray's conclusion about the myriad accusations of wrongdoing by Bill
and Hillary Clinton—from their years in Arkansas to their
years in Washington—was that "the evidence was insufficient
to prove to a jury that they had committed any crime." That
was anything but a testimony to their character. Rush Limbaugh once referred to them as "Bonnie and Clod." That always made me laugh.

In the first presidential debate in Boston, I called Al Gore
rude and cocky and said Bush won because he did not live
down to lower expectations. Gore kept repeating a familiar
Democrat line: "the wealthiest 1 percent." Sound familiar?
It's been a Democrat talking point for decades.

I wrote a review of Frank Rich's highly readable autobi-
ography, *Ghost Light*, which is a reference to the single light
left on the stage after the conclusion of a play. Rich, the former chief drama critic for the *New York Times* and later a columnist for that newspaper, became a good friend after we
learned we have many things in common outside of politics.
Isn't this a lesson more people should learn?

In the second presidential debate, Gore changed his
hairdo and sported better makeup. This was about all he had

going for him. One of the problems in these debates is that they are not real debates. They are like news conferences with "journalists," who numerous surveys over many years reveal mostly vote for Democrats, asking loaded questions of Republicans and tossing softballs at Democrats.

Bush won the third and final debate on substantive issues. Gore delivered another whopper when he falsely claimed the pharmaceutical industry spent more money on advertising than on research and development of new drugs. He can only have it his way at Burger King.

Another great friend and creator of the *Tonight Show*—Steve Allen—died at age seventy-eight. He never told a dirty joke on TV. He didn't have to. He had talent. He once invited me to dinner at his Los Angeles home, saying, "I know what you want to see." He took me into his library and showed me bound copies of original *Tonight Show* scripts, some of which contained skits that I had seen. No one laughed like Steve, and he made others laugh along with him.

The presidential election was "too close to call" and would remain so for weeks, as lawyers for Bush and Gore battled over vote counts and especially electoral votes. Ultimately the Supreme Court validated the election results in Florida (remember "hanging chads"?), giving Bush the victory. Predictably, Hillary Clinton, who won her race for the Senate from New York, called for elimination of the Electoral College. That would give Democrats a permanent majority and reduce the power of less populated states to nothing, a situation that the Founders had wanted to avoid.

Democrats gritted their teeth and worse. Some claimed the election was "stolen" from Gore, a claim that would be made by Donald Trump in 2020. I headlined the column, "The President-Elect and the President Reject."

Bush said he would nominate former Missouri Governor John Ashcroft to be his attorney general. The Left went nuts, not only because of Ashcroft's view of the law but also his Christian faith, which they regarded as a violation of church-state separation. It's OK by them when people of little or no faith impose their policies on the nation.

So ended my observations on the year 2000. Few could have predicted what was about to happen in 2001 and the changes it would bring to America, though the signs were there for those not deliberately blind to them.

2001

The Year of 9/11

All other events of 2001 are dwarfed by what happened on September 11. Like my grandparents' generation, who experienced the Japanese bombing of Pearl Harbor, 9/11 is a day of infamy.

Bill Clinton beats the rap when the Senate failed to convict him on articles of impeachment. All he suffered was the loss of his Arkansas law license.

Ronald Reagan turns ninety but is unable to appreciate the accolades coming his way because of Alzheimer's disease.

CAL'S TAKE

"To not remember 9/11 is to forget what brought it about."

While visiting Belfast, Northern Ireland, I read in the British press how many regarded President-elect George W. Bush as dumb. As an American, I was asked my thoughts. When I noted his degrees from Harvard and Yale, they were surprised.

When I spoke of his inherent decency in contrast to Bill Clinton, they nodded appreciatively. Bush would prove to be the right president at the right time by September 11, and the world would rapidly change its view of him.

In Dublin, a cabdriver told me prosperity hadn't visited Ireland in a long time. But now the economy was booming. Why? Because the government decided to cut taxes by more than $1 billion and private industry began to flourish.

Linda Chavez withdrew as Bush's labor secretary nominee. Her "crime"? She took in a homeless Guatemalan woman and helped her get back on her feet, spending her own money. The woman turned out to be in the United States without documents (an illegal alien, as we once called them). Considering how Joe Biden in 2021 would virtually eliminate our southern border, allowing tens of thousands of illegals to enter, Chavez's "crime" was nothing.

Reverend Jesse Jackson, who became a "spiritual adviser" to Bill Clinton after the Monica Lewinsky affair, told Maureen Dowd of the *New York Times*, "Sex is not the only string on the guitar. There are nine other Commandments." Years later, it would be revealed that Jackson fathered an out-of-wedlock child with a Los Angeles woman. I guess he ignored the one about adultery, making it "eight other commandments"?

Bush called for education vouchers in his No Child Left Behind policy. He also coined a phrase—"the soft bigotry of low expectations"—and applied it to the attitude many have when it comes to black public-school students. Democrats said there was much they agreed with in Bush's proposals to improve education, just not vouchers. That was because the teachers' unions opposed them and they gave a lot of money to Democrat politicians.

I interviewed the new vice president, Dick Cheney. He told me, "In the interest of 'civility' [the new Washington buzz-word], you can't sacrifice fundamental beliefs." He assured me that President Bush would not.

Civility didn't last long when Democrats attacked President Bush for saying the people, not the government, know best how to spend their money. Bush wanted to cut taxes and Democrats responded it would be "risky" and benefit only "the rich." Honestly, haven't we heard this "song" so many times before—and since?

The ruling Taliban in Afghanistan began destroying pre-Islamic statues of Buddha dating back to the seventh century. The world protested, to no avail. The Taliban then—as now—don't care what the world thinks of their fanatical religion and radical politics.

I received a letter from a federal prisoner, who commented on the unfairness of the legal system. Dale Hill had been recommended for parole after serving a fourteen-year sentence for a "low-level, nonviolent drug offense." Numerous people—including clergy, high school teachers, and friends—testified to his changed life, but in our "tough on crime environment," he was neither paroled nor did he have his sentence commuted. Hill's letter to me mentioned Bill Clinton's pardons and commutations of some bad guys, including Patty Hearst, Marc Rich, and several others. Sentence disparity and inequality have been staples of the criminal justice system for a long time. It is often more criminal than just.

President Bush proposed spending millions of dollars on "character" education in government-run schools as a response to school shootings. I noted my parents gave me my character education and it cost nothing. These shooters seem to be mentally disturbed and are unlikely to be deterred by a teacher telling them what is right and wrong. Why do even some Republicans think government is the answer to so many things that used to be the responsibility of parents?

The Dutch parliament gave final approval to a new euthanasia law that would allow doctors to end a life when it had been subjectively determined that life was no longer worth living. Eugenicists everywhere rejoiced. Why so much focus on death instead of life?

After his first one hundred days in office, I wrote in comparison to his predecessor that Bush was not defining decency down, but up.

A professor of psychiatry at Columbia University, who in 1973 persuaded the American Psychiatric Association to remove homosexuality from its official diagnostic manual of mental disorders, said, "Contrary to conventional wisdom, some highly motivated individuals, using a variety of change efforts, can make substantial change in multiple indicators of sexual orientation." He was mostly ignored in favor of the "conventional wisdom" of the secular progressives who didn't want to hear it.

The notion of "traditional families" changed rapidly. Only 51 percent of Americans were married. That number would soon fall under 50 percent.

I was amazed at the Left for their opposition to the execution of Oklahoma City bomber and murderer Timothy McVeigh, who deserved to die, while they continued to support abortion on demand, killing babies who deserve to live.

Attorney General John Ashcroft and I met in his Department of Justice office. Asked about those who oppose the death penalty under all circumstances, yet favor no restrictions on abortion, Ashcroft responded with one of the best comments I've heard on the issue: "I believe there is a difference between innocent life and the predicate on which a person's life is ended in capital punishment. . . . We respect life so profoundly that we say to individuals who take life that you will suffer the loss of your own. . . . There's an irony in individuals who favor taking innocent life and protecting guilty life."

Justice Sandra Day O'Conner told a Minnesota lawyers' group that she thought the death penalty was "unfair" and that innocent people likely have been executed. This from a judge who voted to not only uphold *Roe v. Wade*, but expand abortion "rights" to encompass any stage of fetal growth.

The big media started focusing on Fox News, often referring to it as a "right-wing" network. They never acknowledge that their worldview is left-wing and secular. Fox's ratings continued to climb while those of the broadcast networks declined. That ought to have told them something, but it didn't.

A debate raged over stem cell research. I referenced an article by Ronald Reagan in 1983 for *Human Life Review* called "Abortion and the Conscience of a Nation." In it, Reagan wrote these simple yet profound words: "[A]nyone who does not feel sure whether we are talking about a second human life should clearly give life the benefit of the doubt. If you don't know whether a body is alive or dead, you would never bury it. I think this consideration itself should be enough for all of us to insist on protecting the unborn." Reagan then got to the heart of the issue: "The real question today is not when human life begins, but what is the value of human life? The real question for (the baby) and all of us is whether that tiny human life has a God-given right to be protected by the law—the same right we have."

President Bush announced what he thought was a compromise on stem cell research. He would allow federal funding of research on sixty genetically diverse stem cell lines that "already exist" and have "already been destroyed." That seems reasonable, until one realized that having established a principle would make it impossible to stop the march to include stem cells from aborted babies, not to mention a later revelation of the sale of body parts by abortionists, including allegations that Planned Parenthood engages in the slimy practice.

And then came 9/11. Nothing else seemed to matter. In a rare moment of unity, Democrats joined Republicans in support of President Bush. Patriotism was everywhere. Much of the world supported us. People who may not have attended church in years crowded services to pray for America. Kindness broke out everywhere. Drivers stopped honking at each other in New York City.

What was most surprising in retrospect was how many signals were missed. The hijackers had trained at an American flight school where they wanted only to learn how to take off and fly, not land. That and the fact that they were Middle Easterners should have been a clue.

How did airport security miss the box cutters they used to slit the throats of pilots? Why didn't officials take threats from Osama bin Laden seriously?

I did thirteen columns in a row on the attack that killed nearly three thousand people. The first was titled "Another Day of Infamy." I wrote: "Tough words will not be enough. A single retaliatory strike will not suffice. There needs to be a decision by free nations everywhere to rid the planet of people and organizations that engage in such acts." Unfortunately, several of those nations—most especially the United States and the United Kingdom—allowed these organizations and radical preachers to endure so they could recruit a new generation of fanatics.

In a second column I wrote: "Something else died . . . in addition to thousands of innocent people. It was also the doctrine of moral equivalency—the idea that people everywhere are just like us, or can be made so by meeting their demands."

Bush distinguished himself by going to Ground Zero. On September 14, Bush gave his "bullhorn address" standing next to retired firefighter Bob Beckwith. Bush called out to the first responders surrounded by wreckage as they mourned the loss of the thousands who had perished just days before: "I want you all to know that America today, America today is on a bended knee, in prayer for the people whose lives were lost here, for the workers who work here, for the families who mourn. This nation stands with the good people of New York City and New Jersey and Connecticut as we mourn the loss of thousands of our citizens." Bush continued his speech amid the rubble that was the World Trade Center, but rescue workers yelled back: "We can't hear you!" Responded Bush: "I can hear you! I can hear you! The rest of the world hears you. And the people who knocked these buildings down will hear all of us soon."

Seeing troops on our streets and at American airports was both comforting and frightening. I wrote, "Before we consider suspension of civil liberties, let's get serious about enforcing American immigration laws already on the books and empowering our leaders to fight the war that has been all but officially declared."

The Department of Homeland Security was created. Metal detectors proliferated at airports in the United States and around the world. It seemed to be, to invoke an old analogy, closing the barn door after the horses had escaped. But it has worked and America has not been attacked since 9/11 (at least not yet).

The media flipped on President Bush. After first denouncing him as dumb and an illegitimate president, he suddenly became, even for some liberal journalists and columnists, the equivalent of "The Incredible Hulk."

Other media people, including Oprah Winfrey, busied themselves trying to persuade us that not all Muslims are terrorists. That is true, but it doesn't take a majority to kill you. The fanatics claimed their religion ordered them to conduct such acts. Oprah did a show about modern Muslim women, none of whom were allowed to dress in contemporary clothes, receive an education, or even appear on TV if they lived in radical Muslim states. For a different perspective, I asked someone who knew the subject, Right Reverend Bullen Dolli, an Episcopal bishop in Sudan. He told me what he believed about the nature and intent of contemporary Islam: "It is a militant religion." He laughed at those who serve as its character witnesses.

Seven days after the terrorist attacks of 9/11, anonymous letters laced with deadly anthrax spores began arriving at media companies and congressional offices. Over the ensuing months, five people died from inhaling anthrax and seventeen others were infected after exposure. I also got a letter that contained a powdery substance. When I called the FBI, a huge truck containing men in hazmat suits showed up outside my house. After examining the envelope, an agent concluded it is not anthrax. He told me, "We know this guy. He's in a state prison and thought by doing this he would get an upgrade to a federal cell."

I walked down a long avenue in New York City toward Ground Zero. Two images will always stick in my mind. One was the pictures of the missing that have been taped to store windows, along with their descriptions. The other was of cars near ground zero. Their insides were full of dust from the force of the collapse of the Twin Towers.

In a speech in Atlanta that was broadcast nationally (and interrupted 36 times by my count from his audience), President Bush declared, "We wage a war to save civilization itself." Unfortunately, he claimed, "When the terrorists and their supporters are gone, the people of Afghanistan will say to the rest of the world, 'Good riddance.'" If only. Still, the speech was inspirational. Even most media people started wearing American flag lapel pins.

President Bush encouraged all Americans to return to a normal life and some politicians did by resuming their stupidity. I referred to the Washington, DC, suburb of Montgomery County, Maryland, where the county council passed a law that would fine smokers up to $750 for allowing their fumes to penetrate a neighbor's home. Does this prove political overreach can cause brain damage?

Most networks avoided talking about 9/11 this Christmas, but not Martha Williamson, the writer and executive producer of *Touched by an Angel* on CBS. Titled "I'll Be Home for Christmas," the episode of the popular program centered on a young boy who lost his favorite teacher when the World

Trade Towers collapsed. The teacher was also a choir director who headed up the annual Fourth of July parade in a
small New York town and directed the Christmas pageant at
a local church. The boy was in denial about his teacher, believing he would come home. He left phone messages on the
teacher's answering machine. They were discovered by the
"angels" and the boy's mother, who was the mayor of the little town and also in denial about a lot of things in her life. I
won't give away the emotional ending (you can buy the DVD
and see it for yourself), but I wrote, "If you're not crying and
loving this country and the real meaning of Christmas more
than you ever have before, then you're a computer chip." If
only we had more good TV.

The daily portraits in the *New York Times* of people who
lost their lives on 9/11 read like a yearbook of sadness and
unrealized hopes. And yet, Christmas offered ultimate hope
to all who believed in its central message of God becoming a
man and giving his Son's life that we might live if we accept
his sacrifice on our behalf. Is there any greater hope?

2002

The Year of Guantanamo Bay and Beltway Shootings

Camp X-Ray is established at Guantanamo Bay, Cuba, for captured suspected terrorists. I visit the prison and find their cells cleaner than most American prisons. Prisoners are given Korans and Halal food, and on each bunk is an arrow pointing in the direction of Mecca. The Left claims they are being abused. Some abuse!

In his State of the Union address, President Bush vows to expand the fight on terrorism and labels Iran, Iraq, and North Korea "an axis of evil." How the Left hates the word "evil." It also reacted negatively when Ronald Reagan called the Soviet Union an "evil empire."

Kenneth L. Lay, chairman of bankrupt Enron, resigns. The company is under federal investigation for hiding debt and misrepresenting earnings. Several former Enron executives will be indicted, convicted, and sentenced to prison terms.

Republicans retake the Senate in midterm elections and gain additional House seats.

Wall Street Journal reporter Daniel Pearl is kidnapped in Pakistan. His captors accuse him of being a CIA agent and behead him.

NASA's *Mars Odyssey* space probe begins to map the surface of the red planet using its thermal emission imaging system.

American forces invade Afghanistan in the start of a war that would last twenty years.

Elizabeth Smart, fourteen, is kidnapped from her bedroom in Salt Lake City. She is rescued nine months later.

At Los Angeles International Airport, Egyptian immigrant Hesham Mohamed Hadayet kills two and injures six before being killed by a security officer. The incident is called an act of terrorism.

"American Taliban" John Walker Lindh pleads guilty to aiding the enemy and possessing explosives during the commission of a felony. Lindh agrees to serve ten years in prison for each charge.

Kelly Clarkson wins the first *American Idol* competition.

The Beltway sniper attacks begin with five shootings in Montgomery County, Maryland. They eventually end after ten have been killed and three others wounded. John Allen Muhammed and Lee Boyd Malvo are arrested and charged with the crimes.

Congress passes a joint resolution that authorizes the president to use the armed forces as he deems necessary and appropriate against Iraq.

Republicans gain a majority in the Senate and a larger majority in the House in the elections. What will they do with it?

President Bush signs the Homeland Security Act, establishing the Department of Homeland Security.

United Airlines, the second largest airline in the world, files for bankruptcy.

CAL'S TAKE

"No nation can survive without passing its heritage, language, and, yes, faith to the next generation. A country must be built on something substantial, and if the cultural elitists think it can be built on 'diversity,' that is a foundation of shifting sand."

The euro was established throughout Europe, replacing the French franc, German deutsch mark, Dutch guilder, and other currencies. Only Britain and Switzerland refused to go along, maintaining their traditional pound sterling and Swiss franc. I wrote that the euro looks like Monopoly money with no faces of kings or queens, only nondescript images reminiscent of a Rorschach test. It was ugly, and the coins were hard to read. Bogus euros hit the streets within twenty-four hours of the release of the real thing. Counterfeiters were prepared.

A "bipartisan" agreement was reached that increased the amount of money spent on public schools. I repeated myself: if there was a relationship between spending and achievement, we would have National Merit Scholars all over the country.

The media sought to tie the Enron scandal to President Bush, though it is a private company and Bush had no financial interest in it. Unlike the numerous Clinton scandals, which the media mostly explained away, they went full bore against Bush.

On Bush's first anniversary as president, I wrote that he had brought honor and decency back to the White House by treating the office as public property to be tenderly guarded and respected, not as his personal spoil of political war.

President Bush said he believed "our enemy intend[ed] to hit us again." If so, why were we not deporting illegal aliens from the country who came from nations that bred anti-American ideology and religion that threatened us? This would turn out to be a continuing problem for many years.

As part of its welfare reform campaign, the Bush administration wanted to spend $100 million annually to promote marriage among the poor, who accounted for the largest percentage of out-of-wedlock births and what we used to call "broken homes." Why is money always considered the solution to everything when it solves so few problems? If government could solve them, would it not have by now?

Citizens Against Government Waste uncovered examples of wasteful spending on things that were not the business of the federal government. They included a $20,000 grant to the Twin State Women's Network (TSWN) for a weekend retreat featuring such seminars as "Toys 4 Us" and "Self-Loving/Self-Healing: Discussing the Role of Masturbation as a Tool of Healing." TSWN also received $1,500 for long-distance phone calls, $1,000 for books, including the *New Good Vibrations for Sex* manual, and $250 for videos, including *Fire in the Valley: A Guide to Masturbation for Women*. Your tax dollars at work.

Billy Graham was heard on a thirty-year-old tape agreeing with President Richard Nixon that Jews have a "stranglehold" on American media. Graham, who was eighty-three and in declining health when the tapes were revealed, said he had no recollection of the conversation, but apologized anyway. I said it should be another lesson about the corrupting nature of politics, especially when it came to religious leaders, whom politicians on both sides like to use to advance their policies and ideologies. Meanwhile, the Roman Catholic Church suffered another scandal involving pedophile priests and efforts to cover up the incidents.

President Bush told a United Nations conference on global development in Monterey, Mexico, that Americans have an obligation to "share our wealth" with poor nations. No, we don't. Where is that in the Constitution? We ought to be encouraging poor nations to follow our example and become prosperous themselves.

In another example that crime does pay, Bill Clinton earned between $200,000 and $300,000 per speech as well as a $12 million book advance as he and Hillary continued as the nation's most famous grifters. Clinton told *Newsweek* that, in hindsight, be probably shouldn't have pardoned financier Mark Rich and his brother, Roger. He said nothing and did nothing for people who went to jail for him, including Webster Hubbell, Susan McDougal, and many others. It did not always pay to be a "friend" of Bill and Hillary.

I reviewed the new Broadway musical *Sweet Smell of Success* and met composer Marvin Hamlisch at Sardi's in New York. Marvin was mystified because the show was panned by critics. I think it was because the storyline was so cynical, and following 9/11, people were looking for things more uplifting and optimistic. Still, it was a great show. In the opening-night audience were Steven Spielberg and his wife Kate Capshaw. I introduced myself and told Spielberg that as the head of the "Gentile wing" of American supporters of

Israel I had been thrilled by what he had done in filming the stories of Holocaust survivors. He looked very pleased and thanked me. I returned to my seat in time for the curtain to go up, feeling I had met a person of genuine accomplishment. Same for Marvin. I love the theater.

Two members of the Senate Intelligence Committee—Republican Richard Shelby of Alabama and Democrat Bob Graham of Florida—agreed there were "one hundred terrorist sleeper cells" inside the United States. Graham said they present an "immediate threat to our security." On a visit to Washington, Egyptian President Hosni Mubarak said much the same.

General Electric released a TV ad touting its new 4-D machine that showed a baby developing inside its mother. Over the song "The First Time I Ever Saw Your Face," an announcer said, "When you see your baby for the first time on the new GE 4D Ultrasound, it really is a miracle." GE may not have intended its new device to act as a powerful pro-life statement, but that's what it became. Surveys showed that when abortion-minded women see an image of their child, they mostly choose to give birth. It is why the pro-death cult wants to exterminate them before they start looking "human."

FBI Director Robert Mueller—who would later become a controversial figure—shook up the agency after receiving a thirteen-page memo from Special Agent Coleen Rowley in which she alleged that agents were blocked from investigating terrorists. Sometimes we are our own worst enemy.

The 9th Circuit Court of Appeals in San Francisco (naturally) ruled that the Pledge of Allegiance was unconstitutional because Congress, in 1954, had inserted the words "under God." According to the liberal court, the phrase violated the First Amendment clause prohibiting the "establishment of religion." Under whom, then?

A study by a Rand Corporation security analyst found that our "friend and ally" Saudi Arabia was "active at every level of the terror chain from planners to finances, from cadre to foot soldier, from ideologist to cheerleader. . . . Saudi Arabia supports our enemies and attacks our allies." The only reason we papered over their role is because we needed their oil. It's a Devil's bargain.

I favored removing Saddam Hussein from power because "experts," including Vice President Dick Cheney and Secretary of State Colin Powell, claimed to have seen evidence that he had and was developing more weapons of mass destruction. The evidence ultimately proved wrong, but Bush ordered troops into Iraq and Saddam was deposed, arrested, and eventually hanged. The move left a vacuum in leadership that Iran and terrorist groups sought to fill.

The new policy of the Bush administration was to fight terrorism "over there" so we don't have to fight it "over here." Sounded good, but would it work?

Republicans shocked the political world in the fall elections by gaining enough seats in both houses of Congress to win majorities. An incumbent president usually loses congressional seats in the first election after his own. Call it a spill-over from 9/11. Republicans seem uncomfortable when they have power. They hold a "retreat" (not the word I would have used—advance is better) to decide what to do.

Store owners were told to wish customers a "Happy Holiday" rather a "Merry Christmas" or even "Happy Hanukah" to Jewish patrons. It was another attempt to dilute America's traditions, discount faith, and make all ideas equal.

2003

The Year of the Iraq War

Sky marshals are introduced on American airlines in an attempt to prevent hijackings.

The newly created United States Department of Homeland Security begins operations.

Space shuttle *Columbia* disintegrates over Texas upon re-entry, killing all seven astronauts on board.

Fred Rogers, host of the children's television show *Mister Rogers' Neighborhood*, dies of stomach cancer, at age seventy-four.

The United States and the United Kingdom begin their shock-and-awe campaign, with a massive air strike on military targets in Baghdad.

American forces seize control of Saddam International Airport, changing the airport's name to Baghdad International Airport.

American forces defeat the Iraqi Army and the Iraqi Republican Guard in the Battle of Baghdad.

President Bush accuses Syria of possessing chemical weapons.

President Bush delivers his "Mission Accomplished" speech on the aircraft carrier *USS Abraham Lincoln*.

Martha Stewart and her broker are indicted for using privileged investment information and then obstructing a federal investigation.

The Supreme Court upholds affirmative action in university admissions.

A senior Department of State chemical and biological weapons expert testifies before the House of Representatives Intelligence Committee that he was pressured to modify intelligence reports about Iraq.

The Supreme Court declares sodomy laws unconstitutional.

Washington Post columnist Robert Novak publishes the name of Valerie Plame, blowing her cover as a CIA operative.

Uday and Qusay Hussein, sons of Saddam Hussein, are killed by the American military in Iraq after being tipped off by an informant.

President Bush concedes there is no evidence linking Iraqi President Saddam Hussein to the September 11, 2001, attacks.

End of Operation Red Dawn, resulting in the capture of Saddam Hussein in Tikrit.

CAL'S TAKE

"In a world that has gone global, we no longer have a choice. If we don't export freedom, we risk importing the viruses which have corrupted other nations. . . . Some critics complained that President Bush was arrogant when he suggested America can and should export freedom to other countries. This implies the people of unfree countries may not wish to be free. Which is the greater arrogance?"

When Rush Limbaugh began his radio program and Fox News was launched, the secular Left at first mocked the radio host and the new cable network. They didn't laugh for long. As Limbaugh's show grew (topping six hundred radio stations and millions of listeners) and as Fox News ratings eclipsed CNN and sometimes that of the broadcast networks, the Left went into a panic and began denouncing both as right-wing and extremist. In fact, they were simply giving voice to people who believed their ideas were censored and/or stereotyped by the major media. It was the same when it came to my newspaper column. People told me they started reading their local paper again because I was in it.

Democrats reprised their familiar class warfare scenario as Bush proposed tax cuts. To Democrats, government is the only entity that can make your life better. The successful must be punished, because if initiative, hard work, and taking care of yourself catch on, people might wake up to the lies they've been told by the Democrat Party and start taking care of themselves.

Want to know what's wrong with a lot of polling and why so many are wrong when it comes to predicting election results? Consider a Gallup Poll on President Bush's popularity. The question asked was, "Based on what you have heard or read, please say whether you favor or oppose each of the following economic proposals." Based on what they have heard or read? A better question would have been, "Where did you read or hear what you believe to be true? *New York Times*? *Washington Post*? NPR? *Washington Times*? *National Review*?" When it comes to opinion, it does make a difference to know the source.

Secretary of State Colin Powell made his case before the United Nations Security Council that Saddam Hussein breached UN resolutions. He did a "show and tell" with pictures and objects he said proved Saddam had weapons of mass destruction. It would later emerge that the Iraqi dictator did not, and the United States and United Kingdom had deceived themselves. Many—including me—drew the wrong conclusions from the available data. It is why no president should unilaterally be able to declare war on another country, absent the most extreme emergency. It is why the Constitution gave Congress the ultimate authority to declare war, a fact too often ignored, which gets us into trouble. Vietnam was another example. While President Bush did persuade Congress to issue a "public law" that "authorized" him to use American troops in the region, it fell short of a constitutional declaration of war.

The government created color coding to alert people to the level of terrorist threats.

The 9th Circuit Court of Appeals re-affirmed its decision that saying "under God" in the Pledge of Allegiance violated church-state separation. Politicians on both sides (though more Republicans than Democrats) trashed the decision. I noted they find God a convenient tool to persuade people they are doing His will in Washington, when it often appears just the opposite.

Nicholas Kristof, a *New York Times* columnist, wrote that even though a Gallup Poll found 46 percent of the country identified as evangelical Christians and/or born again, "Offhand, I can't think of a single evangelical working for a major news organization." That tells you a lot, doesn't it? Years later Kristof would ask me if I was still writing my column. Clearly, he lives in a liberal bubble, which is shameful for someone claiming to be a journalist.

The Supreme Court heard arguments about a Texas law that forbade sodomy. Already I knew where this was headed and asked if the Court overturned the law and on what basis did it favor restrictions on any other form of human behavior? Why not legalize everything? If not, why not and according to whom? There's a difference between liberty and license.

After Saddam, what's next? The United States made a major mistake by completely dismantling the Iraqi Army, leaving a vacuum that terrorists from Iran were eager to fill.

Scott Peterson was arrested in California for murdering his wife and "unborn child," which brought up an interesting question: How can the unborn be a "child" and not be protected in law? Easy for the secular progressives who believe an unborn "fetus" is a child only if the woman considers it to be.

On Father's Day, I missed my Dad who died twenty years ago. I wrote, "I remember when he took me to buy my first suit, at age fourteen, and told me I was becoming a man." I recalled baseball games we attended together, the smell of hot dogs and real grass, and how good it felt doing "guy stuff" with him. I inherited no money, but got his fishing tackle box and his character. Priceless.

David Brinkley died. He was eighty-two. I called him the greatest broadcast journalist ever. It was not an exaggeration. The greatest compliment I ever received was when he told me, "I read your column. You write well." It was like being called a good Catholic by the Pope.

Actor Gregory Peck died. In addition to his wonderful films, I remembered him for his virulent anti-Robert Bork TV ads done for the liberal People for the American Way.

The Supreme Court tried to have it both ways when it came to racial preferences and college admissions. In a 5–4 ruling, the majority say minority students who apply for university admission may be given an edge, but it limits how large a role race can play in a university's selection of students. I wondered if the Court still believed the Fourteenth Amendment to be valid?

The Supreme Court ruling striking down that Texas law outlawing sodomy was written by Justice Anthony Kennedy. He was taking us on a journey with no fixed origin and no map but a sure destination. I predicted the next step would be same-sex marriage and so it was.

This is funny—and pathetic. The American Psychological Association published a study of why conservatives are the way they are. A press release said, "At the core of political conservatism is the resistance to change and tolerance for inequality." Well, yes, conservatives are resistant to change for the sake of change, believing that certain ideas about life, relationships, and morality are true for all time.

I was among a small group of fifty people who attended a screening of Mel Gibson's film *The Passion of the Christ*, covering the last twelve hours in the earthly life of Jesus. It was bloody, and for that reason, powerful and realistic about what scourging and crucifixion actually looked like in Roman times. I told Gibson, who attended the screening, that it was the most powerful depiction of a biblical event I had ever seen. People in the audience wept.

President Bush endorsed Arnold Schwarzenegger for governor of California. Bush said he would make a good governor. Based on what? The president couldn't possibly know what Schwarzenegger stood for because no one else seemed to know, including Arnold.

I met and interviewed the great Johnny Cash after he rehearsed for a performance later that night at Wolf Trap Farm Park in Vienna, Virginia. He spoke openly about his wrestling matches with temptation. He said he overcame it with Scripture memorization. He had become a frequent guest speaker for Billy Graham's crusades. Later that evening he broke up the audience when he said, "A lot of people in the business as long as I've been say they still feel like they're twenty-five. I don't. I feel like I'm forty-six." How would he like to be remembered? "As a good daddy," he responded. We stood. He shook my hand, thanked me, and left. His presence was unlike any other person I've met.

President Bush asked Congress for more aid for Iraq and Afghanistan. I called on oil-producing countries to foot the bill, not American taxpayers. Shades of things to come with Donald Trump.

Florida Governor Jeb Bush refused to stay executions for those judged guilty of capital murder. Bush also signed a hastily crafted law granting him power to stay a court order that allowed doctors to remove a feeding tube from Terri Schiavo, allowing her to starve to death. The case became a national sensation and highlighted right to life (and die) issues. I wrote that hard cases could make for bad law.

States found it increasingly difficult to pay the bill for inmates in overcrowded prisons. I blamed the "lock 'em up and throw away the key" politicians who believed this approach would control crime. If that worked, wouldn't crime be going down instead of up? Most nonviolent, non-dangerous offenders should not be warehoused but given alternative punishments and opportunities to change their lives. I recalled Andy Dufresne's line to Red in the film *The Shawshank Redemption*: "The funny thing is—on the outside, I was an honest man, straight as an arrow. I had to come to prison to be a crook."

Singer Michael Jackson was accused of having sex with a young boy. Given the spirit of the age, when just about everything is to be tolerated, I wondered what was wrong with that and according to what standard, as long as the kid is OK with it and his parents approved of their son spending nights in Jackson's bed?

President Bush visited troops in Iraq and was wildly applauded. Senator Hillary Clinton (D-NY) also made a trip and found it difficult to find any soldiers to sup with her.

Saddam Hussein was found hiding in a hole in the ground in Iraq.

In a column called "Keeping Christmas," I noted the rapid replacement of "the original cast"—that would be Jesus, Joseph, and Mary—with elves, reindeer, and Santa Claus; from a babe in the manger to a babe in the window of Victoria's Secret; from gold, frankincense, and myrrh to Bailey, Banks, and Biddle. No room in the inn had been replaced with no room in the mall parking lot. Some, though, still seek Him.

2004

The Year of Bush-Cheney Reelection

Mark Zuckerberg launches Facebook from his dorm room at Harvard. It quickly becomes one of the most consequential inventions of the modern era.

The Republic of Ireland becomes the first country in the world to ban smoking in all workplaces, including pubs and restaurants.

Islamic terrorists involved in the March 11, 2004, Madrid attacks are trapped by the police in their apartment and kill themselves. If they had only reversed the order.

Massachusetts becomes the first state to legalize same-sex marriage.

Ken Jennings begins his seventy-four-game winning streak on *Jeopardy*. He eventually wins more than $2.5 million.

Ronald Reagan passes away after battling for several years with Alzheimer's disease. His memorial service is held at Washington National Cathedral. Few presidents in modern times have so dominated or changed a nation and the world.

Martha Stewart is sentenced to five months in prison and five months home confinement for lying to federal investigators.

American super swimmer Michael Phelps wins his sixth gold medal at the Athens Olympics.

Presidential conventions are held. Republicans re-nominate George W. Bush. Democrats nominate John Kerry.

The Bush–Cheney ticket wins the election.

CAL'S TAKE

"It is easier to drive a stake through the heart of a blood-sucking vampire than to kill off a money-sucking and useless government program."

John Kerry channeled Bill Clinton (who didn't mean it either) when he claimed he wanted to keep abortion "safe, legal, and rare." Why rare if what is being killed is not human life? But then Kerry has always tried to have it both ways. He was for the war in Iraq before he was against it.

In a column about the death of Ronald Reagan, I wrote: "He was hated for precisely the same reasons he was loved. He had convictions and made those without them look weak. Ronald Wilson Reagan was a colossus of the twentieth century. Ronald Reagan saw the evil of communism and did not try to contain or oppose it. He aimed to defeat it, and did, at least the Soviet brand. Millions breathe free today because of him. It is altogether fitting that the Berlin Wall stands no longer as a monument to slavery but, in its deconstructed state, as a testimony to freedom at his library in Simi Valley, California."

Further adding to the belief of many that the media are promoting an agenda rather than the news, the major networks, newspapers, and other entities—even Fox News—sent representatives to the National Lesbian and Gay Journalists Association convention in New York. Many had booths and contributed money to the group. A CNN spokesman told me the network is committed to "diversity." I felt sure they were not committed to ideological diversity.

A study by the Cato Institute revealed no correlation between the amount of money spent on public school education and achievement. I had been saying this for years. Nice to have proof, although liberal politicians continued to make the false claim of a connection. A Cato analyst noted that education spending had ballooned from $25 billion in 1965 (adjusted for inflation) to $108 billion in 2002. And yet, "math and reading scores have stagnated, graduation rates have flatlined and researchers have shown several billion-dollar federal programs to be failures." Didn't matter because government programs take on a life of their own.

John Kerry picked John Edwards as his running mate. Edwards, dubbed the "Breck Boy" for his perfectly coiffed hair, would later be revealed to be having an extramarital affair while his wife was dying of cancer.

The Senate Select Committee on Intelligence found the Bush administration was presented with bad information in the run-up to the Iraq War. Oops!

Appearing on my Fox News channel program *After Hours*, Secretary of Defense Donald Rumsfeld said there was "no question" that the declaration presented by the United States to the United Nations justifying war against Iraq "was flawed, was inaccurate, was false," but nonetheless President

Bush "made the right decision." Rumsfeld added it is difficult to prove a negative (that Saddam Hussein did not have weapons of mass destruction) but suggested that "going forward, we may very well find that there are things that we don't know today." No evidence was unearthed that proved Rumsfeld correct. Saddam was a bad guy, but there were plenty of bad guys. We couldn't oust them all. His regime brought some stability to the region and his removal did the opposite.

In his acceptance speech for the Democrat presidential nomination, John Kerry said there was a "wealth gap" in America. True. Others make more money than I do, but I don't envy them. I am content in the economic state I am in and have the freedom to move up, if I wish, so long as I make decisions that are helpful in climbing the economic ladder. Kerry tried to enhance the envy, greed, and entitlement mentality he and other Democrats liked to promote.

An editorial in the *Washington Post* lamented the increased security in the capital: "At the rate federal authorities are walling off American buildings and grounds . . . downtown Washington could become a partitioned government enclave in only a few years." Was that ever prophetic!

Kerry criticized Bush for not immediately leaving the classroom on 9/11 and said that if he had been president, he would have politely excused himself. To do what? Kerry in fact was meeting that fateful morning with two Senate colleagues. On *Larry King Live*, Kerry admitted he and his colleagues sat frozen for thirty-four minutes after the planes crashed into the Twin Towers in New York and the Pentagon, and "nobody could think." That is a characteristic Kerry has displayed for years.

Eight years after Bill Clinton announced that "the era of big government is over," President Bush told cheering delegates at the GOP convention in New York that the era of small government was over. In accepting his party's nomination for a second term, Bush talked about what he wanted government to do, instead of what government should not be doing and Americans should be doing for themselves. I wrote that Bush was more in the mold of Richard Nixon than Ronald Reagan when it came to his view of the role of the federal government.

PBS broadcast a two-hour program called *The Question of God*. It featured a "debate" between Sigmund Freud, the atheist and founder of psychoanalysis, and C. S. Lewis, the eminent author, scholar, and Christian apologist. The program was based on a popular course taught by Harvard professor Dr. Armand Nicholi. I called it an honest and exceedingly fair summation of the main arguments for God's existence and non-existence by educated and articulate people. It was real reality TV.

CBS went all in against George W. Bush when Dan Rather aired a segment claiming Bush failed to submit to a physical exam "as ordered" while he was in the Texas Air National Guard. There was also an allegation his father intervened to sugarcoat Bush's performance record. It was a lie, and Rather should have known it. There were other allegations in the "story," but they were also full of holes. The credibility of *CBS News* was further damaged, and Rather would subsequently be removed from his anchor chair.

I showed up on a "terrorist watch list" and couldn't fly without "enhanced screening." Some guy with a similar name was a wanted criminal and TSA thought it could be me. After months of calling, emailing, and appealing my case to the secretary of transportation, I was finally removed from the list. If only I wasn't a white male, I could shout "discrimination." Ted Kennedy was on a similar list, but I think he got off faster than I did.

A Cato Institute study concluded what I have thought for a long time—that voters were ignorant about the candidates and their positions and do not know enough about the issues to make informed choices on Election Day. No wonder we often get bad leadership.

Bush won the election by a wider margin than Ronald Reagan. Also defeated was Senate Minority Leader Tom Daschle (D-SD), who had consistently thwarted legislation and court nominees he didn't like. Republicans picked up two Senate seats but squandered an opportunity to reform Social Security and Medicare, the two biggest drivers of debt.

Yasser Arafat died. I wrote that his legacy was one of murder, deceit, and corruption. As part of its obituary, the *New York Times* wrote, "Arafat led a long and failed effort for (Palestinian) statehood." He did no such thing. Arafat led a long reign of terror, the purpose of which was to kill Jews and eliminate the state of Israel.

Senator Mitch McConnell (R-KY) told me he was pleased that Congress had reduced the "rate of the increase in spending." I wonder if this is the new standard for the Republican congressional majority?

Senator Kay Bailey Hutchison (R-TX) wrote a highly readable and fascinating book titled *American Heroines: The Spirited Women Who Shaped Our Country*. The book was ideologically diverse and filled in a lot of gaps in history books.

My first job in radio at WINX in Rockville, MD, as disc jockey and news reader at sixteen.

NOTE: SPECIAL THANKS to Emilce Gomez of egozphotography in Miami, FL, for organizing and digitizing these photographs.

At an armed forces radio interview in New York City circa 1964.

Receiving an award for radio documentary from the Texas Heart Association circa 1969.

Taking a nap with one of my favorite magazines, *Texas Monthly*.

Reporting on a prison riot in outside the Texas State Penitentiary in Huntsville, Texas.

Channel 2 crew in Houston, TX, circa 1976 (Located in back with mustache).

Reporting live for Big 2 News at a chemical spill.

With colleagues Ray Miller, long-time news director at Channel 2 in Houston, TX, and anchor Steve Smith.

With President Ronald Reagan at the White House circa 1985.

With Ted Kennedy on the way from Washington, DC, to Lynchburg, VA, to speak at Liberty University about religious freedom.

With Secretary of Transportation Elizabeth Dole.

In Israel.

With Vice President George H. W. Bush in his office.

With President George W. Bush at the White House.

With President Barack Obama at the Gridiron Dinner in Washington, DC.

At Trump Tower with presidential candidate Donald Trump circa 2015.

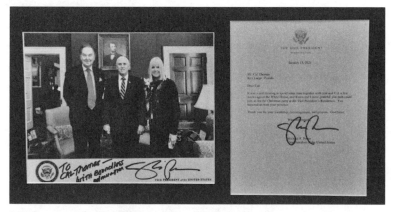

With my wife CJ and Vice President Mike Pence in the vice president's office in December 2016.

With President Donald Trump at the White House.

A journalist's life in press passes.

With Barbara Cook, the original Marian the Librarian in *The Music Man* in Philadelphia, PA, circa 1999.

With actress Roma Downey in Malibu, CA.

With Rachel Maddow in New York City.

With American World War II veteran and Olympic distance runner Louis Zamperini.

With singer Paul Anka at The Music Center at Strathmore in Bethesda, MD.

With my wife CJ (far left), friend Lesley Burbridge, and Kathy Lee Gifford (far right) in Ocean Reef, FL.

My daughter, Caray, at seventeen. This book is dedicated to her memory.

2005

The Year of Hurricane Katrina

North Korea announces that it possesses nuclear weapons as a protection against the hostility it feels from the United States. Few are surprised.

The Internet site YouTube goes online. Slogan is "Broadcast yourself."

The United States Court of Appeals for the 11th Circuit refuses by a vote of 2–1 to stop the euthanasia of Terri Schiavo, who has been in a "vegetative state" since 1990. She dies at age forty-one after her feeding tube is removed in Pinellas Park, Florida.

Mark Felt reveals himself to be the "Deep Throat" source for Bob Woodward in the Watergate affair.

President Bush nominates John Roberts to the Supreme Court to fill a vacancy left by the resignation of Justice Sandra Day O'Connor. After William Rehnquist dies, Bush nominates Roberts to replace him as chief.

Hurricane Katrina hits the Gulf Coast, killing at least 1,836 and causing severe damage affecting most of the eastern portion of the country. It would prove to be the costliest hurricane in American history with an estimated $108 billion in damages.

United States Army Reservist Lynndie England is convicted by a military jury on six of seven counts in connection with the Abu Ghraib prisoner controversy.

Civil rights activist Rosa Parks, who made headlines when she refused to give up her seat on a Montgomery, Alabama, bus, dies of natural causes in Detroit at ninety-two. She becomes the first woman to lie in honor in the United States Capitol rotunda.

Vice presidential adviser Lewis "Scooter" Libby resigns after being charged with obstruction of justice, perjury, and making a false statement in the CIA–Plame leak investigation. He would later be pardoned by President Donald Trump.

President Bush nominates Samuel Alito to the Supreme Court.

CAL'S TAKE

"The worst thing the federal government could do is to increase the size, reach, and cost of government. If government failed in its response to the hurricane, the answer is not more inefficient government."

An independent commission found *CBS News* guilty of "myopic zeal" in its airing of possibly forged documents that suggested President Bush lied about his service in the Texas National Guard. The 224-page report blamed pressure of getting the story, not political bias. Sure, and Watergate was just a "third-rate burglary." Four employees were fired but the ideological tilt continues.

Iraq held elections. Real elections. People who voted display a purple thumbprint.

I sat in the Oval Office with President Bush for a lengthy interview. I asked him about a timetable for the withdrawal of troops from Iraq. He responded, "I think timetables are a mistake." (Note to future presidents Obama, Trump, and Biden, who set timetables for the withdrawal of forces from Iraq and Afghanistan.)

When he was governor of Texas, Bush and I had lunch together at the mansion in Austin. I asked him for some of his favorite Bible verses and he mentioned two or three. During our White House interview, he said: "I don't see how anybody can be president without prayer and belief in the Almighty. . . . I recognize that, in my feebleness, I need support from the Almighty . . . and I love the support of people through prayer." When did you ever hear of a recent president acknowledge his "feebleness"?

Bush said he, along with his wife Laura, read the *Daily Bible*, a collection of verses from both Testaments, Psalms, and Proverbs, and also the devotional writings of Oswald Chambers.

What standard will he use after leaving office that will tell him whether his presidency was a success? "(That) will be judged by others, not by me. I suspect the true history of any administration won't really be known until years down the road, particularly in an administration like ours (that) tries to do big things."

Bush submitted a $2.57 trillion budget to Congress. I wrote that a major reason government had grown so large was that too many Americans had ceded personal responsibility to the state.

While the media and the Left touted research and cures for the AIDS epidemic, I wrote that changing the behavior that caused AIDS was key, but few others wanted to talk about that because we lived in a culture that said you ought to be able to do whatever you want with whomever you wish and pay no penalty for bad outcomes.

Border control was a big issue, even in 2005. I traveled to San Antonio, Texas, where I interviewed a rancher named Kerry Morales. He was not buying the defenders of illegal immigrants that claimed they are just looking for a better life and taking only jobs Americans don't want. "Maybe twenty years ago the illegals were innocent," Morales said, "but not anymore. Now they're extremely dangerous. They mean violence."

Associate Supreme Court Justice Anthony Kennedy opined that we have "evolving standards." That's the problem, isn't it? The statement prompted a column about a plan for a new curriculum about sex in public schools. Among other things, it taught kids how to put a condom on a cucumber. That's sure to boost sales in the produce section of the supermarket, but I doubted it would have much effect on teen pregnancy, absent self-control.

Some evangelicals went all in on battling what was then called "global warming." Richard Cizik, vice president of government affairs for the National Association of Evangelicals, told the *New York Times*, "I don't think God is going to ask us how He created the Earth, but He will ask us what we did with what He created." Really? How did Cizik know this? It was pure supposition on his part and a distraction from what ought to have been his primary message about salvation.

Breaking news! The Project for Excellence in Journalism (if only), an affiliate of Columbia University, said there was not enough reporting of facts in the news and too much opinion. Who knew?

President Bush flew back to Washington from an out-of-town trip to symbolically sign a bill created for the express purpose of inviting a federal court to review the case of Terri Schiavo. The issue was whether the state can intervene to "pull the plug" by removing her feeding tube and allowing her to die, or bend to the wishes of some of her closest relatives who want to artificially keep her alive. Hard cases should not be used to open the door to euthanasia.

Baseball returned to Washington after a thirty-four-year absence. I was thrilled and attended the first game. Memories flooded back of my dad and me attending old Washington Senators games.

More shocking news. A study by professors at three universities found that college faculties are not only mostly liberal but also lean even further to the Left than conservatives had thought. The professors (72 percent) labeled themselves liberal. It has only gotten worse since then.

Pope John Paul II died. I wrote that he was part of a "trinity"— Reagan and Thatcher being the other two—who helped bring down communism in the Soviet Union and Eastern Europe. Even former Soviet President Mikhail Gorbachev said so. Gorbachev told the Italian newspaper *La Stampa* in 1992: "What has happened in Eastern Europe in recent years would not have been possible without the presence of the Pope."

Little was done to protect the southern border as an increase in invading "migrants" continued. Wouldn't you want free stuff you can't get in other countries?

They were once called "junkets" but were now dubbed "fact-finding" trips. A study by Political MoneyLine found that, during the last five years, out of the $16 million spent on congressional travel paid for by private funds, more than half came from tax-exempt organizations and their lobbyists.

What happened to all the communists after the collapse of the Soviet Union? Anyone know? Perhaps they got teaching slots at American universities.

I acquired my first GPS. Like other men, I could now justify never again having to ask for directions. Besides, it is a woman's voice that still told me where to go.

The Pentagon acknowledged five instances in which guards or interrogators at Guantanamo Bay, Cuba, handled the Koran in a way that caused offense to some who believe it is the revealed word of Allah. Too bad the terrorists aren't as sensitive to Christian beliefs and Scripture.

At an Asian security conference in Singapore, Secretary of Defense Donald Rumsfeld delivered a blunt critique of China and its military buildup: "Since no nation threatens China, one wonders why this growing (military) investment?" I answered: Rather than feeling threatened, China intended to threaten others, especially the United States.

Kenneth Tomlinson, chairman of the Corporation for Public Broadcasting, said he believed PBS and NPR slant too far to the Left and need to be brought into balance. Lefties like Bill Moyers were fine with the current slant.

The Supreme Court did a legal version of The Twist. In one case, it ruled that a display of the Ten Commandments at the Texas capital building in Austin was constitutional, because it had been there since 1961, and no one had previously complained about it. The court also ruled framed copies of the Ten Commandments at two rural schools in Kentucky were unconstitutional because they were of more recent vintage and were displayed for the express purpose of advancing a particular religion. No wonder people have so little trust in federal courts.

Muslim terrorists bombed London. British Prime Minister Tony Blair invited Muslim "leaders" to a meeting. My suggestion as to what he should have told them (but never did): "The onus is on you, guys. You find and shut down the terrorists and their network. You turn those who incite, plan, and encourage violence over to the authorities. If you don't act, we will by closing and bulldozing the mosques and schools that incubate and instruct the killers and close our borders to anyone from countries that harbor and teach terrorists. Those who are British citizens will be stripped of their citizenship." To his credit, Blair did try to deport one of the more fanatical Mullahs who preached hate at a London mosque, but the legal system prevented him from doing so.

Israel announced a unilateral withdrawal from Gaza. I predicted it would be used by terrorists for new attacks against the Jewish state. One didn't have to be a prophet to know such attacks were inevitable. They happened, but much of the world still believed in the false notion that Israel relinquishing land would bring peace. It took just twelve days following the withdrawal for terrorist rockets to begin raining down on the Western Negev area. More would come.

I still like the title of this column: "When Gas Was Cheap and People Were Valuable."

The media misreported many things about Hurricane Katrina, including the number of deaths and the supposed slowness of aid to the New Orleans region. Bush's approval numbers fell. Mission accomplished.

Bush nominated Harriet Miers for a seat on the Supreme Court. Like Sandra Day O'Connor, her record was thin, and conservatives didn't want another stealth liberal like David Souter, so they opposed her, and she later withdrew.

I wrote about historian David McCullough's book *1776* and how what was said about George Washington was some of the same rubbish that had been said about a current "George W.," as in Bush.

Bush learned his lesson after the Harriet Miers mistake and nominated a solid conservative, Samuel Alito, to the Supreme Court.

Muslim immigrants rioted in the suburbs of Paris, France. Are the French learning anything from their willing acceptance of people from radical Muslim nations? Later they do, but it could be too late.

One of the reasons I preferred to be known as a conservative and not a Republican was that Republicans too often compromise their ideals, hoping the Left will like them. It never works. The Left despised them anyway, and in the end, they sold out for nothing.

Bush learned a lesson, but one too late. False allegations must be responded to, or they become truth in the minds of many. So, it was about the Iraq war when the narrative of critics was believed by many and Bush's approval numbers fell.

After saying he welcomed people who come to America, no matter how they got here (meaning legally, or illegally), President Bush announced a new "get tough" policy on those who break immigration laws. He was a bit tardy.

William Raspberry retired as a columnist for the *Washington Post*. As a black American, Raspberry never indulged in bitterness or name-calling. Rather, he sought to persuade people when it came to injustices in society. In a 1995 Alf Landon lecture at Kansas State University, Raspberry lamented the loss of community in America that led to violence in our streets, apathy in our schools, and hopelessness among our young people. He said a lot of these things resulted from "our crisis of community."

2006

The Year of Terrorists and Border Security

The Human Genome Project publishes the last chromosome sequence, in *Nature* magazine. Now that's significant!

Israel launches an offensive in the Gaza Strip in response to rocket fire into Israeli territory. Told you so.

Seven bombs go off in Mumbai, India. More than two hundred are killed.

Israeli troops invade Lebanon in response to the kidnapping of two Israeli soldiers and the murder of three others by the terrorist group Hezbollah. Hezbollah declares open war against Israel two days later. Told you so again.

North Korea claims to have conducted its first-ever nuclear test. There would be more.

Google buys YouTube for $1.65 billion.

Former Iraqi President Saddam Hussein is sentenced to death by hanging for crimes against humanity.

CAL'S TAKE

"Evil cannot be accommodated. Evil must be defeated if peace on Earth is to exist."

Britain's Labour Party exhibited the same tendencies of putting government first as America's Democratic Party. In a section of the liberal newspaper *The Guardian*, I noticed a long list of "help wanted" ads. They were all for government jobs. The average annual pay for these jobs was ten thousand pounds higher than comparable wages for private sector jobs. The reason for their existence was to shift more power from individuals and the private sector to the state. Sound familiar?

New British Prime Minister David Cameron sounded more like the British Left than the party of his predecessor, Margaret Thatcher. Cameron promised to put the interests of the poor above the rich. That's code for more government spending on programs that do not make the poor un-poor. Why do so-called conservatives try to out-promise the Left with programs that don't work but cost a lot? It's all about image and feelings.

On a visit to Paris, I noted that French Prime Minister Dominique de Villepin had fallen into the trap of apologists for Islamic terrorists. He blamed the riots in Muslim neighborhoods last year on "racial bias, lack of business opportunities, and insufficient education for immigrant children." Nowhere did he blame their twisted religion. This denial only increased the possibility of more riots and more terrorism.

During the early stages of his confirmation hearings, prospective Justice Samuel Alito assured senators that he had "no agenda." Why is that statement never required of liberal nominees? Turned out his only "agenda" was the Constitution, as written, and not what judges wished it said.

Following the lobbying scandal involving Jack Abramoff, congressional Democrats blamed Republicans for the "culture of corruption." That was a laugh since Democrats were part of the same "swamp" culture. Term limits would fix this, but the swamp dwellers were not about to harm their careers and benefits.

John McCain told me he was seriously thinking of running for president in 2008. In an interview in his Senate office, McCain said while he lauded Bush's response to the terrorist attack on 9/11 and his subsequent efforts to protect the homeland, he opposed the president on more spending and bigger government. He declared immigration reform to keep terrorists from sneaking into the country must be a "prime issue." How did that work out? McCain made a good point on spending when he noted Bush had not vetoed a single bill—including spending bills—in his five years in office.

A Republican Senate voted to raise the debt ceiling to nearly $9 trillion. Senators then quickly passed a record (at the time) $2.8 trillion budget. I recalled the words of Ronald Reagan about debt: "The federal deficit is outrageous. For years I've asked that we stop pushing onto our children the excesses of government." Those excesses and debt would only grow worse because politicians didn't want to say no to anybody, and the result was more addiction to an ever bigger and costlier government that ultimately led to a loss of liberty.

More evidence—if any was needed—on the worldview of most who work in journalism. ABC News suspended for one month without pay John Green, executive producer of the weekend edition of *Good Morning America*, after two emails Green sent came to light. In one, Green wrote to a colleague during the first 2004 presidential debate: "Are you watching this? Bush makes me sick. If he uses the 'mixed messages' line one more time, I'm going to puke." In the second, leaked to the *New York Post*, Green said former Secretary of State Madeleine Albright should not be booked on the show because 'Albright has Jew shame.'" Albright was raised Roman Catholic, but had a Jewish heritage. Green issued an apology, but the emails were revealing.

Just in time for Easter, officials in St. Paul, Minnesota, banned the Easter Bunny from City Hall. They said it might offend some non-Christians, as if the bunny had anything to do with the resurrection of Christ. I guess they never gave a thought that the bunny, like Santa Claus, might offend some Christians.

I wrote a review of perhaps the best male-bonding book I had ever read, Bob Greene's *And You Know You Should Be Glad*. It's about a group of boys who went through school together and go their separate ways. Later, one of them was diagnosed with terminal cancer, and the others came back to the small town of Bexley, Ohio, where they all grew up, to be with him. It was powerful, emotional, and wonderful. If you haven't read it, get it. You will be more than glad.

Border security remained such a controversial issue that President Bush addressed the nation and called on Congress to approve his plan to hire thousands of additional border patrol agents and to authorize the National Guard as backup.

I wrote about the "death of ideology" and lamented the demise of real debates that produced results from policies that worked instead of the tired, rehearsed, and poll-tested soundbites that both parties regularly tossed at each other.

President Bush felt compelled to issue a public statement in which he said marriage should be reserved for men and women marrying each other, not members of the same sex. Opponents said to deny same-sex marriage was "discrimination." Some discrimination is good because it preserves what used to be called cultural norms. If anything goes, then everything potentially goes.

The new leader of the Episcopal Church in America, Bishop Katharine Jefferts Schori, said she does not believe homosexual sex is a sin and that homosexuals were created by God to love people of the same gender. She cited no Scripture to back up her claim because there is none. No wonder this and other liberal denominations continue to bleed members.

Katie Couric, the newly minted anchor of *CBS Evening News*, announced a "listening tour" (shades of Hillary Clinton) to find out what real people were thinking. You had to fill out an application to be admitted so she could listen to the select few.

House Republicans were told by their leaders to run their fall campaigns on a platform of fiscal discipline that included cutting spending. This from a party that had given us new entitlement programs resembling Lyndon B. Johnson's Great Society; this from a party that had set new records in "earmarks" for pork barrel projects in their home districts and states; this from a party that under Ronald Reagan at least tried to eliminate the Department of Education, but under President Bush had thrown new money at it with no appreciable improvement in academic achievement. Yes, I can be critical of both parties when they do wrong.

Oliver Stone, a committed liberal and critic of America, produced a patriotic movie titled *World Trade Center*. What? The Oliver Stone who hung out with and praised Fidel Castro; the Oliver Stone who indulged in conspiracy theories and was a dues-paying member of the Hollywood Left? Yes, *that* Oliver Stone. The film was about five men who volunteered to enter the Twin Towers on September 11, 2001, in their role as officers of the Port Authority Police Department. Three of them died. The film (which starred Nicholas Cage) was a triumph of patriotism, heroism, and hope. Stone appeared on *Larry King Live* and said that if conservative Cal Thomas liked it, the film must be good.

Actor Mel Gibson delivered a slur against the Jewish people. Later he was seen at a bar. I asked: "What is a married man with seven children doing at a bar at two o'clock in the morning with young women hanging all over him?"

An alleged attempt by terrorists to hijack multiple flights from Britain to the United States produced the clearest statement yet from President Bush about the problem confronting us: "We are at war with Islamic fascists."

I met again with the president in the White House. He said he knew some people considered him stubborn, but "if you believe in a strategy . . . you have to stick with that strategy." He believed the struggle with what he called "Islamo-radicalism" would be a long one. He was right about that, though he wouldn't admit that the intelligence behind the Iraq War was flawed. He hoped to leave his successors "foundations" for fighting terrorism and interrogating suspects that would allow future presidents to successfully wage the battle. He probably never anticipated a President Joe Biden.

School violence was the subject of a "summit" in Chevy Chase, Maryland, not far from where some of the "Beltway snipers" conducted their indiscriminate shootings outside of school. When life became cheap and humans were disposable (as with abortion), it explained what was behind some of the violence.

A poll finds 78 percent of those surveyed believe "our system of government is broken." That's because politicians and judges no longer adhere to the Constitution, which is as perfect a document ever written by human minds.

I met again with Secretary of Defense Donald Rumsfeld in his Pentagon office. He said, "Terrorism is growing. In the thirty days ending last week, it is estimated there were thirty-seven terrorist attacks, by thirteen different organizations, against the property or citizens of twenty different countries." He said much of it is state-sponsored.

I also met separately with Secretary of State Condoleezza Rice. I asked her why she thought there were so many trouble spots threatening the United States and the world at the same time. She replied: "We are at the beginning of a big historic transition. When I was here the last time working for President George H. W. Bush, we were at the end of fifty years of containing the Soviet threat and ultimately defeating it. And so, we got to harvest the end of that. . . . This time we're at the beginning of a new, big historic transition where we're trying to lay the foundation for the ultimate victory of democracy and triumph against the ideology of hatred and the defeat of terrorism and the rogue states." Rice and I disagreed on a Palestinian state. She said she didn't believe most Palestinian mothers wanted their sons to become the first suicide bombers. "I think mothers want their children to go to university." She concluded: "If human beings don't want a better future, don't want their children to grow up in peace and have opportunities, then none of this is going to work anyway." Exactly!

I asked a cynical question: If God was on the side of conservative Christians and conservative Christians were on the side of the Republican Party, shouldn't Republicans have done better in the elections?

Milton Friedman, the "grandmaster of free-market economic theory," died at age ninety-four. Friedman and his wife, Rose, were advocates and supporters of school choice as a means of liberating poor and minority children from failing government schools. They put their money where their beliefs were and paid for many scholarships so kids could get a real education and hope for a better future.

In my (almost) annual Christmas column, I wrote: "As we approach the day once known as Christmas, before it became 'holiday,' there is a sense that the Messiah, whom the day is supposed to acknowledge, is rapidly being supplanted in the public consciousness by a new American religion called politics."

2007

The Year of Bitter Politics

Rep. Nancy Pelosi (D-CA) becomes the first female Speaker of the House. A liberal is a liberal no matter the gender or race, but the media rejoice.

American warplanes conduct air strikes in Somalia against suspected terrorists.

Steve Jobs announces the release of the first iPhone and continues a revolution in communication. Instead of heads turning, more heads look down.

President Bush announces a plan to station twenty-one thousand five hundred additional troops in Iraq.

Senator Barack Hussein Obama announces he's running for president.

Bagram Air Base is hit by a homicide bomber during a visit by Vice President Dick Cheney. Cheney is unhurt, but twenty-three are killed.

Thirty-two people are killed at Virginia Tech in Blacksburg, Virginia. The gunman bought the firearms legally, despite having a record of mental illness.

Bob Barker hosts his final show for *The Price Is Right*.

The Dow Jones Industrial Average closes above 14,000 for the first time in history.

Barry Bonds of the San Francisco Giants breaks Hank Aaron's home run record, hitting his 756th home run.

The Texas Rangers score thirty runs in one game, setting the modern (post-1900) Major League Baseball (MLB) record for most runs by one team in a single game. Final score is 30–3 victory over the Baltimore Orioles.

The recession officially begins. Unemployment rate is 5 percent.

CAL'S TAKE

"America's most dangerous diseases have developed an immunity to politics. We suffer not from a failure of political organization or power, but a failure of love."

The doctrine of "just deserts" has been effectively abandoned in modern times. It meant if you knowingly do something wrong and get caught, you deserve the punishment. The Old Testament principle put it this way: "An eye for an eye; a tooth for a tooth." Gilbert and Sullivan expressed it in an entertaining way when they wrote in *The Mikado*: "Let the Punishment Fit the Crime."

Saddam Hussein got what he deserved when he was hanged in Iraq. In a final blasphemy, Saddam, who spent most of his life as a murdering secularist, went to his death holding a Koran and offering his soul to God, if God would accept it. I said that if God did, He would have to commute the "sentences" of other mass murderers, including Hitler, Stalin, Mao, and Pol Pot.

In 2004, Nancy Pelosi issued a "minority bill of rights" in which she promised that if Democrats won back a House majority, she and her fellow Democrats wouldn't treat Republicans the way she claimed they treated Democrats. Now they have one. How did that work out?

House Democrats touted an "ethics reform" package. It was amusing to watch people who created the problem claim to be able to fix it.

Barack Obama announced the formation of an "exploratory committee" to consider whether he should run for president. In a video accompanying his announcement, he said, "How hungry we all are for a different kind of politics . . . our leaders in Washington seem incapable of working together in a practical, common sense way. Politics has become so bitter and so partisan, so gummed up by money and influence, that we can't tackle the big problems that demand solutions." When Democrats speak of unity, they mean Republicans should acquiesce to their point of view. Obama would prove to be a very divisive president.

Hillary Clinton declared her candidacy for president. I wrote that on the Left, feminists would likely portray her as the reincarnation of suffragette Susan B. Anthony. On the Right, conservatives would portray her as a cross between Lady Macbeth and Bonnie Parker.

At an appearance in Iowa, Hillary Clinton lied about her vote in the Senate to authorize the war against Iraq. Fortunately, we have a YouTube video that showed her casting a "yes" vote. She should take lessons from husband Bill, who not only was an expert at lying but could make you believe he was actually telling the truth.

North Korea agreed to take steps toward nuclear disarmament. This was like Bill Clinton embracing fidelity. Neither happened.

After voting in favor of the war in Iraq when they were in the minority, House Democrats now voted in favor of a "non-binding resolution" to oppose President Bush sending twenty thousand additional troops to stabilize the new government.

The Clintons have always been grifters. Recall Bill once sold his underwear. Now, the *Washington Post* revealed Bill had taken in nearly $40 million in speaking fees since he left office.

White House Press Secretary Tony Snow spoke at a dinner for media people I have sponsored for years in Washington. It was just revealed his cancer had returned. Among other things, Tony said the disease had caused him to ask where he would go with faith: "For a lot of us as kids, having faith is like sitting on Santa's lap; you pray because you want things and you want outcomes. But instead, when you're faced with death, you don't really die; you get to go to a cooler place with maybe a sterner teacher. It's not that big a leap, and you're going to go see a lot of friends there." Now that's a sermon. Tony died a few months later. I miss him still and always regarded him as a great friend and colleague.

In England, a new government-backed study found that British schools were dropping the Holocaust from their history lessons. Teachers were afraid to teach about the Nazi atrocity because Muslims might take offense. Will that also include not teaching about Muslim atrocities?

To just about everyone's surprise, Northern Ireland Protestant leader Reverend Ian Paisley and Sinn Fein's

Gerry Adams, reached an agreement to form a new local government in which Protestants and Catholics would share power. It effectively ended decades of sectarian violence in the province. I interviewed Paisley and asked him if he had any regrets over his own rhetoric that critics said contributed to the violence known as "The Troubles." He responded: "I may have said and done things that, if I had to say and do them again, I might have said and done them differently. But I have no regrets that the line I took was the right line. I think that has now been vindicated by what has happened (the peace agreement). We have got a deal we were told we couldn't get. It is quite clear to everybody there is going to be no united Ireland for one hundred years, at least."

CBS Radio and MSNBC suspended Don Imus for two weeks because he made remarks some regarded as disparaging to black Americans. I noted that a lot of hip-hop music disparaged black women far more than what Imus said. Jesse Jackson criticized Imus, apparently forgetting his own use of "Hymietown" in a reference to New York City Jews. You have to love the Left's double standards.

A one-man massacre occurred at Virginia Tech University, in which thirty-two people died. I wonder what difference it would have made if one person had been armed and taken down the killer?

The Supreme Court, by a narrow 5–4 vote, upheld a law banning partial-birth abortion. It was the first restriction on abortion the court had allowed since *Roe v. Wade* in 1973.

Liberals wanted to resurrect the fairness doctrine in response to the success of talk radio hosts like Rush Limbaugh and Fox News. They refused to understand that the success of Limbaugh and Fox were a result of the unfairness toward conservatives practiced by the big media.

Jerry Falwell died at age seventy-three. I called him a central figure in the rise of what liberals called the "Religious Right." His crowning achievement, however, had less to do with politics than with his vision for Liberty University, which endures.

President Bush and several senators claimed to have fixed the problem of illegal immigration. It looked more like amnesty to me. The new law—get this—allowed for the construction of three hundred seventy miles of fence along the southern border, two hundred miles of vehicle barriers, ground-based radar, camera towers, and aerial vehicles. An additional eighteen thousand border patrol agents were to be hired. How did that work out in light of future events and a future president?

The British education system is giving up classical teaching in history, science, and English literature in favor of trendy things to make the subject matter more "popular." It's a form of national suicide when a nation refuses to remind future generations of its founding and sustaining principles.

The *New York Times* did a puff piece on Hillary Clinton's "faith." There were pictures of her in Sunday school as a young girl, of two ministers who "influenced Hillary Rodham on faith and social responsibility," and of her praying. The story was in line with liberals who tried to pry some of the "Christian vote" away from Republicans. One of the ministers of her youth, Reverend Donald Jones, said of his messages: "I wouldn't have focused so much on personal salvation. I would have focused more on social responsibility." That is a works-based attempt to achieve salvation, and if one could work their way into Heaven, why did Jesus bother to come and die for sinners?

On the continuing opposition to our presence in Iraq and the support of a stable government, I noted that we never hear Democrats speak of victory. They embraced defeat, unwilling to wait for Bush's "new strategy" to work. The anti-war crowd owned their party, and to them, no war was worth fighting.

So cynical have our politics become that a spokesman (yes, he was a man, I think) for Speaker Nancy Pelosi said Democrat leaders are "not willing to concede there are positive things to point to" in Iraq. Most seemed to be so invested in defeat that they had no plan B, which should have been victory and success.

I called "global warming" (now re-named "climate change") the secular religion of our day. It was like a cult. No dissenting ideas were to be considered. *Meet the Press* host Chuck Todd said he would no longer have a guest on his program who didn't believe in climate change. No bias there, right?

After months of claiming we were losing the war in Iraq and President Bush's surge of troops was not working, some Democrats re-positioned themselves, saying that the surge appeared to be working. Just in time for the coming election, so they can claim to support the troops.

Oh, for the good old days when Jimmy Carter only lusted in his heart. Deviancy's downward spiral reached the level where a United States Senator—Larry Craig (R-ID)—plead guilty to cruising an airport men's room in search of an anonymous "quickie." He was forced to resign.

At a debate among Democrat presidential candidates in Philadelphia, Senator Barack Obama promised that as president he would "convene a meeting of Muslim leaders" to confront Iran's nuclear threat. One might as well convene a meeting of anti-Semites to combat anti-Semitism.

A *Washington Post*–ABC News poll revealed nearly three-quarters of those surveyed believed the country was on the wrong track. How often have we heard this before, especially when a Republican was in the White House?

There used to be a bumper sticker that said: "Fight Crime: Shoot Back." That's what forty-two-year-old volunteer security guard, Jeanne Assam, did at the New Life Church in Colorado Springs. When a twenty-four-year-old gunman with a declared grievance against Christians walked into the church, Assam confronted him. The gunman then committed suicide. Who doubts he would have killed many church members had Assam not stepped in? It proved once again that a good person with a gun can stop a bad person with a gun.

In Washington over tea, I interviewed former Pakistani Prime Minister Benazir Bhutto. She was about to return to Pakistan despite death threats. She was a strong woman, and I wrote that strong women are a threat to men who are weak. She knew the risks of returning home but told me, "I love my country and my people." Weeks later she was assassinated. I shall never forget her courage and her amazing beauty.

2008

The Year of the Subprime Mortgage Crisis

Joe Biden drops out of the 2008 election. It's the second time he has given up. So, too, do Rudy Giuliani and John Edwards.

President Bush announces an economic stimulus package, proposing $800 per individual and $1,600 per couple in tax refunds.

Stock markets around the world plunge amid growing fears of an American recession, fueled by the 2007 subprime mortgage scandal.

Actor Heath Ledger, twenty-eight, is found dead at his New York City home. He would later be awarded a posthumous Academy Award for Best Supporting Actor for his role as the Joker in *The Dark Knight*. The film becomes the highest-grossing film of the year.

United States stock market indices plunge more than 3 percent after a Non-Manufacturing ISM Report on Business shows signs of economic recession in the service sector.

The S&P 500 falls 3.2 percent, and the Dow Jones Industrial Average drops 370 points.

The Senate passes a $170 billion economic stimulus package by a margin of 81–16.

John McCain secures the 2008 Republic presidential nomination.

New York Democratic Governor Eliot Spitzer (a.k.a. "Client number 9") announces his resignation days after being linked to a high-priced prostitution ring.

California becomes the second state after Massachusetts in 2004 to legalize same-sex marriage after the state's Supreme Court rules a previous ban unconstitutional. What's next?

Senator Ted Kennedy announces that he has a malignant cancerous brain tumor.

Barack Obama secures the 2008 Democratic presidential nomination.

After three decades as the chairman of Microsoft Corporation, Bill Gates steps down from daily duties to concentrate on the Bill and Melinda Gates Foundation.

Former United States senator and vice-presidential and presidential candidate John Edwards admits to an adulterous affair with former campaign worker Rielle Hunter after months of tabloid speculation, but he denies being the father of her baby. Edwards would later say he was the baby's father. Politicians lie.

Barack Obama and Joe Biden are declared the Democratic presidential and vice-presidential candidates at the Democratic National Convention in Denver.

Republican presidential candidate John McCain chooses Alaska Governor Sarah Palin as his running mate. Both are declared their party's nominees at the GOP convention in St. Paul, Minnesota.

The Rachel Maddow Show premieres on MSNBC.

Wall Street investment bank Lehman Brothers files for Chapter 11 bankruptcy protection.

The Dow Jones Industrial Average falls 777 points due to the financial panic.

Barack Obama is elected president.

The unemployment rate soars to 7.3 percent, the highest since December 1992.

O. J. Simpson is sentenced to thirty-three years in prison for participating in an armed robbery. Simpson would be granted parole and released in October 2017.

Bernie Madoff is arrested and charged with securities fraud in connection with what would later be revealed to be the largest Ponzi scheme in history.

CAL'S TAKE

"Prosperity without a soul is like a corpse whose heart has stopped breathing. There is no life, only consumption."

I fell into the category of people who were excited by the potential of Barack Obama. I allowed my joy at the possibility of seeing a black man elected president (when just forty years earlier he would have been barred in some places from public facilities), to overcome my natural skepticism that any liberal Democrat would change his spots, regardless of the color of his skin.

At an aptly named Republican "retreat," President Bush argued in favor of his "bipartisan stimulus package." Why do so many Republicans appear to be "Democrat-lite"?

A group called Exodus Mandate began placing literature in scores of Southern California church lobbies, urging parents to take charge of their children's education and oppose attempts by liberal activists to shape their worldview. The final straw for many came when Governor Arnold Schwarzenegger, a Republican, signed a bill requiring "nondiscrimination" against sexual orientation and other characteristics.

Obama campaign manager David Plouffe asked Hillary Clinton to release her tax returns, calling her "one of the most secretive politicians in America today." I love it when Democrats go after each other.

Eliot Spitzer (a.k.a. "Client number 9"), having literally been caught with his pants down (while keeping his socks on) with a prostitute in an upscale Washington, DC hotel, was advised by me that he should have looked at the Gideon Bible in the bedside table. Then he would have found this warning: "A prostitute is a deep pit; an adulterous woman is treacherous. She hides and waits like a robber, looking for another victim who will be unfaithful to his wife" (Proverbs 23:27–28 NIV).

Barack Obama ludicrously claimed never to have heard any of the anti-Semitic and anti-American sermons preached by Reverend Jeremiah Wright, his pastor. Wright even claimed the United States was complicit in the 9/11 terrorist attacks. Only Fox News tried to hold him accountable for his remarks, and not the mainstream media. Their agenda was clear.

The Obama campaign went after Roman Catholic and even Protestant evangelical voters by forming a National Catholic Advisory Council. I called it a sham because Democrats, even many Catholic Democrats, are not about to oppose their church's teachings when it comes to sex and marriage.

Time magazine published another of its "100 Most Influential People in the World" lists. It never tells us why they are "influential," or even what the word means to them. Most are aligned with political power, wealth, and influence. No mothers who influence their children to make the right decisions are selected. Neither are pastors who preach about the possibility of a changed life, which is real influence.

Gas prices exceeded $4 a gallon in some places.

Senator Ted Kennedy announced he had a brain tumor. It's serious. I wrote about my twenty-five-year friendship with him and—issues aside—how I came to regard him as a friend. I urged people to pray for him.

Victimhood and a "can't do spirit" (at least without government) characterized the Democratic Party and the rhetoric of Barack Obama and Hillary Clinton. Listening to them made me feel I was living in a Third World country, not the United States of America, where the poorest person had more benefits and opportunities than any other country. I quoted the main character from the film *Auntie Mame*: "Life is a banquet, but most poor suckers are starving to death."

Hillary Clinton and Barack Obama go on a "unity tour" after he secured his party's presidential nomination. I recalled something Clinton said about him on *The 700 Club* program only weeks earlier: ". . . there is a certain phenomenon associated with (Obama's) candidacy. (He) dangerously oversimplifies the complexity of the problems we face, the challenge of navigating our country through some difficult, uncharted waters." Hillary flip-flopped faster than a fish out of water.

It is a truism in politics that you are supposed to lower expectations if you want to boost your political stock. Obama did the opposite. He raised expectations so high that there was no way he could meet them. Remember that promise to lower the ocean levels and "we are the ones we've been waiting for" malarkey?

Both Obama and McCain promised, if elected, to reach out to "the other side." Obama turned out to be one of the most divisive presidents in recent history. Why were so many surprised?

Aleksandr Solzhenitsyn died at age eighty-nine. He truly was a prophet for our times, repeatedly warning the West about the cracking of its fundamental foundations. He also warned the West not to be deluded by the notion that all nations desired to be like America. He called this "the blindness of superiority" and warned against thinking that only "wicked governments" temporarily prevented other nations from "adopting the Western way of life." Unfortunately, like many of those Old Testament prophets, Solzhenitsyn was ignored by the elites.

Obama picked Joe Biden as his running mate. Biden had been in the Senate for thirty-six years and yet he and Obama criticized Washington and its politics. If it was so bad, what role did Biden play in its decline?

House Speaker Nancy Pelosi, an "ardent, practicing Catholic," defended her pro-choice position on abortion because, according to her, her church had held its pro-life position for only fifty years, and for the two thousand preceding years, it had reached different conclusions about when life began. In an unusual public rebuke of a leading political figure, Archbishop Donald W. Wuerl said Pelosi was "incorrect" in her statement. Wuerl quoted from the Catechism of the Catholic Church which he said had been clear for two thousand years: "Human life must be respected and protected absolutely from the moment of conception. . . . Since the first century, the Church has affirmed the moral evil of every procured abortion. This teaching has not changed and remains unchangeable. Direct abortion, that is to say, abortion willed either as an end or as a means, is gravely contrary to the moral law." That seemed clear to me, but apparently not to Pelosi.

I spoke with Florida Governor Jeb Bush, who complimented Palin for bringing enthusiasm to the ticket, "which was the one element of the campaign that was completely missing." That enthusiasm faded as the media did a hatchet job on the vice-presidential nominee. Unfortunately, Palin too often handed them the hatchet.

The Supreme Court legitimized same-sex marriage. I wondered if there was anything the Court wouldn't tolerate. If there was, I wanted to know what standard they would use.

Reverend Jesse Jackson told columnist and author Amir Taheri that the foreign policy would improve in an Obama administration because "decades of putting Israel first" would come to an end. Jackson said this in Evian, France, the home of the preferred water of Volvo-driving liberals.

A seven-year-old audio recording of Barack Obama surfaced in which he strongly suggested the United States Constitution was an impediment to his desire to redistribute the nation's wealth. Thank goodness for the Constitution. A major reason that document was written was to constrain the powerful from infringing on our liberties, including economic liberty.

The ombudsman for the *Washington Post* acknowledged that conservatives had a point when they claimed an imbalance in coverage of Barack Obama and John McCain. Talk about a gift for the obvious, but it's a little late.

Obama won the election, and the media and liberal America went orgasmic. The power of the so-called "Religious Right" seemed depleted.

O. J. Simpson got his "just deserts," not for murdering two people but for his role in an armed robbery and kidnapping at a Las Vegas hotel. Simpson was sentenced to between nine and thirty-three years in prison.

The CIA was revealed to have given Viagra to an older Afghan leader who had four wives. When the agent made a return visit, the Afghan had a big smile on his face and handed over information about the Taliban. One longtime CIA operative said, "Whatever it takes to make friends and influence people, whether it's building a school or handing out Viagra." It sounded like we were taking "foreign affairs" to a different level.

2009

The Year of the Great Recession

The worst month of the Great Recession sees nearly eight hundred thousand jobs lost; the unemployment rate rises to 7.8 percent—the highest since June 1992.

Congress is back with Democrats increasing their majority to 256 seats in the House and to fifty-nine seats in the Senate.

US Airways Fight 1549 loses power in both engines shortly after takeoff from LaGuardia, forcing the pilot to ditch the aircraft in the Hudson River. All 155 passengers and crew are rescued with no casualties, and the pilot, Chesley Sullenberger is hailed as a hero.

Circuit City, the number two electronics retailer in the United States, announces the closing of all 567 of its American stores and the termination of thirty-four thousand jobs.

Barack Obama is sworn in as the forty-fourth president of the United States.

President Obama signs executive orders to close the Guantanamo Bay detention facility within one year and to prohibit torture in terrorism interrogations. It never happens.

Illinois Democratic Governor Rod Blagojevich becomes the first state governor in a quarter century to be impeached and removed from office.

President Obama orders the deployment of seventeen thousand additional troops to Afghanistan.

In an address to Congress, President Obama defends financial bailouts as necessary to economic recovery, and vows stricter regulation of financial institutions and health care reform. He also warns that future bailouts may be necessary.

Insurance giant AIG reports nearly $62 billion in losses during the fourth quarter of 2008, and the American government gives it $30 billion more in aid in a new bailout. Federal Reserve Chairman Ben Bernanke says AIG took huge, irresponsible risks.

Bernie Madoff pleads guilty to his Ponzi scheme investment scandal.

A report by the Federal Reserve says American families lost a record 18 percent of their wealth in 2008.

AIG announces it will pay $450 million in bonuses to top executives despite its central role in the global financial meltdown and despite receiving a $173 billion government bailout. A massive public outcry follows, with Obama calling AIG greedy and reckless.

The unemployment rate hits 9 percent for the first time since September 1983; it will not drop below 9 percent again until late 2011.

Obama visits Cairo, Egypt, and delivers a speech to the "Muslim world" that is full of apologies for America's "flaws." Critics decry it as "the apology tour."

Pennsylvania Republican Senator Arlen Specter switches parties to become a Democrat, giving that party a fifty-nine-seat Senate majority.

President Obama announces vehicle emissions and mileage requirements. Under the new federal rules, vehicles will use 30 percent less fuel and emit one third less carbon dioxide by 2016. The changes will add $1,300 to the cost of each new vehicle.

The Great Recession officially ends, but job losses continue through December, though at a slower pace. The unemployment rate hits 9.5 percent for the first time since August 1983.

Entertainer Michael Jackson dies. A public memorial service is one of the most watched funerals of all time, potentially reaching over 2.5 billion people worldwide. Does this reveal where our priorities lie?

Sonia Sotomayor becomes the third woman and the first Hispanic to serve on the Supreme Court.

The Department of Justice announces the largest health care fraud settlement in history, $2.3 billion, involving Pfizer. The company will later develop in record time a COVID-19 vaccine.

The unemployment rate peaks at 10.0 percent, the highest since June 1983.

President Obama is awarded the Nobel Peace Prize, which surprises many, including Obama.

Fort Hood becomes the scene of the worst mass shooting at a United States military base when Army psychiatrist Major Nidal Malik Hasan opens fire, killing thirteen and wounding dozens.

Ongoing are wars in Afghanistan and Iraq.

CAL'S TAKE

"Victimhood and a 'can't do' spirit is what the Democratic Party has mostly been about since the Great Depression."

I interviewed Louisiana Governor Bobby Jindal at the governor's mansion in Baton Rouge. He told me there are at least three lessons that Republicans should learn from their wipeout in the last election: 1) "the party must consistently do what it says. You can't be the party of fiscal discipline and tolerate the kind of spending that our party has accepted in the last several years; 2) We've got to consistently oppose corruption in our own party. It's not enough to make excuses that 'the other side does it'; 3) We have to apply our ideas to the problems Americans care about. For too long the Republican answer (to health care) for example, has been dumb."

I wrote a "Welcome to town" letter to incoming President Obama, expressing the hope that he would offer minority children opportunities to escape from failing public schools and not embrace a left-wing agenda. I don't think he read it, or if he did, he ignored it. Too bad. He squandered many great opportunities and the goodwill of many who wanted the first president of color to do well.

Obama had promised to end politics as usual and create a new bipartisanship to get things done for the American people. Most politicians say that, but never do. Obama proved to be no exception.

Obama dispatched his special envoy to the Middle East, former Democratic Senator George Mitchell, in hopes of forging a peace deal between Israel and the Palestinians. I compared his mission to the faith of *Peanuts* character Linus

van Pelt, who believes each Halloween that the Great Pump-
kin will rise out of the patch and bring gifts with him. I said
the mission would fail because peace is not about us but
about them, and especially about the Palestinians who refused to accept Israel as a Jewish state.

Obama's nominee for secretary of the treasury, Timothy
Geithner, and his nominee for secretary of health and human
services, former Senator Tom Daschle, caused heads to spin
when Geithner claimed to have "forgotten" to pay $43,000
in back taxes and penalties to the IRS, and Daschle remembered to pay $128,000 he owed plus $12,000 in interest—only
six days before his confirmation hearing.

Struggling General Motors (GM) and Chrysler applied for
federal bailout money. Ford decided to fend for itself. While
GM and Chrysler would eventually pay back the money to
Washington, I believed a bad precedent had been set. A private business should succeed or fail on its own. This policy
happened to save jobs and the auto industry, but it should
have been seen as an exception, not a rule.

Financial adviser Ric Edelman said on his syndicated radio
show the reason so many people were panicking during the
recession was that they had lived only in prosperous times.
Edelman noted that thirty years ago, just 20 percent of the
country was invested in the stock market. Now, 70 percent
were invested and most had lived only during periods when
the market (and home values) always increased.

A rule approved in the waning days of the Bush administration established broad protections for health care workers whose religious faith, conscience, or moral misgivings
forbade them from participating in an abortion. The Department of Health and Human Services (ironically named)

announced its intention to rescind the rule. What is it about abortion that makes some social liberals consider it a sacrificial rite, through which only the killing of an unborn child can truly liberate a woman from the clutches of paternalism?

Rush Limbaugh ignited the Conservative Political Action Conference in Washington with a speech imploring Republicans to recall what they said they once believed that had won them elections. Instead, he said, too many of them have tried to cozy up to the liberal elites, hoping they will praise them for being "reasonable" and "moderate." Michael Steele, chairman of the Republican Party, made Limbaugh's point when he called the talk show host's rhetoric "incendiary" and "ugly." In truth, it was educational and inspirational, even entertaining.

Tom Brokaw hosted a show on the Discovery Channel called *Global Warming: The New Challenge*. Brokaw claimed there was a "growing consensus that global warming is real and getting worse." Actually, there was a growing body of opinion that it is a fraud perpetrated by liberal politicians and their scientific acolytes who want more grant money and more control over our lives. I always refer people to the excellent website climatedepot.com.

Susan Boyle, a plain-looking middle-aged woman, astounded the *Britain's Got Talent* program with her amazing singing voice. The panel and audience had already judged her negatively because of her appearance, but when she sang "I Dreamed a Dream" from the musical *Les Misérables*, people were stunned and many began to cry. All of those hypocrites who thought nothing good could come from this dowdy, forty-eight-year-old woman—because our narcissistic culture has taught us the only thing that matters is physical beauty and not depth of character—suddenly wanted to embrace what seconds before they had instinctively rejected. One hopes that they learned a valuable lesson not to judge by appearances.

If more evidence were needed that the media were "in the tank" for Obama, this comment by *Newsweek* editor Evan Thomas (no relation, thankfully) should remove all doubt. On MSNBC, Thomas said: ". . . in a way, Obama's standing above the country—above the world. He's sort of God."

South Carolina Republican Governor Mark Sanford acknowledged that all those times he claimed to be hiking along the Appalachian Trail, he was actually keeping company with his mistress. I once asked Billy Graham if he ever experienced temptations of the flesh. He said, "Of course." How did he deal with them? "I asked God to strike me dead before He ever allowed me to dishonor Him in that way."

Obama pressured Congress to pass a "stimulus package." We would hear similar language from his successors (Democrats, that is). The best stimulus is a growing economy that occurs when taxes are low and unnecessary regulations repealed.

Reverend Jesse Jackson said, "I have to admit it, but I have reached a stage in my life that if I am walking down a dark street late at night and I see the person behind me is white, I subconsciously feel relieved . . ." Make of that what you will. Jackson was not charged with being a racist.

A USA Today–Gallup Poll found that 57 percent of adults believed President Obama's $787 billion economic stimulus package was having "no impact on the economy or making it worse." With government, results matter less than "intentions." Vice President Joe Biden would later say, "I guess all those shovel-ready jobs weren't shovel-ready." Yuk-yuk. Why should they care? It's not their money being spent. They're just trying to buy votes.

There was a bully in my neighborhood where I grew up, and he only attacked people he thought were weak and wouldn't defend themselves. I likened this to foreign policy. Totalitarian bullies fear and try to avoid confrontations with those who are stronger. War through weakness, I call it.

David Letterman acknowledged having had sex with female subordinates and fathered a child out of wedlock with his live-in "girlfriend." Letterman admitted only to "creepy behavior." When there are no standards, anything goes.

The first government "stimulus" didn't work, so naturally President Obama wanted a second one. This only works in government, never the private sector.

Obama was awarded the Nobel Peace Prize, but for what? According to the website globalsecurity.org there were currently "forty-two active conflicts and/or wars in the world today." Obama didn't end any of them. The Nobel Peace Prize is as worthless as the Pulitzer Prize in journalism.

President Obama ratcheted up criticism of Fox News and talk radio. Maybe he should have considered whether they are doing the job journalists used to do before so many became mouthpieces for the Democratic Party.

The Media Research Center published a compilation of reports, editorials, articles, and commentary extending over the last twenty-two years revealing how the mainstream media were handmaidens of totalitarian communism. Just a couple of many examples. *Time* magazine writer Strobe Talbott (who would become a high-ranking official in Bill Clinton's State Department) wrote: "(Soviet leader Mikhail) Gorbachev is helping the West by showing that the Soviet threat isn't what it used to be, and what's more, that it never was." I think I'll trust Aleksandr Solzhenitsyn over Talbott. NBC's John Chancellor refused to see the history of Soviet communism. As the Soviet Union unraveled in 1991, Chancellor said: "The problem isn't communism; nobody even talked about communism this week. The problem is shortages." And guess why there are shortages? It's because of communism. Duh!

A mass shooting at Fort Hood, Texas, by a Muslim fanatic, who was an Army psychiatrist, provoked some government and military officials to issue statements that such actions were not "true Islam." None of these statements were issued by Muslims. That should tell you something. The government worries about alleged racists and homophobes in the military. I worry about jihadists.

I sounded like a prophet when commenting on President Obama's decision to send an additional thirty thousand troops to Afghanistan. I was opposed to establishing a timetable for withdrawal because if this was truly a war, a timetable can only encourage the enemy to hang on until we depart. Which is exactly what would happen in 2021 in a chaotic withdrawal ordered by President Joe Biden.

Just before Christmas, President Obama spoke to a group of children in Washington. He asked them if they knew "why we celebrate Christmas." One child piped up, "The birth of the baby Jesus." Obama devolved into his self-declared role as theologian-in-chief when he claimed Jesus "symbolizes for people all around the world the possibility of peace and people treating each other with respect." What about salvation in and through Him? Obama apparently believed that can only come through government.

A faulty detonator in the underwear of Umar Farouk Abdulmutallab on a Christmas Day flight from London to Detroit, along with some fast-acting passengers, prevented a catastrophe. I wonder how a man who has been on MI5's terrorist watch list was deemed an insufficient threat and allowed on a commercial airline flight? His father warned State Department officials about his son's radical beliefs and extremist connections.

2010

The Year of the Tea Party

A special election is held in Massachusetts to fill the seat of the late Ted Kennedy. To the surprise of most people, Republican Scott Brown beats State Attorney General Martha Coakley.

President Obama, in his first State of the Union address, emphasizes the nation's economy, job creation, ending the "Don't ask, don't tell" policy in the military, and restates his commitment for health care reform.

The job market hits a post-recession bottom of 129,655,000 payroll employees, a decline of 8,710,000 from the peak in December 2007.

The Tea Party movement, which gained momentum in 2009 during the national health care debate, holds its first convention in Nashville, Tennessee.

The Women's Medical Society abortion clinic in Philadelphia is raided by the FBI in an investigation into suspected illegal drug prescription use. The raid uncovers extreme unsanitary operations, use of untrained staff, and eventually leads to charges against a number of staff members for murdering babies at the clinic.

The United States Navy announces it is lifting its ban on women assigned to submarines.

President Obama signs into law the euphemistically named Patient Protection and Affordable Care Act. It ignites a controversy and court challenges that eventually weaken the measure. Twenty-one states announce plans to sue the government.

The last American combat troops leave Iraq.

The United States and other Western nations walk out of the UN General Assembly following claims by President Mahmoud Ahmadinejad of Iran that the "majority of the American people as well as most nations and politicians around the world" say that the 9/11 attacks were the work of the United States government trying to protect Israel.

Julian Assange's WikiLeaks begins releasing confidential diplomatic documents from the United States.

Democrats maintain their Senate majority in the elections, but Republicans gain six seats, reducing the Democrats' numbers. Republicans win control of the House, gaining at least sixty-four seats. It is the largest seat change for any party since the 1948 elections and the largest for any midterm since the 1938 midterm elections. Republicans also win a majority of governorships, adding twelve to the other eleven who won their reelection bids, and a majority of state legislatures.

The San Francisco Board of Supervisors bans the McDonald's Happy Meal over obesity concerns.

The unemployment rate ends the year at 9.3 percent.

A federal judge in Virginia rules that parts of the Affordable Care Act, specifically the individual mandate that would require all Americans to get health care by 2014, is unconstitutional.

The Senate votes to repeal the controversial "Don't ask, don't tell" policy by a vote of 65–31.

The results of the 2010 United States Census are released. The American population grows by 9.7 percent to 310 million, the smallest percentage increase since the Great Depression. Could abortion be a contributing factor?

CAL'S TAKE

"Asking politicians to give up a source of money is like asking Dracula to forsake blood."

Brit Hume shocked the media world when he opined on Fox News that the solution to Tiger Woods's problems is a relationship with Jesus Christ. Hume said, "My message to Tiger would be: Tiger, turn to the Christian faith and you can make a total recovery and be a great example to the world." Woods had said he was seeking help from Buddha who, last I checked, was still dead.

If one lives long enough in Washington, one comes to realize there really is "nothing new under the sun." The same arguments are made by members of each party ad nauseum. Maybe government isn't the answer, after all?

President Obama met with congressional Republicans at their "retreat." It was theater, because he didn't compromise on anything, expecting only Republicans to abandon their principles (Republicans have principles?).

Vice President Joe Biden attempted to take credit for progress in the Iraq War when he had opposed the war from the start. I guess he thought people have short memories. Unfortunately, too many do and the media are no help in recalling his past contradictions.

A thought I have that would have been taken as a self-evident truth by our Founders: "As more Americans come to rely on government to take care of them, we risk losing our independence."

Newly elected New Jersey Republican Governor Chris Christie appointed a commission that would recommend what state government functions could be done better—and at less cost—by the private sector. It was something I had promoted for years at the federal level. It worked for a while in New Jersey, but inevitably the party of government—that would be Democrats—returned to power and grew the government at greater expense and raised taxes.

Pork is the preferred metaphor in Washington for misspending. But pork took a backseat to baloney, which was present in abundance as President Obama and House Democrats tried to convince the public—and themselves—that their takeover of one-sixth of the economy was going to improve health insurance and the availability of medical treatment.

Dan Coates, an Indiana Republican, had retired from Congress after serving four terms in the House and two in the Senate. He voluntarily retired to a comfortable private life, but decided to run again for his old Senate seat. Over breakfast at a local diner in Arlington, Virginia, I asked him why. "I deliberately avoided stopping at a psychiatrist's office on the way to making this decision," he told me. He was motivated to run again after "watching for a year with increasing frustration and anger what is happening to our country and saying to himself, 'Do I want to go quietly into the night and enjoy the fruits of my labors, or do I want to throw myself back in and see if I can do something about it?'" Unfortunately, Coates was only one man, and Washington resists reform. We could have used more men and women like him to help reverse the decline.

Former Speaker Newt Gingrich and I met to discuss the future of the Republican Party. He said he liked what he saw. The intensity and commitment by the tea partiers to "throw the bums out" seemed to him as strong as the 1994 revolution that swept Democrats from power and gave Republicans an opportunity Gingrich readily admitted they squandered. That is a recurring problem for Republicans, but never Democrats, who use power when they get it to advance their agenda. We always hear about how angry people are about the behavior of politicians, but they keep electing the same ones, expecting a different outcome. It's the definition of "insanity."

Unemployment in America hovered just below 10 percent, so President Obama hosted a Summit on Entrepreneurship in an effort to boost economic development . . . in Muslim nations! Obama said he believed such an effort would bring Muslim women to the United States and change Muslim attitudes about America.

President Obama returned to a theme he used effectively during the 2008 campaign. In a commencement address to University of Michigan graduates, Obama said politics had become too divisive; name-calling isn't helpful; labeling people doesn't solve problems. These things have been going on since our founding, so it's nothing new and nothing changes. I looked at the list of commencement speakers and found conservative speakers in short supply.

The president nominated Elena Kagan to the Supreme Court and said she "loves the law." What does that mean? Better for her to love the Constitution as written.

The Anti-Defamation League (ADL) had a full page on its website devoted to church-state separation. Which is why it was remarkable that the ADL's Philadelphia chapter voted overwhelmingly in favor of a resolution endorsing school vouchers that would allow schoolchildren in underperforming government (a.k.a. "public") schools to escape to schools where they would be safer and better taught.

Memorizing musical comedy scores over the years often helped me in critiquing certain politicians. In describing President Obama's first address from the Oval Office, I said it can be summed up with a lyric from the 1951 Broadway show *Paint Your Wagon*: "Where am I going I don't know; when will I get there I ain't certain; all that I know is I am on my way."

Eric Metaxas published *Dietrich Bonhoeffer: Pastor, Martyr, Prophet, Spy*, a major biography about a giant of the Christian faith. Bonhoeffer was executed by Adolf Hitler just before the end of World War II for his role in a plot to assassinate the Führer. It is one of the best biographies I have ever read.

The Supreme Court ruled that a public university was not required to subsidize with student fees campus groups it considered discriminatory. This seemed arbitrary to me since the university could accuse anyone it didn't like of discrimination. The case involved the Christian Legal Society, which excluded practicing homosexuals and non-Christians. Would Jewish groups be banned because they excluded non-Jews? Doubt it.

In a story about increasing government debt—this time in Illinois, but it could easily be applied to other states run by

Democrats and certainly the federal government—the *New York Times* headline summed up the problem: "Illinois Stops Paying Its Bills, but Can't Stop Digging Hole."

NASA administrator Charles Bolden proved he is lost in space when he claimed the agency's "foremost mission" was not returning to the moon, or completing a mission to Mars, but rather it was improving relations with the Muslim world. Does he plan to send the fundamentalists among them to another planet? Doubtful.

Rep. Charles Rangel (D-NY) was accused of violating the House ethics code (who knew they had an ethics code?) for "failing to declare $239,000 to $831,000 in assets and about his effort to raise money for a private center named after himself at City College of New York." It must be hard to make ends meet with such assets.

Newt Gingrich declared radical Islam to be a clear and present danger to America. He was one of a few to boldly state what others fear to say.

In arguing against extending the Bush-era tax cuts for "the wealthy," President Obama claimed the government can't afford to "borrow" the estimated $700 billion he says it will "cost government." If you aren't laughing, you don't get the irony given our current multi-trillion debt.

The film *Secretariat* was released. About the horse that won the Triple Crown in 1973, it contained every value most people overtly or covertly care about. It is a story about overcoming big odds, especially the horse's owner, Penny Chenery Tweedy (played magnificently by Diane Lane), who overcame incredible sexism and opposition from her brother and husband. They claimed that a woman had no business in horse racing. The video of those races can be seen on YouTube. If you haven't seen the film, get a copy. You won't regret it. It's the kind of movie Hollywood makes on occasion to remind us it doesn't have amnesia when it comes to real American values. Directed by Randall Wallace, an openly Christian man, *Secretariat* has subtle touches of faith throughout the movie.

In the past two years, congressional spending increased 21.4 percent, according to the Congressional Budget Office. It will only get worse as long as too many people look to government first and themselves as an afterthought.

Republicans won a House majority and gained seven seats in the Senate, but not enough to win a majority there. They also won ten governorships. Republicans still find it difficult to outmaneuver Democrats even when they have the power to do so.

Once again, the Obama administration pressured Israel to stop building "settlements" in the area called the West Bank. The formula was all wrong. There is no way that people who believe they have direct orders from Allah are about to change their minds about eliminating Israel and killing as many Jews as they can.

At Thanksgiving, I wrote about the woman who cut my hair. She was an immigrant from Vietnam named Kim Vu. She told me how thankful she was to be in America and extolled its virtues. Americans who have never lived under a communist regime could learn much from her.

One solution to the problems Congress creates for itself and us: Make them part time and pay them accordingly.

My colleague Jim Pinkerton said we should be spending whatever it took to find cures for diseases that most ravage humanity, rather than focus mainly on expensive care. He argued that finding cures, while costly upfront, greatly reduces the cost of care. I agreed. Didn't Joe Biden, as vice president, get assigned the task of finding a cure for cancer after his son died of a brain tumor? What happened to that?

"What if the Christmas story is all true?" I asked in a column. What difference would it make? All the difference in the world.

2011

The Year of Occupy Wall Street

A bomb explodes as Coptic Christian worshippers in Alexandria, Egypt, leave a new year service, killing twenty-three.

Egyptian President Hosni Mubarak resigns after widespread protests, leaving control of Egypt in the hands of the military until a general election can be held.

Uncertainty over Libyan oil output causes crude oil prices to rise 20 percent over a two-week period following the Arab Spring, sparking the 2011 energy crisis.

Protests break out in Syria. There are demands for democratic reforms, the resignation of President Bashar al-Assad, and release of prisoners. The government responds by killing hundreds of protesters and laying siege to various cities, beginning the Syrian civil war.

Israel uses its Iron Dome anti-missile system for the first time to intercept a rocket fired from Gaza, marking the first short-range missile intercept ever.

An estimated two billion people watch the wedding of Prince William and Catherine Middleton at Westminster

Abbey. A triumph of celebrity, or just hunger for something pleasant for a change?

President Obama announces that Osama bin Laden has been killed by a Navy Seal Team in Pakistan. Vice President Joe Biden opposes the operation.

In Norway, Anders Behring Breivik kills eight people in a bomb blast that targeted government buildings in central Oslo, then murders sixty-nine at a Youth League camp.

Libyan rebels take control of Tripoli, effectively overthrowing the government of Muammar Gaddafi, who is later captured and killed.

Occupy Wall Street protests begin in the United States, eventually spreading to eighty-two other countries. It appears to me that the spoiled brats of the world once again have no clue as to what they are protesting, or the benefits wealth has brought to them.

Israel and the Palestinian terror organization Hamas exchange prisoners. The terrorists give up Israeli Army soldier Gilad Shalit in exchange for the release of 1,027 prisoners held in Israel. Once again it shows the value Israel places on even one human life.

The United Kingdom severs diplomatic ties with Iran and expels Iranian diplomats, less than twenty-four hours after protesters attacked the British embassy in Tehran.

North Korean dictator Kim Jong-il dies of a heart attack or a stroke.

CAL'S TAKE

"Don't liberal Democrats ever learn economic principles, or does their class warfare trump all else?"

The new House Republican leadership took turns reading aloud the United States Constitution. Now if they and the Democrats would only obey it—especially the Tenth Amendment, which says all powers not specifically granted to the federal government are to be reserved for the individual states and the people.

A senseless shooting in Tucson, Arizona, severely wounded Rep. Gabrielle Giffords (D-AZ) and killed six others, including United States District Judge John Roll and a nine-year-old girl. Democrats claimed there were not enough gun control laws. The shooter was mentally disturbed and lawbreakers don't care how many laws are on the books.

Another year, another Chicken Little "the sky is falling" approach to the debt ceiling, which is not really a ceiling at all. If it were, it would not constantly be raised to accommodate new spending.

President Obama, who once said marriage is between a man and a woman, now said his view of same-sex marriage is "evolving." I called that Darwinian politics.

Conservative activist James O'Keefe recorded several employees of National Public Radio making outrageously biased statements. One said a fictitious Muslim group could make a $5 million donation to NPR and the IRS would not have to know. All resigned, but nothing changed because they just hired more secular progressives.

Spreading the wealth around should focus more on expanding the economy so more people have an opportunity to become either wealthy or at least self-sustaining. That would be counter to Obama's view to take from the successful and give to the unsuccessful unless the goal was to make them successful and no longer in need of government programs. But then they might vote Republican, so never mind!

Ayn Rand's 1957 novel *Atlas Shrugged* was made into a movie, reflecting the book's theme of focusing on self and ignoring social responsibility and spiritual truth. Still, it hit the mark when it came to taxation, over-regulation, and the loss of our liberties to overreaching government.

Donald Trump teased about running for president. He reached out to evangelical voters by having an interview with David Brody of the Christian Broadcasting Network. Trump described Christianity as a "wonderful religion." In answer to a question about his faith, Trump said, "I believe in God," (But so does Satan, I thought to myself). "I am Christian. I think the Bible is certainly, it is 'the' book. It is the thing." To evangelical ears, that statement lacked substance, even sincerity. Trump added that people send him Bibles and that he stores them "in a very nice place . . . and sometimes give them away to other people."

Osama bin Laden, the brains behind 9/11, died a coward in his fortified Pakistan hideout. Credit to President Obama for ordering Seal Team 6 to conduct the operation which, again, Joe Biden opposed. Unfortunately, the terrorist movement lives on.

Robert Woodson, the president of the Center for Neighborhood Enterprise for thirty years, is a black American who doesn't traffic in the belief of liberal white Americans that the solution to the problems faced by black people is big government. He told me, "You can't learn anything by studying failure. If you want to learn anything, you must study the successful." Amen!

The British press went the American media one better in fawning over Barack and Michelle Obama during their European visit. The normally reserved *London Times* columnist William Rees-Mogg compared Obama's speech before

Parliament to those of Winston Churchill. Comparing Obama to Churchill is like comparing Lady Gaga to Ella Fitzgerald.

Laura Hillenbrand's book *Unbroken* was published. It is a biography of Olympic champion Louis Zamperini and an account of his internment in a Japanese concentration camp during World War II. It also includes the story of his conversion at a Billy Graham crusade, a seminal moment that was left out of the film version. I later interviewed Zamperini when he was ninety-four years old and found him alert and as compelling as he comes through in the book. I also interviewed Hillenbrand and praised her for her impeccable research and great writing. I read the 398-page book in two sittings.

Rep. Anthony Weiner (D-NY) was ridiculed by late-night comics and double entendre headlines when it was revealed he texted half and fully naked pictures of himself to women he did not know. His wife, Huma Abedin, an aide to Hillary Clinton, eventually left him with their child. Weiner was sentenced to twenty-one months in federal prison for "sexting" to a minor and promised to get help for sex addition while in prison. Given his behavior after release, it appeared not to have helped.

The State of Alaska responded to media requests and released twenty-four thousand pages of emails from Sarah Palin when she was governor. Media outlets paid $750 for the printed copies. There was "live coverage" of the release in the United States and abroad. Clearly, the Left was looking for something they could use to further demean and discredit Palin. Among the great "revelations" was this from the *Washington Post*: "Palin felt passionately about issues of importance to her state, the documents show, and she waged battle with foes large and small." Furthermore (pant, pant) she showed "concern about alcohol in Alaska governor's mansion because of the presence of young children." This is news?

Another example of why there continues to be declining trust in big media. NBC edited "under God" from the Pledge of Allegiance at the beginning of its coverage of the United States Open.

I met with freshman Senator Marco Rubio (R-Fl). He impressed me when he came into the office, turned the lights on (he was the first to arrive), and made coffee.

I was on a flight with John Glenn, the first American to orbit the Earth and now a Democrat senator from Ohio. The movie shown was about the mission to the moon captained by Jim Lovell on *Apollo 13*, which had to be aborted because of a mechanical failure. At the end of the film, several people came up to Glenn to ask for his autograph. I said, "John, you know they are not asking for your autograph because you're a senator, don't you?" He laughed and replied, "How well I know." What a gentleman!

President Obama and his fellow Democrats enjoyed bashing "millionaires and billionaires." Obama blasted people who fly private, though he flew on the ultimate private jet, Air Force One, which taxpayers pay for. He didn't like yachts, or specifically the people who can afford to buy them. And yet the people who made the private planes and yachts have jobs precisely because others have achieved a level of success that enabled them to afford such luxuries. When President George H. W. Bush agreed to tax hikes that included higher taxes on private planes and yachts, the company owners began laying off the people who built them. It's Economics 101.

According to the Politico website, Vice President Joe Biden agreed with an argument made by Rep. Mike Doyle (D-Pa) at a two-hour, closed-door Democrat caucus that congressional Tea Party members "acted like terrorists" by standing against attempts to raise taxes and force spending reductions as part of a deal to raise the debt ceiling.

The United States Department of State published its annual list on human rights practices in Arab states. It consistently found all are ruled by variations of dictatorial regimes that oppress their people, deny basic freedoms of press, speech, due process, and are all intolerant of any faith other than Islam, punishing converts to other faiths (a capital offense in some of them) and anyone who shares other faiths with their people. It spoke to me of the futility of trying to bargain with a culture that believes we are infidels.

On the tenth anniversary of 9/11, *Variety* reported forty-plus special programs would air commemorating that tragic day. While it is good to remember and honor the victims and heroes of that awful day, it is better to do all that is necessary to avoid a repeat attack. Immediately after 1998, I wrote, "The first step—even before military action is contemplated or taken—is to expel from this country the people and organizations tied to radical terrorist groups in the Middle East." I still feel that way.

Bill Clinton said, "If you live long enough, you'll make mistakes. But if you learn from them, you'll be a better person." I guess Clinton's learning curve was a bit longer than it is for the rest of us.

The Office of Personnel Management admitted that the government has been sending checks to dead people for the last five years. Maybe that explains why so many continued to vote. It's the ultimate absentee ballot.

This summer the national unemployment rate among black Americans increased to 16.7 percent, the highest in 37 tears. And this happened under America's first "black president." And yet black Americans continued to vote in overwhelming numbers for Democrats. Why?

Apple CEO Steve Jobs—one of the great innovators of our time—passed away. Why don't we have the kind of inventors and entrepreneurs we used to have? Could it be that we discourage achievement these days when we used to encourage it with sound tax and regulation policies?

Politics and faith were at issue again in the run-up to the 2012 election. I may care about a person's faith, but I am more interested in whether he can do the job of president and how that faith applies to his policies.

House Minority Leader Nancy Pelosi demonstrated her gift for understatement when she opposed a bill by Rep. Joe Pitts (R-PA) that would prohibit federal funds to be used to pay for abortions. Pelosi said that if Republicans vote for the measure, "they will be voting to say that women can die on the floor and health care providers do not have to intervene." She has such a gift for understatement.

President Obama, who said at the Democratic National Convention in Boston in 2004 that there is not a black or white or Latino or Asian America, but the United States of America, showed he didn't mean it as he became the most racially divisive of any modern president. Some black commentators and show hosts said black Americans should vote for Obama strictly because of his race. A white person who said that about a white president would be called a racist.

Bobby Jindal won reelection as governor of Louisiana with a staggering 65.8 percent of the vote. Most media ignored or buried the story. Why? I think it was because he is a racial minority, a Republican and a pro-life Catholic.

The International Atomic Energy Agency reported Iran was "close" to developing a nuclear weapon. Ten years later, they are still saying the same thing.

The alleged sexual abuse of young boys by former Penn State defensive coordinator Jerry Sandusky was disgusting, outrageous, and immoral. The motto of Penn State's athletic program is "Success with Honor." The cover-up by revered head coach Joe Paterno was also shameful.

Self-described atheist Christopher Hitchens died. He made a career out of bashing especially Christians, and for this and other reasons was a media darling.

The Department of Justice rejected a South Carolina law that required voters to show a valid ID before casting their ballots. It is an issue that will surface again and again in future elections.

2012

The Year of Sandy Hook

The passenger cruise ship *Costa Concordia* sinks off the Italian coast, killing thirty-two. The captain is later found negligent.

Queen Elizabeth observes the sixtieth anniversary of her ascension to the throne.

After 246 years, the Encyclopedia Britannica discontinues its print edition.

Vladimir Putin is elected President of Russia.

The respiratory virus called SARS-CoV-2 is first identified.

Twelve people are killed and fifty-eight injured in a mass shooting at an Aurora, Colorado, movie theater.

The worst power outage in world history leave 620 million people in India without power.

Barack Obama wins reelection, defeating Republican challenger Mitt Romney.

The UN General Assembly, which regularly opposes all things Israel, approves a motion granting non-member observer status to the Palestinians.

Washington State becomes the first jurisdiction in the modern world to officially legalize the possession of cannabis for personal use. This explains a lot.

Twenty-eight people, including the gunman, are killed in an elementary school in Sandy Hook, Connecticut.

CAL'S TAKE

"We tolerate, even promote, many things we once regarded as evil, wrong, or immoral. And then we seek 'explanations' for an act that seems beyond comprehension. Remove societal restraints on some evils and one can expect the demons to be freed to conduct other evil acts."

My brother, Marshall Stephen Thomas, passed away. He was born with Down syndrome and exceeded his life expectancy by nearly four decades. Our parents refused to put him in an institution, and as a result, he taught us much about being handicapped, tolerance, and grace.

Secretary of Defense Leon Panetta announced a 10 percent cut in defense spending. Supposedly this would reduce the federal deficit, but Congress always finds new ways to spend money. The cuts sent a message to our enemies and encouraged "war through weakness" instead of "peace through strength."

For sixty years, the National Prayer Breakfast was a nonpolitical event where speakers put aside their earthly biases to focus on a Higher Authority. President Obama departed from that tradition to claim the endorsement of Jesus for raising taxes. The president quoted from Luke 12:48 NIV: "From everyone who has been given much, much will be demanded;

and from the one who has been entrusted with much, much more will be asked." The website biblestudytools.com said of this verse: "The more knowledge a man has, the more practice is expected from him; and the greater his gifts are, the more useful he ought to be, and diligent in the improvement of them." Obama's social gospel misinterpretation of that verse sounded more like Karl Marx than Jesus Christ.

In a column called "Losing Liberty," I quoted Thomas Jefferson and Patrick Henry, who issued warnings on the topic. Said Jefferson, "Can the liberties of a nation be secure when we have removed a conviction that these liberties are the gift of God?" Said Henry, "The Constitution is not an instrument for the government to restrain people; it is an instrument for the people to restrain the government—lest it dominate our lives and interests."

I publicly apologized for saying something about MSNBC host Rachel Maddow at a CPAC convention in Washington. I called her, and she graciously accepted my apology. I invited her to lunch in New York, and we enjoyed talking and getting to know each other beyond stereotypes. She said on her show that she believed my apology was genuine. I was reminded of a lesson I should have learned before—that civility is better than name-calling if you want to be heard.

Why does Black History Month so often feature mostly black Americans who are liberal Democrats and ignore those who are conservative Republicans and successful?

The *New York Times* carried a story that noted "more than half of births to American women under thirty occur outside marriage." Anyone else think that's a problem?

Rush Limbaugh apologized on air for calling thirty-year-old Sandra Fluke a "slut" and a "prostitute." Fluke had demanded that Catholic Georgetown University, where she was a law student, pay for her contraceptive pills because she claimed she and her friends couldn't afford them. That they are available for pocket change at stores like Target must have escaped her. Limbaugh said, "I acted too much like the leftists who despise me." I know how he felt (see my Rachel Maddow apology).

Democrats succeeded in diverting attention from President Obama's failed record on just about everything and get Republicans talking about sex and morality.

New York City Mayor Michael Bloomberg took government overreach to a new low when he decided to order limits on food donations to city charities, including homeless shelters, because the government was unable to measure the nutritional value of the food. Ask a homeless person if he or she cares.

President Obama suffered from open mike syndrome when he was overheard telling Russian President Dmitry Medvedev he would have "more flexibility" to deal with missile defense after the election and to tell incoming president Putin to have "patience" and give him "space." The statement was mocked by conservatives and rightly so.

Virtually everything said and done in a presidential election year distorts the truth, much like concave and convex mirrors in a carnival attraction alter one's true reflection. That kind of distortion is promoted by especially Democrats who ignore or mock women who choose to stay at home, rather than put their young children in day care and work at paying jobs.

Eleven Secret Service agents and several members of the United States military were accused of consorting with prostitutes prior to President Obama's arrival in Cartagena, Colombia.

Former Nixon aide Charles Colson died at age eighty. Colson's book and the film called *Born Again* (in which I had a tiny role) told of his conversion to Christ. He founded Prison Fellowship to take the Gospel to inmates and their families. That will be his legacy, not the political shenanigans that sent him to prison.

College debt increased while the value of a college education seemed in decline, except perhaps for specialty subjects like medicine and law. Increasing numbers of young people, especially men, were finding alternatives to high-priced institutions of what I call "lower learning." If you can't get a job after graduation, what's the point of a degree?

Finding Your Roots premiered on PBS. Hosted by Harvard Professor Henry Louis Gates Jr., it explored the genealogical and genetic history of a diverse group of people. As I wrote about Gates' earlier series, *African American Lives*, which traced the African and slave roots of celebrities such as Oprah Winfrey and Chris Rock, Gates eviscerated any excuse for racism when he explored the lineage of the black Americans he interviewed. That's because the whitest and blackest among us are a mix of genes formed out of a racial melting pot that included ancestors who were black and white.

President Obama lamented that laws (he didn't mention the Constitution) prevented him from acting unilaterally to push his agenda. That's what the Founders intended— limited government, unlimited people. Obama is not an emperor.

President Obama delivered a line that would be used against him during the rest of the campaign when he told a crowd in Roanoke, Virginia: "If you've got a business, you didn't build that. Somebody else made that happen." Where would we be without government? A lot better off when it becomes larger, more expensive, and intrusive than the Founders envisioned.

The media constantly looks for "proof" that ratifies their biases. Case in point: ABC investigative reporter Brian Ross claimed after the movie theater shooting in Aurora, Colorado, he found a name similar to that of the shooter and discovered he was a member of the Tea Party movement. Ross's rush to judgment was proved wrong, and he was forced to apologize, and for a time, was suspended by ABC.

Chick-fil-A President Dan Cathy got in trouble with the LGBTQ crowd because he committed a cardinal sin in the age of political correctness: He supported traditional marriage. The Left ordered a boycott of his restaurants, and on the day scheduled, thousands of people showed up in support of Cathy and bought his chicken sandwiches.

My friend Marvin Hamlisch died at age sixty-eight. Marvin won a Pulitzer Prize for his Broadway musical *A Chorus Line* and composed many songs, including "Nobody Does It Better" and "The Way We Were." He was the youngest student ever accepted at the Juilliard School of Music in New York. Knowing him was a tremendous privilege and so much fun.

Democrats created a political ad that showed a Paul Ryan "look-alike" pushing an elderly woman over a cliff in her wheelchair. The point was to misrepresent Ryan's serious proposal to reform Medicare, one of the main drivers of national debt. The Left is nothing if not dishonest.

Helen Gurley Brown, the female equivalent of Hugh Hefner, died at age ninety. Brown, who founded *Cosmopolitan* magazine, was known for saying, "Nice girls go to Heaven; bad girls go everywhere." Her theology was as bad as her morality. Brown encouraged young women to "sleep around."

The presidential debates fit the usual mode: Liberal "journalists" asked confrontational questions of Mitt Romney and gave a virtual pass to President Obama. Why do Republican candidates not demand at least one conservative on the panel, or refuse to participate?

Rep. Todd Akin (R-MO) walked into a trap when a St. Louis reporter asked him whether abortion should be illegal in the case of rape or incest. Akin responded that if the rape was "legitimate," the female body "has ways to try and shut that whole thing down"—that "thing" being conception. What he should have said was that rape is a horrible crime that should be prosecuted, but that pregnancy from rape is rare, so what about partial-birth abortion? That OK with you, reporter?

Democrats flogged the poverty issue at their convention in Charlotte, North Carolina. I wondered why they never focus on helping the poor become un-poor. Do you have to ask? They wanted a permanent underclass that will always vote for them so their government benefits will continue.

Testifying before a congressional committee on the failure of the Obama administration to send help to rescue United States diplomats under attack by terrorists in Benghazi, Libya, Secretary of State Hillary Clinton uttered these immortal words about their deaths: "What difference does it make?"

Romney released his tax returns and was immediately attacked by Democrats for taking advantage of lower rates for capital gains available only to "those at the top." Yes, well, people who invested their money wisely would be better off than those who didn't, wouldn't they? It's another classic example of the Left's promotion of envy of the successful.

Vice President Joe Biden debated Republican vice-presidential nominee Paul Ryan. Biden interrupted Ryan more than eighty times and moderator Martha Raddatz broke in at least fifty times. It is a classic leftist tactic—interrupt the conservative to throw him off track and help the audience forget what he was saying. Biden behaved like a bully.

Obama did better in his second debate with Romney than in his first, but the air seemed to have gone out of his messianic balloon as people began to focus more on facts and record rather than his race.

The election choice was familiar: bigger and more expensive government with higher taxes versus smaller government, lower taxes, and more freedom. The results showed the former as Obama was re-elected.

CIA Director David Petraeus resigned when it was revealed he had an extramarital affair while commanding forces in Afghanistan. I was amused at the double standard some reports applied to such things. They mostly defended Bill Clinton, who was impeached for lying (not adultery) but didn't resign. Playing off a popular TV show, I titled my column "Sex and the City (of Washington)."

On a visit to Singapore, I found virtually no unemployment (1.9 percent). A taxi driver told me, "Everyone works here." An earlier article in The Economist said about Singapore: "The state's attitude can be simply put: being poor here is your own fault. Citizens are obliged to save for the future, rely on their families, and not expect any handouts from the government unless they hit rock bottom." Wow!

I visited one of Bangkok's "red light districts" (not as a customer). In the song "One Night in Bangkok," a line described my feelings: "I can feel the devil walking next to me." I visited with two Christian missionaries who sought to help the young women out of the sex trade. They were amazing and sometimes effective, finding jobs for the women and helping them in other ways.

Completing my Asia tour in Hanoi, I saw the communist regime still using TV to spread propaganda, but it appeared that young people were mostly not listening. The government allowed the United States embassy to make available computers so that people could access the Internet. Prosperity seemed to be breaking through much of the poverty that had been a problem for Vietnam for many years.

The massacre of children at Sandy Hook Elementary School in Newton, Connecticut, shocked the nation. The usual blame game was heard—not enough gun laws, too much violence on TV and in movies, talk radio. I said the better explanation is that evil exists.

2013

The Year of the Boston Marathon Bombings

North Korea conducts its third underground nuclear test, prompting widespread condemnation and tightened economic sanctions from the international community. They would be as successful as previous sanctions: not at all.

Benedict XVI resigns as pope, becoming the first to do so since Gregory XII in 1415, and the first to do so voluntarily since Celestine V in 1294. He is succeeded by Cardinal Jorge Mario Bergoglio of Argentina, a noted theological and political liberal. He takes the name Francis and becomes the first Jesuit pope.

Nicolas Maduro is declared winner of the Venezuelan presidential election. There are allegations of fraud. Protests follow.

Two Chechnya-born Islamist brothers (one of whom is a United States citizen) detonate two bombs at the Boston Marathon, killing three and injuring 264 others.

In a study published in the scientific journal *Nature*, researchers describe the first production of human embryonic stem cells from cloning.

Former CIA employee Edward Snowden discloses to news organizations operations engaged in by the United States government. Snowden then flees the country and is later granted temporary asylum in Russia. Any bets the Russians extracted as much information as he had before sending him away?

The Supreme Court overturns a key section of the Defense of Marriage Act, granting federal recognition to same-sex marriage. Ronald Reagan appointee Justice Anthony Kennedy writes for the majority.

Amid mass protests across Egypt, President Mohammed Morsi is deposed in a military coup, leading to widespread violence. The West calls it part of the "Arab Spring."

Following the coup in Egypt, two anti-coup camps are raided by the security forces, leaving 2,696 dead. The raids are described by Human Rights Watch as "one of the world's largest killings of demonstrators in a single day in recent history." Iran must rank a close second.

Almost fifteen hundred are killed in a chemical attack during the Syrian civil war.

CAL'S TAKE

"In business, poor performance leads to bankruptcy or, at a minimum, a restructuring of the company. In American education, failure entitles the bankrupt system to even more taxpayer dollars."

A "fiscal cliff" bill was passed by Congress (don't you love the names they give these things to obscure higher taxes and more spending?). It was 153 pages long, and most members did not read it before voting. Same old same old.

Diane Sawyer gushed on *World News Tonight* about the "record number" of female United States senators (twenty). Two female Democrats—Barbara Boxer of California and Barbara Mikulski of Maryland—praised the Senate female population, with Boxer saying she wouldn't be satisfied until there were fifty. The four female Republican senators were mostly ignored. It is not about gender, any more than it is about race. It is about ideology. There is little difference between a liberal female and liberal male when it comes to policy.

More talk by liberal politicians about gun control laws. I noted that self-control and self-defense are better. Anyone who wanted to find a gun to kill someone will find a way because if laws stopped people from committing crimes the prisons would be empty.

Barack Obama increasingly resembled an emperor. All that he needed was a scepter, a crown, and a robe trimmed in ermine. "The American people agreed with me," he told a news conference. Sorry, but nearly half of voters didn't vote for you, and they are American people (well, those who aren't illegal immigrants and dead, that is).

On the fortieth anniversary of *Roe v. Wade*, President Obama signed "executive actions" designed to combat "gun violence." He knew he couldn't get anything through Congress, ergo executive actions. Obama said ". . . when it comes to protecting the most vulnerable among us, we must act now." Never mind protecting the unborn. Since he signed the executive actions, shootings increased in his hometown of Chicago and other major cities. It appeared the shooters were not impressed.

Louisiana Governor Bobby Jindal got it right when he told the Republican National Committee winter meeting in Charlotte, North Carolina, that the GOP loses when it plays on the liberal Democrats' turf. "America is not the federal government," he said. Amen to that!

House Budget Committee Chairman Paul Ryan (R-WI) told me he believed a majority of Americans would come to understand how bad the debt was after the rhetoric gave way to reality. Ryan had many talents. Predicting the future was not one of them. The debt grew and grew and . . .

Given his track record on marital fidelity, former President Bill Clinton was not the person I would consult about "committed, loving relationships." Clinton used those words in a *Washington Post* op-ed, urging the Supreme Court to overturn the 1996 Defense of Marriage Act, which defined marriage as the legal union of one man and one woman, which Clinton signed into law!

Former Secretary of State Henry Kissinger said he neither saw hope in the "Arab Spring" nor was he optimistic about peace in the region following the rise of the Muslim Brotherhood. He was correct, and we were on the same page.

Why do liberals fear success? Many liberals are successful. I thought it had to do with their fear that if more people succeed without government help, they will need government less and thus not vote for the party of government. That would be the Democrats.

Seven teachers in an Atlanta, Georgia, public school were accused of altering standardized test scores to make it appear students performed better than they actually did. According to investigators, the seven sat in a locked room without windows, erasing wrong answers and inserting correct ones. It's bad enough when a child cheats. It's worse when a teacher cheats. Compounding the scandal—the elementary school children were mostly poor and black.

Former British Prime Minister Margaret Thatcher died at eighty-seven. "Thatcher Saved Britain" said a headline in the *London Daily Telegraph*. No, Thatcher inspired British citizens to have less faith in government and more in themselves. In this, she was a lot like Ronald Reagan. Thatcher's legacy included demolishing Britain's welfare state, breaking up state monopolies, and confronting powerful unions. She was called "The Iron Lady" by her critics, but what they hated was her spine of steel. I titled my column, "The Lady Was a Champ."

Addressing a meeting of Planned Parenthood, President Obama accused pro-lifers of wanting to "turn back the clock to policies more suited to the 1950s than the twenty-first century." Apparently, he didn't care that more black babies were born in the '50s than today, when most are aborted.

The *Washington Post* obtained documents from an audit conducted by the IRS inspector general that indicated the agency targeted conservative groups for special scrutiny with "tea party" and "patriot" in their names as well as nonprofit groups that criticized the government and sought to educate Americans about the Constitution. Lois Lerner, who was responsible for overseeing nonprofit groups and their tax status, could not explain why organizations with "progressive" in their names were not also targeted. She denied the nonprofit designation was a result of partisanship. Uh-huh.

I praised Obama's commencement addresses to two black colleges in Georgia for their inspirational tone. He said black American men needed more role models and encouragement to counter the reality, reinforced by much of the media, of too much failure, crime, imprisonment, out-of-wedlock births, a disproportionate abortion rate and other social maladies. He didn't mention conservative black men who have lived the kinds of lives he thinks the graduates should admire and emulate, but still . . .

The Pew Research Center found trust in government remained mired in a historic low, while frustration with government remained high. And yet voters continued to send the same people to Washington who were responsible for their frustration. Explain this to me.

More evidence of standards evaporating everywhere was a story that one of the prostitutes visited by Secret Service agents advancing a trip to Colombia by President Obama had written a tell-all book titled *Room Service*. She said she is opening a nonprofit to "help hookers" and "has a modeling contract plus a deal to bring her story to television." Of course she does.

After twelve years of fighting, the Taliban announced they were ready to talk peace with the United States. To see how that worked out, flash forward to 2021.

Having abandoned the Scripture as life's ultimate guide and increasingly turn to the Constitution when it came to law, I asked what standard—if any—was useful for deciding right from wrong. Saying it is up to each individual invites anarchy.

George Zimmerman was acquitted of murdering Trayvon Martin. Reactions depended largely on one's race and politics, less so any evidence.

The BBC and Sky News carried an inspiring speech by Malala Yousafzai, a sixteen-year-old Pakistani girl shot in the head by the Taliban for promoting education for girls, something Islamists oppose. Addressing a youth gathering at the United Nations and wearing a scarf once owned by assassinated Pakistani President Benazir Bhutto, Malala said: "The terrorists thought that they would change our aims and stop our ambitions, but nothing changed in my life except this: Weakness, fear, and hopelessness died. Strength, power, and courage was born."

It was something of a mystery why President Obama continued to speak of racism when he is an argument against it. Didn't a large number of white people vote for him—twice?

I visited the hiding place of Anne Frank in Amsterdam. It was an overwhelming experience, and I quoted from her diary, which at that time had sold 30 million copies and been translated into seventy-five languages.

On a National Review cruise in Norway, I was pleased to quote from the great Thomas Sowell: "Most of the social history of the Western world over the past three decades has been a history of replacing what worked with what sounded good." I couldn't improve on that.

Actor Ashton Kutcher delivered a surprising address at the Teen Choice Awards. Following screams from his young female fans, Kutcher told them: "I believe that opportunity looks a lot like hard work. . . . I've never had a job in my life that I was better than. I was always lucky to have a job. And every job I had was a stepping stone to my next job, and I never quit my job until I had my next job." Kutcher wasn't through: "The sexiest thing in the entire world is being really smart and being thoughtful and being generous. Everything else is crap . . . that people try to sell to you to make you feel like less. Be smart, be thoughtful, and be generous." That this made news said a lot about where we were as a country. Such things used to be self-evident not that long ago.

Attorney General Eric Holder attempted to block Louisiana's popular school voucher program that primarily benefited and was popular with black children and their parents. Holder's rationale was that the program "impedes the desegregation process." Black parents preferred to have their children well educated and not pawns in a political process. The Obama girls went to a pricey Washington private school. Again, why won't his administration allow the same opportunity for poor black kids?

President Obama pledged to end partisanship (hah!). Instead, he exacerbated it. He accused House Republicans of extortion for their opposition to raising the debt ceiling and wishing to defund Obamacare. Nothing like using harsh language to bring people together.

Democrats prepared to engage in the same old tactics over threats of a government "shutdown." The media collaborated with them, warning of national park closures, children who can't visit the Lincoln Memorial, and (gasp) late or no delivery of Social Security checks. Talk about extortion!

As plans proceeded for the withdrawal of United States forces from Afghanistan—which were delayed with surges and other decisions by succeeding presidents—I wondered what would happen to Afghan women and girls when it was completed. We had only eight years to wait until Joe Biden's botched pullout and the Taliban again running and ruining the country, denying equal rights for women and education for girls.

The United States stupidly sought a nuclear deal with Iran, which I compared to the Munich Pact. There was no way Iran would abide by such an agreement as subsequent years proved.

Obama tried to ruin Thanksgiving by suggesting politics be discussed around the family table, including immigration reform and Obamacare. Let the bickering begin!

Nelson Mandela died. When released from prison he took on the role of a statesman and was elected president of South Africa. Upon his death, President F. W. de Klerk said, "South Africa has lost one of its founding fathers and greatest sons." No person could ask for higher praise or a better epitaph.

I confessed I suffered from "income inequality," a theme President Obama liked to sing. Yes, there are always people who make more money than me, but I don't envy them. As long as I have the freedom to work hard, invest wisely, and live within my means, then I am content. The rest just fuels political ends and divides us as a people.

2014

The Year of Michael Brown and Riots in Ferguson

Colorado becomes the first jurisdiction in the modern world to officially begin state-licensed sales of cannabis for recreational use.

West African Ebola virus epidemic begins, infecting at least 28,616 people and killing at least 11,310 people, the most severe both in terms of numbers of infections and casualties.

Belgium becomes the first country in the world to legalize euthanasia for terminally ill patients of any age.

Russia formally annexes Crimea after President Vladimir Putin signs a bill finalizing the process.

During an emergency meeting, the United Kingdom, the United States, Italy, Germany, France, Japan, and Canada temporarily suspend Russia from the G8, recognizing Crimea within Ukraine's international borders and rejecting the validity of the 2014 Crimean referendum.

The Catholic Church canonizes Popes John XXIII and John Paul II.

The Islamic State of Iraq and Syria (ISIS) declares itself a caliphate.

The shooting of Michael Brown, after he was accused of shoplifting and wrestling with a police officer in Ferguson, Missouri, triggers riots.

Scotland votes against independence from the United Kingdom.

The United States and several Arab partners begin their airstrike campaign in Syria.

President Obama announces the resumption of normal diplomatic relations with Cuba and travels to the island.

CAL'S TAKE

"In violent streets and broken homes, the cry of the anguished soul is not for more laws but for more conscience and character."

The Senate Intelligence Committee, chaired by Senator Dianne Feinstein (D-CA) blamed the State Department and intelligence community for failing to prevent the attacks on the United States consulate in Benghazi, Libya, that killed Ambassador Chris Stevens and three other Americans.

In a radio interview, Democratic Governor Andrew Cuomo told conservatives to leave New York because they don't represent "who we are." So much for inclusion, diversity, and other buzzwords liberals like to use.

Jay Leno left as host of *The Tonight Show*. I wrote about our friendship and noted he was one of the nicest people I have known in show business.

Republicans on an appropriately named "retreat" announced they are open to offering some kind of legal status to 11 million people who broke our laws to get to the United States. One doesn't have to be a prophet to know this would only encourage more and more to come, which it has.

Former *CBS News* anchor Dan Rather went on Bill O'Reilly's Fox News show and said even though Bill Clinton lied about having a sexual relationship with Monica Lewinsky, Rather still believed Clinton to be an honest man. "I think you can be an honest person and lie about a number of things," said Rather. He should know.

Too many Republicans wanted to go back to the past (a perennial fault). Kathleen Willey, who claimed Bill Clinton sexually harassed her twenty years ago, published a book titled *Target: Caught in the Crosshairs of Bill and Hillary Clinton*. Willey told anyone who would listen that Hillary "is the real war on women." Maybe so, but voters put all that behind them and wanted to focus on the future.

The Obama administration showed it could be tough on foreign policy. Unfortunately, that toughness was not directed at Russia for its incursion into Crimea, but at Israel, America's ally. On the eve of a visit by Israeli Prime Minister Benjamin Netanyahu, Obama told an interviewer he planned to tell Netanyahu that "his country could face a bleak future—one of international isolation and demographic disaster—if he refuses to endorse an American framework agreement for peace with the Palestinians." No similar pressure was applied to Israel's implacable enemy, of course. In math and in foreign policy, if the formula is wrong, the outcome will also be wrong.

New Jersey Governor Chris Christie spoke at the Conservative Political Action Conference (CPAC) in Washington and had good advice for Republicans and conservatives (not always the same): "Start talking about what we're for and not what we're against."

What is it about some Western leaders who wanted to find good in men of bad character? George W. Bush once said of Vladimir Putin that he had looked Putin in the eye and "was able to get a sense of his soul." In a 2010 interview with Hugh Hewitt, Bush was asked about that remark. He responded: "The reason why I said that is because I remembered him talking movingly about his mother and the cross that she gave him that she said she had blessed in Jerusalem." Didn't Bush realize that Putin and his henchmen did a background check on Bush, including his faith, and told him what he wanted to hear? I'm sure a number of mothers of communist leaders took them to church. The question is, did faith take in them, and if it did, how could they embrace atheistic communism?

ABC White House correspondent Jonathan Karl said freshman Senator Ted Cruz (R-TX) was so hated by his fellow Republicans that "he's going to need a food taster." I wrote that might have been because Cruz was sticking to his principles and, by doing so, exposed other Republicans as having none worth fighting for.

The Hobby Lobby case went to the Supreme Court. At issue was whether the Christian-owned organization should be forced to provide for employees' contraceptives in its insurance policies when these go against the company's religious beliefs. The government argued that the religious exception in the Affordable Care Act applied only to churches and not businesses, thus allowing government to define where religious beliefs can be expressed.

Critics of the film *Noah* claimed the movie didn't accurately reflect the biblical account. Breaking news for the critics: Noah didn't speak English, as Russell Crowe did, so right there we have a departure from biblical accuracy. One should not turn to Hollywood for theological truth, but I'm glad they made the movie because it might send people to the "original cast."

The "global warming" cult was getting hot under the collar. People seemed to have stopped paying attention and polls showed "climate change" barely registered on a list of voters' concerns. This despite almost nonstop media hype and their refusal to carry any opposing views, including from experienced climatologists.

The Supreme Court, by a 5–4 vote, said prayers at public meetings were not unconstitutional. If we could only get government to stop "preying" on us with higher taxes, more debt, and increased regulations on business. I think public prayers are largely for show. Jesus said to go into our "closets" and pray in secret.

Pope Francis came out in favor of wealth redistribution. He had it backward. He should favor the creation of new wealth.

Michael Sam became the first "openly gay" player to be drafted by a National Football League (NFL) team—the St. Louis Rams. The media and the gay rights movement treated him like an American pioneer. He was drafted in the 249th round.

Hillary Clinton sustained a concussion after a fall and spent thirty days in the hospital. When discharged she was seen wearing large glasses. Former Bush adviser Karl Rove said wearing large glasses was characteristic of people who had traumatic brain injury. Bill Clinton said she was in better shape than he was, which is not comforting. The

Clintons are experts at covering up things they don't want others to know.

Euphoria over the Taliban's release of Army Sgt. Bowe Bergdahl was quickly tempered by media reports that Bergdahl had abandoned his post and that his father made comments opposing the wars in Iraq and Afghanistan. Bergdahl's father tweeted, "I am still working to free all Guantanamo prisoners. God will repay for the death of every Afghan child." Did that include those children killed while being used as human shields by the Taliban? Apparently Bergdahl's father's wrath was saved only for his own country and its effort to free Afghans—especially women—from the grip of the Islamic fanatics. Obama released several prisoners from Guantanamo prison, apparently in exchange for Bergdahl. I called it a bargain with the devil.

President Obama ordered the last American troops out of Iraq but then was forced to send back a small contingent to push back Islamists who had moved to fill the vacuum.

It should be a lesson to Republicans that when Democrats gained power, they use it. Republicans in power seemed to care more about winning approval from the Establishment than promoting policies that worked and benefited the most people.

A *Washington Post* editorial claimed "climate change deniers" were guilty of a "nihilistic refusal" to address the issue. The actual nihilists were those who refused to accept any scientific information that undermined their claim the globe was warming and if we don't spend trillions of dollars and force everyone into electric cars we were doomed. Various scenarios said we had only a few years, a few months, or a few weeks to turn things around. We are still waiting for the apocalypse. The real "hot air" was coming from the *Post* and their fellow cultists.

How many people have read *The Federalist Papers*? These were the writings of the Founders. They told us their philosophies—not a judge's philosophy—behind our founding documents. Today's government bears little resemblance to what they created, and that is why it has become so dysfunctional and costly.

Weekend shootings in Chicago killed sixteen and wounded dozens more in fifty-three separate incidents. Democrat politicians who have run the city and state for years issued meaningless statements about more gun control laws, but voters kept electing them. Are they nuts? Doesn't the question answer itself? Gang members should be rounded up and sent to an island for re-education. My kind of town, Chicago is not.

An Obama administration official came out in favor of a fence between Israeli and Palestinian territories to quell (Palestinian) violence. Unfortunately, the administration won't build a fence along the US–Mexico border. I called for all aid to the Palestinian Authority to be cut off so long as violence continued.

Robin Williams committed suicide. He was a comedic genius, but his inner demon—clinical depression—overcame him.

Eighteen-year-old Michael Brown was shot dead by a police officer in Ferguson, Missouri. He was seen on a video shoplifting from a store and then intimidating the store owner. The officer said he wrestled with Brown, who was trying to grab his gun. The media and the civil rights establishment took the side of Brown. Riots followed.

The Chinese government promised it would allow Hong Kong its freedom for fifty years after the British turned it over to the Beijing government. On a visit to this vibrant city, I find that Beijing was falling thirty-three years short of its promise as it pressured and censored media and jailed human rights advocates and politicians who did not toe the communist line. I title the column, "Breaking News: Commies Lie!"

Comedienne Joan Rivers died. She was a "surprise friend." We met following a *National Enquirer* "story" in which the writer made up a quote from me denouncing her after I refused to speak with him. I wrote her a letter care of *The Tonight Show* where she guest hosted, saying I never said any such thing and I admired her tenacity and talent. She wrote back, enclosing a "Can we talk?" pin. We subsequently met and kept in touch. Her book, *Enter Talking*, in which she inscribed a beautiful sentiment, was a testimony to what vision and persistence can do for virtually any person. She wrote: *To Cal—With lots of good wishes—Thank you for being so terrific over the years. XXX Joan Rivers.*

The Ebola virus invaded America. It was a preview of an even worse virus to come.

Forget the race "card." In the 2014 elections, Democrats played the entire race "deck." The *Wall Street Journal* listed some of the more outrageous ads and flyers designed to frighten black Americans into believing that all opposition to President Obama's policies and the Democratic Party was a sign that lynch mobs may soon return. Shameless doesn't even begin to describe it.

More talks with Iran over its certain development of nuclear weapons capability went nowhere. No surprise since Iran viewed America as "the great Satan."

Jonathan Gruber, one of the architects of the Affordable Care Act (a.k.a. Obamacare), told an audience the measure passed because of "the stupidity of the American people." Now you know what the elites think of you.

President Obama unilaterally granted legal protection to five million illegal immigrants. Shades of things to come.

A black store owner, whose shop was torched by rioters following a decision by a grand jury not to indict officer Darren Wilson for shooting and killing Michael Brown in Ferguson, Missouri, asked, "How am I going to feed my kids?" I suggested that the rioters and looters be forced to pay restitution to those (mostly black Americans) whose livelihood they ruined.

President Obama dropped sanctions against Cuba imposed fifty years ago by President Kennedy. The United States got nothing in return—no easing of press censorship, or more religious freedom, and no release of political prisoners from Cuban jails.

The film version of Laura Hillenbrand's best seller *Unbroken* was incomplete, because it left out the conversion of Louis Zamperini and his attempt to meet and forgive the man who tortured him in a Japanese internment camp during World War II. Producer Angelina Jolie said it would have made the film "too long." I said leaving out this central part of Zamperini's story would be like leaving out the civil rights activism of Martin Luther King Jr.

2015

The Year of the Charlie Hebdo Attack

Two gunmen belonging to Al-Qaeda's Yemen branch kill twelve people and injure eleven more at the Paris headquarters of satirical newspaper *Charlie Hebdo*. Muslims are angry that the publication depicted an image of Mohammed.

Cuba and the United States end fifty-four years of hostility and re-establish full diplomatic relations. The United States gets nothing in return except a speech in Havana by President Obama.

Justin Trudeau becomes prime minister of Canada.

The 2015 UN Climate Change Conference is held in Paris. Leaders from 147 nations attend and most will do nothing about it, though they contributed to air pollution by their transportation choices.

Two gunmen open fire at a workplace in San Bernardino, California, killing fourteen before dying themselves in a shootout with police. ISIS claimed responsibility.

CAL'S TAKE

"America's most dangerous diseases have developed an immunity to politics. We suffer not from a failure of political organization or power, but a failure of love."

Former New York Governor Mario Cuomo died at eighty-two. He was a model of what we now call "progressivism" (a.k.a. liberal), a gifted rhetorician and consummate politician. He said his Catholic faith compelled him to suspend the death penalty in New York, but that same faith said nothing to him about stopping the slaughtering of the innocents through abortion. Cafeteria theology?

It is from Aesop's fable we get the phrase: "A man is known by the company he keeps." The British and American media were carrying the first stories of Prince Andrew keeping company with Jeffrey Epstein, who was accused of keeping underage girls as "sex slaves" for prominent men. Buckingham Palace issued a vehement denial on Andrew's behalf. We would later see the truthfulness of that claim not worth the paper on which it was written.

Following the *Charlie Hebdo* shootings, I recalled the late *Los Angeles Times* cartoonist, Paul Conrad, who frequently used religious symbols, including the cross, to make political points. If he were alive, would he put himself at risk by drawing a cartoon depicting Mohammed? I doubt it.

George Clooney offered a tribute to his new wife, Amal, at the Golden Globe Awards. In an age when people had "relationships" and "partners," it was refreshing to hear a man swoon in public over his wife, even though they had been married for only four months! Ain't love grand?

President Obama, in his State of the Union address, called for—wait for it—higher taxes on the wealthy and successful in order to pay for programs for the poor and middle class. Honestly, don't Democrats ever sing a different tune? Politicians never have enough of our money, while not having to make any of their own.

President Theodore Roosevelt said, "Speak softly and carry a big stick." More than a century later, President Obama spoke loudly (and often incessantly) and carried a twig. The president was mismatched to the times in which we lived. He was unserious when seriousness was required. The tyrants of the world took notice and rightly calculated they could pretty much do what they wanted without paying a heavy penalty. Shades of worse to come when Joe Biden became president.

It isn't often that a member of the media revealed the philosophy behind his political ideology, but that happened when Chris Cuomo (son of Mario and brother of Andrew) outed himself as he was interviewing Alabama Chief Justice Roy Moore. Moore had just asserted that our ultimate rights came from God. Chris Cuomo responded, "Our laws do not come from God, your honor, and you know that. They come from man." I guess that meant that Jim Crow laws were OK when they were imposed against black Americans, as well as laws penalizing anyone who helped slaves escape their masters? Martin Luther King Jr. didn't believe our rights came from man. Neither did John F. Kennedy, who said in his Inaugural Address in 1961: ". . . the rights of man come not from the generosity of the state, but from the hand of God." The modern Democratic Party became the party of, by, and for secular progressives.

Obama loyalists were dispatched to Israel to try to defeat Benjamin Netanyahu in the Israeli elections. Over opposition from the administration, Netanyahu addressed Congress and blew them away with the power of truth about the adversities Israel, the United States, and the West would face from rogue and terrorist regimes.

Pop star Taylor Swift donated $50,000 to the New York City public school system. It was a bad investment. Her money would have been better spent on scholarships for poor children to attend private schools.

It was the fiftieth anniversary of the civil rights march in Selma, Alabama. President Obama joined many others in the march. Unfortunately, all the marches and laws have not lived up to their promised results, otherwise things would be different for poor black Americans. The Bureau of Labor Statistics reported black unemployment stood at 10.4 percent, a slight increase from the previous month. Why do race hustlers never talk about the real problem—which begins with unstable or non-existent families, crime, drugs, and poor education, thanks to rotten inner city government schools?

A question that was being asked by people who follow politics: How do you solve a problem like the Clintons? Their incessant vacuuming of cash and skirting (no pun intended) of laws and regulations would place lesser mortals in danger of prison, yet they manage to escape accountability while others go to prison or die under mysterious circumstances.

In a column titled "Another signpost on our road to destruction," I wrote: "When future historians analyze the decline of America, they need look no further than the trivialities increasingly occupying our time and concerns instead of substantive matters seriously threatening our existence."

The latest in a long list of examples is a two-hour ABC special devoted to former Olympic athlete Bruce Jenner and his coming out as a transgender person. Two hours! Neither ABC nor any other media giant had paid that much attention to international threats from Russia, China, or the rapid rise of Islamic fanaticism, not to mention Bill and Hillary Clinton's financial empire.

Anybody can be labeled or self-identify as a journalist these days. No rules or experience need apply. Example: Former Clinton administration official George Stephanopoulos became an ABC "journalist" because the president of that network said he was. It is later revealed Stephanopoulos donated $75,000 to the Clinton Foundation but neglected to disclose that information while interviewing Peter Schweizer, author of *Clinton Cash*, a book critical of the foundation and the Clintons.

Stephanopoulos apologized and his bosses at *ABC News* said no disciplinary action would be taken, except that he removed himself from moderating or appearing on any debate panel during the 2016 election cycle. It didn't matter because anyone who replaced him would likely have the same worldview—Republican candidates bad; Hillary Clinton and all Democrats good.

Too many people appear to "worship" the false god of politics. It reminded me of something the late comedian George Carlin said: "Never underestimate the power of stupid people in large groups."

In a commencement speech to the United States Coast Guard Academy, President Obama attempts to draw a connection between "climate change" and "terrorism."

It is such a rare act that most did not know how to respond, except in stunned silence. Relatives of the nine people murdered while attending a Bible study and prayer meeting at Emanuel A.M.E. Church in Charleston, South Carolina, told the accused killer they forgave him.

By a vote of 5–4 with Reagan nominee Anthony Kennedy casting the decisive vote, the Supreme Court OKed same-sex marriage. I asked what would be next, and would the Court ever say no to anything? If it did, on what would it base its decision? The Constitution? Scripture? Hardly. Those two documents have long been ignored in jurisprudence and culture.

What was most shocking was an undercover video of a conversation between Deborah Nucatola, a Planned Parenthood executive, and two pro-life activists from the Center for Medical Progress posing as employees from a biotech firm. ABC, CBS, NBC, and CNN ignored the story on their Sunday morning political talk shows, but not Fox. The discussion centered on the sale of donated tissue from aborted fetuses. Nucatola said in the video, "We've been very good at getting heart, lung, liver . . . so I'm not gonna crush that part, I'm gonna basically crush below, I'm gonna crush above, and I'm gonna see if I can get it all intact." I recalled this quote from Dr. Leon Kass: " . . . if we come to see ourselves as meat, then meat we shall become."

"The British Invasion" used to mean The Beatles, Rolling Stones, and other musical groups who came to and sold plenty of records and concert tickets in America. A different "invasion" took place in Britain. On a single day, at least fifteen hundred migrants attempted to storm inadequate fences in Calais, France. Outnumbered police could only stop a few. Some migrants interviewed vowed to return as many times as it took to get into a country they see as providing jobs, health care and other benefits. In response, the

Home Office confirmed "it was planning to strip families of the automatic right to benefits if their asylum applications were rejected." The government moved forward with a plan to evict illegal immigrants without a court order from rental properties "under new laws designed to make Britain a tougher place to live in." Theresa May, the home secretary and later prime minister, warned in a *Telegraph* article written with Bernard Cazeneuve, France's minister of the interior, that Britain's "streets are not paved with gold." They wrote, "Tackling this situation is the top priority for the UK and French governments." America should pay attention, but didn't.

Germany, which in the last century twice invaded other countries, contributing to two world wars, was being invaded by hordes of Muslims. According to Pew Research Center, there were 4.76 million Muslims in Germany, about 5.8 percent of its population, and that number was steadily growing. The *Wall Street Journal* reported, "The government estimates that about eight hundred thousand foreigners will seek asylum in Germany this year, almost four times as many as last year."

The announcement by House Speaker John Boehner that he was retiring at the end of October stunned Washington, where life is all about grabbing power and holding on to it, often until death do part. At a meeting with reporters, Boehner said, "My first job as Speaker is to protect the institution." Really? Is that why Ohio voters sent him to Washington in sixteen elections and his Republican colleagues elected and re-elected him Speaker? Did he take an oath to preserve, protect, and defend the institution of the House, or the Constitution, which, if followed, offered protection enough?

In Washington, most stories that made the newspapers and evening newscasts were about scandals and political infighting. Rarely was there one about redemption.

In his new book, *I Should Be Dead: My Life Surviving Politics, TV, and Addiction*, Bob Beckel, the longtime political operative, told a deeply personal story about searching for life's meaning through political power, drugs, physical abuse as a child, womanizing, hardball politics and finally a change of heart and direction.

I have been asked about my friendship with Bob more than about myself. People were curious how two men who come from different backgrounds and hold different political views on most, but not all, issues could be close friends without compromising their beliefs. Partially it had to do with refusing to be defined by labels. Shared faith was also a bond between us.

In my Christmas column, I wrote: People speak of "the spirit of Christmas," or when observing some special act with which they approve or seek to inspire, refer to "the true meaning of Christmas." They are never asked what they mean by either. The true meaning of Christmas is this: God took on human form in the Person of His Son, Jesus Christ, to die in our place, paying for our sins, so that humans who receive Jesus might be forgiven and be with Him forever. You are free to reject that message and the One who delivered it, but what you are not free to do is redefine or change the message into something different.

2016

The Year of Donald Trump's Election

Agunman claiming allegiance to the Islamic State opens fire at a gay nightclub in Orlando, Florida, killing forty-nine people and injuring fifty-three others.

The United Kingdom votes to leave the European Union. It is quickly labeled "Brexit."

Hillary Clinton is nominated for president, becoming the first woman to be nominated by a major political party.

The United States and China formally join the Paris Agreement on global climate. Why do I think China won't live up to its promises? Oh, that's right. They're communists, and commies lie! But then again, climate change is also a lie, so they fit well together.

Three events that played a significant role in the 2016 presidential election all take place on the same afternoon: (1) United States intelligence agencies publicly accuse the Russian government of using computer hacking to interfere with the United States election process; (2) the *Washington*

Post releases a videotape showing candidate Donald Trump privately bragging about sexual improprieties; (3) WikiLeaks releases thousands of private emails from inside the political campaign of candidate Hillary Clinton.

The Chicago Cubs win the World Series for the first time since 1908, ending the longest championship drought in American sports history.

Businessman and television personality Donald Trump is elected the forty-fifth president of the United States, much to the shock of all except those who voted for him.

CAL'S TAKE

"This attitude that government is better at making decisions than you are because you are too stupid to know what is good for you is a hallmark of patronizing, arrogant, and condescending liberalism."

The "inevitability" of Hillary Clinton's presidential candidacy was not so inevitable after all. Not only was she unlikable, the FBI expanded its investigation into her use of private email as secretary of state and possible links to the Clinton Foundation.

I wrote an essay for *National Review*, along with many others, opposing Donald Trump's candidacy. I was called all sorts of names by letter writers, but I changed my mind later when the choice was between him and the "deplorable" Hillary Clinton.

Pro-choicers were angry at a Doritos commercial aired during the Super Bowl and called for a boycott of the chip. The ad featured a pregnant woman receiving a sonogram while lying in her hospital bed. The screen showed the baby. The father was snacking on Doritos and he noticed the child's arms moving in the direction of a chip as dad took it from the bag and put one in his mouth. Finally, the baby could stand it no longer and emerged from the womb to grab his own chip. The last thing the pro-choicers wanted was for women to look at a sonogram and see their baby, and that's why the ad angered them. While they boycotted, I went out and bought several bags.

President Obama nominated Merrick Garland to the Supreme Court to replace Antonin Scalia. The media called him a "moderate," but never defined the term. Senate Majority Leader Mitch McConnell (R-KY) refused to hold hearings, quoting Joe Biden, who once said under different circumstances that no one should be confirmed to the Supreme Court in an election year. Never mind! Given Garland's record as an attorney general, McConnell was right to block his nomination.

"I am not a dictator, I am the president," claimed Obama. That statement became inoperative in light of the administration's diktat to the nation's public schools that they must accommodate transgendered students when it comes to restrooms, showers and changing areas. Why are your kids still in these re-education camps?

The popularity of the Broadway musical *Hamilton* offered an opportunity to re-visit the thinking of our most prolific founding father. Hamilton, like the rest of the Founders, knew that government governs best when it governs least. In a speech to the New York Ratifying Convention in 1788, Hamilton said: "Good constitutions are formed upon a comparison of the liberty of the individual with the strength of the government. If the one is too high, the other will be weakened too much. It is the happiest possible mode of conciliating these objects, to institute one branch peculiarly endowed with sensibility, another with knowledge and firmness. Through the opposition and mutual control of these bodies, the government will reach, in its regular operations, the perfect balance between liberty and power."

I agreed with the rapper Snoop Dogg, who said he is tired of seeing movies about slavery and would prefer a series "about the success that black folks are having." He was singing my song!

I interviewed Donald Trump in his Manhattan office. I asked him to define himself. He told me he went to great schools and thought he understood education. He said his father didn't want him to move from his homes in Brooklyn and Queens to Manhattan, "and I have done a great job in Manhattan." He told me about his "bestselling books," his TV show (*The Apprentice*), and "now I'm doing something else." He meant running for president. He said President Obama had "been an unbelievable divider of this country, whether it's rich or poor, black or white."

I mentioned the criticism of his divisive language as opposed to sticking to issues, and at first, he said he agreed and would switch, but never did. "I've had great success at everything I've done," he said with no sign that humility was one of those "successes." He said his first executive order as president would be to control the border, a promise he fulfilled but was abandoned by Joe Biden to our detriment.

I asked him about faith and he responded that he had a lot of evangelical support. I followed up by quoting him as saying he didn't need to seek forgiveness. He responded: "I will be asking for forgiveness, but hopefully I won't have to be asking for much forgiveness. As you know, I'm a Presbyterian and a Protestant. I've had great . . . relationships with ministers. . . . I'm going to treat my religion, which is Christian, with great respect and care."

I gave him a signed copy of my book *What Works: Common Sense Solutions for a Stronger America* and wished him good luck as I left and descended in his gold elevator to the crowded Manhattan streets.

President Obama endorsed Hillary Clinton to be his successor. He said, "I don't think there's ever been someone so qualified to hold office." Presumably he didn't mean himself, or maybe he did.

FBI Director James Comey gave Hillary a "get out of jail free card" when he said he would not recommend she be prosecuted for her staff's "extremely careless" handling of emails on private servers that included documents classified as "top secret," "secret," and "confidential." Comey's use of "extremely careless" was significant because if he had used the word "negligent," that's covered under federal law 18 U.S.C. 793.

I described Trump's choice of running mate, Mike Pence, as "salt" to Trump's "pepper." Pence was the polar opposite of Trump—a serious Christian, one who thought before he spoke, calm, controlled, and married to the same woman he started with. Trump needed him, in part to mitigate his acerbic personality.

Hillary Clinton denied a "pay-for-play" arrangement granting contributors to the Clinton Foundation access to her when she was secretary of state." She said, "I know there's a lot of smoke, and there's no fire." I asked my son,

Jay, about this as he had been a firefighter most of his professional life. He told me, "Where there is smoke, there is, or was, fire. Smoke is a byproduct of combustion. There are three stages of fire: smoldering, incipient and free burning. Each one (emits) smoke." The Clintons' behavior over many years resembled a forest fire.

In a line that would haunt her long after she made it, Hillary Clinton told an LGBT fundraiser in New York, "You can put half of Trump supporters into what I call the basket of deplorables," adding that some were "irredeemable," meaning they had strong convictions opposite her own.

Prior to a presidential debate I liked to suggest questions I would ask of the candidates if given the opportunity. The problem was too many members of the "panel" asked their questions from a mostly liberal perspective. Still, I posed these questions:

For Clinton: You once supported traditional marriage, but now favor same-sex marriage. Polygamists now want to be next to receive legal and cultural approval. Do you oppose polygamy, and if so, according to what standard? Follow-up: What is your standard for deciding right from wrong?

For Trump: You were once pro-choice until you said you heard about a baby that was going to be aborted, but wasn't. You called the child a "total superstar." Is a baby only valuable when it becomes a superstar, or is every life valuable?

For Clinton: You appear to have an interventionist foreign policy record. What is your standard for sending American forces into battle, especially in the Middle East where nothing ever seems to get resolved? Follow-up: In one of your emails, you praise Sidney Blumenthal's son, Max, for his virulent anti-Semitic and anti-Israel comments, favoring the dismantling of Israel. Since Israel's enemies have also vowed to destroy the only one democracy in the Middle East, would you support the Jewish state, or demand that it give up more land to Palestinians when the land Israel already relinquished has brought it no closer to peace?

For Trump: Why do you so often praise Vladimir Putin, who routinely behaves like the KGB agent he once was?

For Clinton: The federal government took in record amounts of tax money in 2015—$3.18 trillion—but the debt is approaching $20 trillion and you want to spend more. Why won't you propose cutting programs that aren't working?

For Trump: What agencies and programs would you cut?

Admit it. These questions would have been far more interesting than the ones the panel asked.

What would you think of an individual or a company that earned a pre-tax profit of $29.9 million in one year, paid no taxes, and still received a $3.5 million refund? Am I speaking of Donald Trump? No, it is the New York Times Company, whose newspaper constantly advocated for higher taxes on "the wealthy."

In the final presidential debate before the election, Hillary Clinton recycled the line Democrats used for sixty years, that "the wealthy" aren't paying their "fair share" in taxes, but said nothing about cutting spending. Trump promised to cut taxes, advocate for more school choice. The smears kept coming against Trump, including the "Access Hollywood" tape in which Trump used a vulgarity to describe women. As usual, the hypocritical media ignored Hillary's enabling of Bill and his numerous extramarital affairs, as they did with John F. Kennedy and Lyndon B. Johnson.

The *New York Times* allowed Hillary to edit her own quotes before publishing some of her emails uncovered by WikiLeaks. If this didn't prove the big media were in the tank for her, what would?

I now call myself an "Ever-Trumper," considering his proposals rank higher than his personality, and the disaster of a president Hillary Clinton would create. Among others is novelist and former Jack Kemp and Rush Limbaugh aide, Joel Rosenberg. He listed ten reasons why he intends to vote for the Trump–Pence ticket. They were mostly about stopping Hillary and her secular-progressive agenda, which he believed would complete the moral, economic, and political destruction of the country. Me, too.

Trump won, stunning not only the media, but the world. He might even have surprised himself.

The Left thinks it had a "divine right" (if it believed in the Divine) to always control the government and our lives. When it lost, it couldn't accept that a majority didn't want their agenda. Case in point: When Vice President-elect Mike Pence and his wife attended a performance of the hit Broadway musical *Hamilton*, Brandon Victor Dixon, the actor who played Aaron Burr, criticized Pence during the curtain call. Dixon lectured Pence about diversity and the "fear" of people like himself, a black American, about a Trump–Pence administration. It reminded me of when Joe Biden told a black audience that Republicans wanted to put them "back in chains." Desperation was a terrible thing to observe.

It's the 500th anniversary of the Protestant Reformation. I recalled a message preached by Martin Luther (no, I didn't hear it in person), who began that Reformation by nailing his ninety-five theses to the All-Saints church door in Wittenberg, Germany. After underscoring the humble backgrounds of Mary and Joseph and noting how rich travelers stayed in far better surroundings than the stable that the world's most famous couple were forced to occupy, Luther commented: "See, this is the first picture with which Christ put the world to shame and exposed all it does and knows. It shows that the world's greatest wisdom is foolishness, her best actions are wrong, and her greatest treasures are misfortunes." That's about as good as it gets for Christmas sermons.

2017

The Year of Jerusalem Becoming the Capital of Israel

Donald Trump is sworn in as the forty-fifth president of the United States. He is the first person to be elected to the presidency without a political or military background.

Millions of people worldwide join the Women's March in protest of Trump's inauguration. Some people can't handle elections that don't turn out the way they prefer.

North Korea prompts international condemnation by test firing a ballistic missile across the Sea of Japan. Kim Jong-Un doesn't seem to care.

Kim Jong-nam, the eldest son of deceased North Korean leader Kim Jong-il and the half brother of the current North Korean leader, is killed after being attacked by two women with VX nerve agent at Kuala Lumpur International Airport in Malaysia.

A major late-season blizzard affects the northeastern United States, dumping up to three feet of snow in the hardest hit areas. Climate change activists who usually blame "global warming" for seasonal changes assert this is another example that the planet is in peril. Memo to the activists: It's called winter.

In response to a suspected chemical weapons attack on a rebel-held town, the United States military launches fifty-nine Tomahawk cruise missiles at an air base in Syria. An Indigenous American group protests the word "Tomahawk." Just kidding, but wait a while.

President Trump fires FBI Director James Comey.

Former FBI Director Robert Mueller is appointed special counsel, taking over the investigation of purported Russian interference in the 2016 election. The "story," though touted as true on virtually every media platform, proves to be completely false, and the entire ruse is connected to the Hillary Clinton campaign and Democratic Party, but not before the damage to Trump is done, which is the point.

An ISIS terrorist bombing attack at an Ariana Grande concert in Manchester, England, kills twenty-two people and injures more than five hundred others.

President Trump announces the United States will withdraw from the Paris Climate Accords.

Eight people are murdered and dozens of civilians wounded by Islamist terrorists in an attack on London Bridge. Three of the attackers are shot dead by the police. ISIS claims responsibility.

A Unite the Right rally is held in Charlottesville, Virginia, by a variety of white nationalist and other far-right groups. Heather Heyer, a counter-protester, is killed after being hit by a car. Media hype of a small minority of white supremacists make them look like the majority of the crowd.

Sixty people are killed and 867 more injured when Stephen Paddock opens fire on a crowd at a concert in Las Vegas.

A Leonardo da Vinci painting, *Salvator Mundi*, sells for $450 million at Christie's in New York, a new record price for any work of art.

Russia is banned from the 2018 Winter Olympics following an investigation into state-sponsored doping.

The United States officially recognizes Jerusalem as the capital of Israel. Thank you, President Trump! Guatemala follows by announcing they will also move their Israeli embassy to Jerusalem, as do Honduras and Panama.

CAL'S TAKE

"If a state, or nation, has laws it will not enforce for political reasons, it mocks both the law and politics, to say nothing of the cultural order."

According to CNN (and where else would you go for trusted information?), Chicago experienced a surge in violent crime in 2016. There were 762 murders, 3,550 shootings and 4,331 shooting victims. This is a city with some of the most restrictive gun laws in the nation. Once again, it wasn't exactly breaking news that criminals don't obey laws. That's why they're called criminals. Democrats ran Chicago for years, but people kept electing them, expecting different results . . . the definition of insanity. Things will only get worse.

At the Golden Globe Awards, actress Meryl Streep spent six minutes trashing president-elect Donald Trump. She urged journalists to hold him accountable. Given the media's poor job of holding Barack Obama accountable (especially when it came to his broken promises on health care insurance), Streep was driving on a one-way street.

Newly inaugurated President Trump signed a flurry of executive orders that delighted those who voted for him. They included withdrawing the country from the Trans–Pacific Partnership, reinstating the Mexico City Policy, which prohibited tax dollars going to fund abortions in other countries, advancing the Keystone XL and Dakota oil pipelines. All of these would be reversed by future President Biden in 2021, which is why I think executive orders should be limited. Better to go the congressional route, especially if the incumbent's party controls both houses on Congress.

The Left went nuts, saying Trump was an "illegitimate president" because he didn't win the popular vote; he only won the most states with their collective electoral college votes. Let's not forget the charges of "racism" and "immorality," as if the Left had a standard for what was moral and its opposite. The major media engaged in introspection as to what they did wrong because Trump beat Hillary.

My wife of fifty-one years, Charlotte Ray (nee Heath) Thomas passed away. I owed her much, especially when it came to encouraging my faith.

The new secretary of education, Betsy DeVos, is an old friend. She and I were in prison together in Jackson, Michigan. It was part of a Prison Fellowship program. DeVos became a lightning rod for the public education establishment, partly because she was a strong advocate for school choice. She also believed top-down policies from Washington had not contributed to higher test scores. She told me "This department has invested $7 billion trying to improve failing schools and there were literally no results to show for it."

Trump created the term "fake news," and the media went wild. *Editor and Publisher* magazine claimed that newspapers could use his attacks to their advantage and increase circulation and advertising dollars. Why? Because, said the magazine, their "unbiased reporting" can be used as "a sales strategy." That line made me laugh out loud.

President Trump submitted his first budget to Congress, I recalled a quote from Ronald Reagan that told you a lot about "the swamp" that is Washington: "No government ever voluntarily reduces itself in size. Government programs, once launched, never disappear. Actually, a government bureau is the nearest thing to eternal life we'll ever see on this earth!"

Personality is not policy. While Trump won the election in large part because of his personality, advancing one's policies was a completely different game. In the end, Trump's personality would not be enough to win reelection (and, no, I don't believe the election was "stolen"). I pleaded with him to stop insulting others. He didn't take my advice.

Roger Ailes passed away. He and Rupert Murdoch changed the media and much of the political landscape when they founded Fox News Channel. Roger was a friend and a great encourager who twice gave me my own shows—first when he was head at CNBC and later at Fox.

The religious left felt left out. According to an article in the *New York Times*, liberal clergy felt excluded from the political arena and blamed the religious right for occupying what they once believed was their exclusive territory. They were, according to the story's headline, "seeking to break the right's grip on nation's moral agenda." Left out of what? Abortion for any reason? Marriage to anyone? Gender fluidity? Best to leave them out. They should focus on why they are bleeding members.

Less than forty-eight hours after the shooting rampage targeting Republican members of Congress and their staff on a baseball field in Alexandria, Virginia, Republicans and Democrats knelt in prayer at Nationals Park before their annual charity game. Things quickly returned to normal . . . or abnormal. A *Drudge Report* headline read: "Shots fired at a truck flying 'Make America Great Again' flag"; "Starbucks staff harasses Trump supporting customer"; "Time Warner defends funding assassination play," in which Julius Caesar is presented as a Trump look-alike in Shakespeare's classic.

The white supremacists marching in Charlottesville said they wanted to "take America back." Take it back from whom and for what purpose? The Left and the Right occasionally conveyed a similar message. What is it about America that made some people want to seize it from other people? Among other things, the demonstrators were upset that streets and statues memorializing men who led the South during the Civil War were being removed and replaced by those honoring men and women untainted by the stain of slavery. Three people died and nineteen were injured. Democrats used the tragedy to smear Republicans as "racists."

After promising to get out of unending Middle East wars, President Trump did a slight pivot. The president admitted that reality had caught up with him after his inauguration, and that America must ensure al-Qaida did not again gain a foothold in the country from which it could plot another massive terror attack on the United States. A Trump administration official said the Pentagon would send an estimated four thousand additional American forces to Afghanistan—a plan reminiscent of the Iraq "surge" ordered by President George W. Bush and successfully led by Gen. David Petraeus.

I visited Budapest, Hungary. On Jan. 1, the government of Prime Minister Viktor Orban lowered the corporate tax rate from 19 percent to 9 percent, the lowest rate among the 28 member states of the European Union. By comparison, the United States' top marginal tax rate is 38.92, just behind Puerto Rico and the United Arab Emirates. The result? Seven hundred thousand new jobs created, only one hundred fifty thousand of which were government jobs.

About the Clintons, I wrote: "How do they do it? I am not the first to compare the Clintons to Harry Houdini, the great magician and escape artist, but Bill and Hillary make him look like a rank amateur. No law seems to touch them. No regulation seems to control them. No prosecutor wants to take the risk of holding either Clinton accountable for any-thing." OK, Bill was impeached by a Republican House, but not convicted in the Senate.

In a year-end column titled, "The UK's Consequential Em-brace of Secularism," I wrote from Wales: The UK *Daily Mail* has again published a story about a subject that has become a recurring theme this time of year. No, not Christmas, but rather drunkenness, though the holiday is used as its pri-mary excuse. Pictures accompanying the story show young people collapsing in gutters and vomiting on the sidewalks. It is not a pretty sight.

2018

The Year of Government Shutdowns

The government enters another of those phony "shut-downs" as a result of a dispute over Deferred Action for Children Arrivals (DACA). Democrats have used this extortion strategy for years and Republicans never seem to be able to counter it.

Space X successfully conducts its maiden flight of its most powerful rocket to date.

A school shooting occurs at Marjorie Stoneman Douglas High School in Parkland, Florida. Seventeen are killed and seventeen more injured. Why do these things keep happening? Could it have anything to do with the cheapening of human life?

Former Russian double agent Sergei Skripal and his daughter, Yulia, are poisoned by the Novichok nerve agent in Salisbury, England. UK counter-terrorism police investigate amid speculation the Kremlin (meaning Vladimir Putin) was behind the incident.

Donald Trump accepts an invitation from North Korea's Kim Jong-un for a meeting in May to discuss the denuclearization of North Korea. Lots of commentary about who is using whom.

China's government approves a constitutional change that removes term limits for its leaders, granting Xi Jinping the status of "president for life." Sounds like the way some members of Congress think of themselves.

In response to school shootings thousands of high school students across the country participate in an organized protest they call the National School Walkout. Symbolism over substance. Armed security guards and metal detectors, along with emergency gates that would shut when any threat is noticed, would be better.

Vladimir Putin "wins" a fourth term as Russian president. No one dares ask for a recount.

The United States, the United Kingdom, and France conduct bombing raids on Syrian military bases in response to the sarin attack allegedly by the Bashar-al-Assad regime on civilians in Ghouta.

Cinemas open in Saudi Arabia for the first time since 1983 with the American film "Black Panther" chosen as the first to be screened. I would have picked a musical.

Kim Jong-un steps across the border with South Korea to meet with President Moon Jae-in, becoming the first North Korean leader to cross the DMZ since its creation in 1953.

President Trump announces the United States will withdraw from the nuclear agreement with Iran. They weren't going to abide by it anyway since the Mullahs claim their "god" wants them to kill Jews and what they call "cross worshippers" and "polytheists."

Prince Harry and "gold digger" and social climber Meghan Markle get married. I don't care. An estimated 1.9 billion watch on TV, apparently because they have nothing better to do.

Nicolas Maduro "wins" reelection in the lowest voter turnout in Venezuela's modern history. That's because a lot of voters stayed home, believing it to be a sham election, which it was. Now try to find basic staples like toilet paper and peanut butter. Ah, the joys of socialism and communism.

Leaders of North Korea and the United States meet for the first time in Singapore.

The United States announces it will withdraw from the UN Human Rights Council. Good, because some of those on it are the worst practitioners of human rights.

Canada becomes the first major industrialized country to legalize cannabis for recreational use. Don't we already have enough people who are living in alternate mental states (think Washington politicians).

Saudi Arabia allows women to drive. In that country, it's considered progress.

Seven members of a Japanese terrorist group who were convicted in 1995 for a sarin gas attack in the Tokyo subway are hanged. What took them so long?

American tariffs on $34 billion worth of Chinese goods come into effect, as President Trump suggests the final total could reach $550 billion. China accuses the United States of starting the "largest trade war in economic history" and announces immediate retaliatory tariffs. A better solution: start making more things in America again. It will also solve the supply chain problem that will confront us in 2021.

Apple, Inc. becomes the world's first public company to achieve a market capitalization of $1 trillion.

The United States reimposes sanctions on Iran. Hooray!

Fifteen-year-old Swede Greta Thunberg stays out of school in an attempt to give attention to the "climate change" issue. Anyone else think she is just repeating the propaganda she has been taught in that school and elsewhere? The media turn her into a star, but who thinks a fifteen-year-old knows anything?

Jamal Khashoggi, who occasionally wrote columns for the *Washington Post*, is murdered inside the Saudi consulate in Istanbul, triggering a diplomatic crisis for Saudi Arabia. Somehow this doesn't pass the "smell test."

The Intergovernmental Panel on Climate Change (IPCC) releases its Special Report on Global Warming. In what has become a familiar litany ("the end is near"), the agency says "rapid, far-reaching and unprecedented changes in all aspects of society" are needed to ensure that global warming is kept below 1.5 degrees centigrade. I again refer readers to my favorite website on the subject: climatedepot.com

President Trump announces that the United States will "terminate" the Intermediate Range Nuclear Forces Treaty over alleged violations by Russia. Nice to have a president who holds other nations accountable for breaking treaties.

Eleven people are killed in a terrorist attack by what authorities labeled a "white supremacist" at the Tree of Life Synagogue in Pittsburgh.

France experiences its worst civil unrest since 1968. Protests in Paris turn into riots. Hundreds of people are injured and thousands arrested; over one hundred cars are burned, the Arc de Triomphe is vandalized and numerous other tourist sites are closed, both in the capital and elsewhere in the country. The issues? Rising fuel prices, high taxes, uncontrolled immigration, and government indifference.

The United States government enters a second government shutdown in a dispute over funding for the US–Mexico border wall. The shutdown, which lasted until January 25, 2019, is the longest in American history. And we've seen how failure to finish the wall has contributed to a massive influx of migrants breaking our laws to get here and getting free stuff. Democrats are the modern Al Capone, using extortion to get what they want.

In the biggest event of the year for me, God brings into my life a former high school classmate, who now goes by the name "CJ." We are married twice—first in a ceremony in Florida and later at a fifteenth-century villa in Rome, Italy. I am so grateful.

CAL'S TAKE

"The difference between the more traditional sports clubs and Congress is that Congress doesn't really compete against another."

"When prosperity comes, do not use all of it."—Confucius. I just threw that in to remind politicians not to spend us into oblivion. Oops, too late. How about this from Charlie Chan: "When money talks, few are deaf."

One reason Democrats seem so fixated on importing illegal immigrants and allowing their children to stay and become citizens may be the exodus from high-tax and traditionally Democratic states. One can't escape federal taxes, but we can escape state taxes. More and more people work remotely, which allows them to live just about anywhere. I recalled a quote from Florida Republican Governor Ron DeSantis: "Governor Cuomo (of New York) says I'm stealing his people. I'm not stealing them. He's driving them out."

In his State of the Union address, President Trump touched on a subject that is not usually thought of as a Republican issue: "As America regains its strength, opportunity must be extended to all citizens. That is why this year we will embark on reforming our prisons, to help former inmates who have served their time get a second chance at life." Having been in many prisons (as a visitor) and known several ex-cons whose lives have been changed, I endorsed his objective.

Responding to the Chicken Little scaremongers that "climate change" is about to destroy us, Costco announced it has a doomsday meal kit for sale. The cost is $6,000. The online listing says the kit contains thirty-six thousand servings of food that will feed a family of four for one year. Yum!

Not so long ago, using vulgar words would get you ostracized from what we used to refer to as "polite company." Not today. At the White House Correspondents' Dinner in Washington, in the very ballroom where the annual National Prayer Breakfast is held, a previously obscure "comedian" named Michelle Wolf climbed out from under a rock to spew words and personal insults at President Trump, his press secretary, Sarah Huckabee Sanders, and top aide Kellyanne Conway, obliterating any remaining standard of conduct and decency. Wolf also made grotesque references to abortion and used words to describe in vulgar terms female genitalia. It was the last dinner of its kind I cared to attend.

Hillary Clinton and I happened to be in Melbourne and Sydney, Australia, at the same time. Unlike me, she arrived with a huge chip on her shoulder, still steaming over her 2016 election loss to Donald Trump. As with almost everything else the Clintons do, it cost to hear her bitterness. Those who went to hear Clinton speak, more than five thousand people, paid between $200 and $500 Australian dollars (about $147 to $339 USD).

What they heard was criticism of President Trump and his foreign and domestic policies. Not that long ago, Americans made an effort to stop "partisan politics at the water's edge," but no more.

In a 7–2 ruling, the Supreme Court decided the Colorado Human Rights Commission had failed to take into account the religious beliefs of a Lakewood baker who refused to make a wedding cake for a gay couple. Justice Anthony Kennedy was highly critical of the commission, which he said had written its anti-discrimination regulations in ways that were hostile to the faith of the baker, Jack Phillips.

Charles Krauthammer passed away. It is a great loss to the country, to journalism and to me. What I found most amazing about Charles was that despite an accident in his youth that left him paralyzed, he never complained. Neither did he accept or embrace pity. He scooted around in his powered wheelchair and into and out of a van especially configured for him. While he was unable to exercise his limbs, he exercised his mind to the great benefit of all those who have read his syndicated columns and watched him on TV. He spoke slowly, partly from physical necessity, but also because it helped him make his points. In the rapid-fire speech characteristic of cable TV, one was more likely to remember what he said. That he appeared in the *Washington Post* provided a great counterweight to that paper's liberal editorial policy and other mostly liberal columnists.

President Trump nominated Brett Kavanaugh for the Supreme Court. Kavanaugh believed in the Constitution as written, which always sparked outrage from leftists who think judges should read into that founding document what conforms to their political outlook, or ignore it altogether.

Kavanaugh was smeared by Christine Blasey Ford, who claimed he raped her but can't remember where she was or any other details. In announcing her decision to vote for Kavanaugh's confirmation, Senator Susan Collins (R-ME): "We have come to the conclusion of a confirmation process that has become so dysfunctional it looks more like a caricature of a gutter-level political campaign than a solemn occasion." Kavanaugh was ultimately confirmed, mostly along party lines.

Alexandria Ocasio-Cortez won the New York Democratic primary for a seat in Congress. Voter turnout was low, but the former bartender would win the fall election and become a media darling, while demonstrating that she knew little about anything, especially economics.

A Pittsburgh, Pennsylvania, grand jury released a report after a two-year investigation into six of the state's Catholic dioceses. It found 301 "predator priests" had raped little boys and girls. There could hardly be a better argument in favor of capital punishment, or at least castration.

George H. W. Bush, "41," died. I had known him since he was a congressman from Houston and I worked there at a TV station from the late 1960s until 1977. Bush was a letter writer like no other. I think I have an almost complete collection of his notes and letters, some typed, some handwritten, from every position he held in public life. These included as congressman, Republican National Committee chairman, chief liaison officer to the People's Republic of China, UN ambassador, CIA director, vice president, and president. When he became president, I wrote him a congratulatory note and he responded on White House stationery. I later told him I was keeping the letter "just in case you amount to something." He laughed. He was one of the kindest and most honorable political leaders I have ever known. We don't have enough of his kind. The major media, which trashed him during his presidency, did a 180 and praised him in death. For them the word "hypocrisy" was invented.

The Boy Scouts of America was the subject of several lawsuits charging scoutmasters with sexually abusing young boys. What did they expect when they began allowing admitted gay men to become scout masters? Should heterosexual men be allowed into the Girl Scouts? The organization eventually was forced to file for bankruptcy and parents interested in the original purpose of the Boy Scouts began enrolling them in scouting programs associated with their local church.

President Trump announced his intention to withdraw American troops from Syria and Afghanistan. Osama bin Laden was right when he said the United States would not have the staying power, as in Vietnam, while Muslims are patient and can wait one hundred years, if necessary, to achieve their goals.

In an end-of-year column in the *New York Times* titled "Why I'm Still a Never-Trumper," Brett Stephens listed the accomplishments of the Trump administration: tax cuts, deregulation, more military spending, cuts for the United Nations, defeat of the Islamic State in Syria, more troops to Afghanistan, arms for Ukraine, getting tough with North Korea, recognizing Jerusalem as Israel's capital, decertifying the terrible Iran deal, yes to Keystone, no to Paris Climate Accord, huge gains on Wall Street and higher consumer confidence, plus more conservative judges on federal benches, including Neil Gorsuch on the Supreme Court. Still, he said, he opposed Trump because of what he saw as his bad character. I'll take success on issues I care about over his character analysis. Those presidents with what Stephens would probably call good character never accomplished as much in so short a time as did Trump.

2019

The Year of the Trump Impeachment

President Trump and North Korea dictator Kim Jong-un meet in Hanoi for the second time.

WikiLeaks founder Julian Assange is arrested after seven years hiding out in Ecuador's embassy in London. And Swedish prosecutors reopen the rape allegation against Assange, attempting to seek extradition of Assange from the United Kingdom after he has served his fifty-week prison sentence for skipping bail. American prosecutors take note. You should be pursuing rape allegations made by Juanita Broaddrick and other women against Bill Clinton.

President Trump visits London and meets with Queen Elizabeth II and outgoing Prime Minister Teresa May. It is the first official state visit to the United Kingdom by a sitting American president since 2011.

Over 1 million people in Hong Kong protest against proposed legislation regarding extradition to the mainland. It is the largest protest in Hong Kong since the 1997 handover by Britain. The Hong Kong government subsequently announces it will indefinitely suspend the bill, but protests continue.

President Trump becomes the first sitting American president to cross the Korean Demilitarized Zone (DMZ) and enter North Korea. Trump and Kim also agree to restart stalled denuclearization negotiations. Symbolic? Maybe. Sometimes symbolism works, though probably not with North Korea.

The International Atomic Energy Agency confirms that Iran has breached the limit on its stockpile of enriched uranium. Why is anyone surprised? Don't people read what the Mullahs say about nukes being a gift from Allah to destroy Israel and America?

Boris Johnson becomes prime minister of the United Kingdom. Worst hair of any British prime minister, but apparently it works for him. He eventually marries his longtime mistress.

Speaker of the House Nancy Pelosi announces the start of a formal impeachment inquiry against President Trump. It's a hoax and witch hunt over phony Russian "collusion" as future developments will reveal.

President Trump announces that the leader of the ISIS in Iraq, Abu Bakr al-Baghdadi, has been killed in an American special forces operation. It is reported that al-Baghdadi detonated a suicide vest after being chased into a tunnel. First words after death? "Uh-oh" (I made that up).

The United States formally begins the process to pull out of the Paris Agreement. Applause, applause!

Speaking of political moves, Israeli Prime Minister Benjamin Netanyahu is indicted on charges of bribery, fraud, and breach of trust. When the Left fails to win an election, they go this route. Shameless!

First known human case of Coronavirus disease, or COVID-19, is detected in Wuhan, China.

House Democrats announce formal charges against President Trump, accusing him of abusing power and "obstructing Congress"; he becomes the fourth American president in history to face impeachment.

CAL'S TAKE

"One of the reasons people hate politics is that truth is rarely a politician's objective. Election and power are."

The major media went gaga over the number of women newly elected to Congress and those announcing their run for the White House in 2020, with more female candidates likely to follow suit. But the media's bias was again exposed when they focused on mostly liberal women with barely a mention, if they are mentioned at all, of women who are conservative.

The annual March for Life in Washington recalled an article I read in 2012 by bioethicists Alberto Giubilini and Francesca Minerva. It was printed in the *Washington Post*. The two claimed killing babies after they are born is not out of bounds. "After-birth abortion (don't you love the euphemisms?) . . . could be ethically permissible in all the circumstances where abortion would be. . . . We propose to call this practice 'after-birth abortion,' rather than 'infanticide,' to emphasize that the moral status of the individual killed is comparable with that of a fetus (on which 'abortions' in the traditional sense are performed) rather than to that of a child." Staggering, isn't it? But who can argue against it in a nation and world that became indifferent to God and sought to take His place?

Rep. Ilhan Omar's (D-MN) comment that the influence of the Israeli lobby in Washington pushed lawmakers to take a pledge of "allegiance to a foreign country" was bad enough. A watered-down House resolution condemning not Omar but "all-hatred" was as tepid as denouncing drunk driving. After heated debate within their caucus, Speaker Nancy Pelosi and the Democratic leadership released a separate statement: "Congresswoman Omar's use of anti-Semitic tropes and prejudicial accusations about Israel's supporters is deeply offensive. We condemn these remarks and we call upon Congresswoman Omar to immediately apologize for these hurtful comments." That didn't happen. Surprise!

In the category of Mad magazine's "scenes we'd like to see" came President Trump's threat to transport migrants to cities and states that have declared themselves sanctuaries. If only.

After more than two years of investigations, subpoenas, witness testimony and millions of dollars wasted, Special Counsel Robert Mueller's report concluded, "The investigation did not establish that members of the Trump campaign conspired or coordinated with the Russian government in its election interference activities." As for Democrats' charge that Trump was guilty of obstruction of justice, how does one obstruct something that is not a crime?

It was Oscar Levant who uttered the famous line: "I knew Doris Day before she was a virgin." In a way it was a backhanded compliment to a woman who represented in most of her film roles an image of chastity and virtue that was once promoted in American culture, though not always practiced in private lives, including hers.

Day, who passed away at ninety-seven, became a friend late in her life. It was for me a "Sentimental Journey."

Democratic presidential candidates, the media and economists such as Paul Krugman of the *New York Times* refused to give President Trump any credit. It was Krugman, a Nobel Prize winner, who predicted that Trump's election would trigger "a global recession." One waited in vain for an "I was wrong" statement from him.

Questions I would have asked during the Democratic presidential debates included:

1. Some of you have, or had, the power to change many of the things you now say are wrong with America. Why didn't you?
2. (for Joe Biden): You and Barack Obama, for a time, had a Democratic majority in Congress. Why didn't you reform immigration laws and address homelessness? Your administration deported a lot of people who were in the country illegally, so why criticize President Trump for wanting to follow your example? Do our laws mean nothing?
3. During the second debate, all of you raised your hands when asked if you would provide free health care to immigrants who are here illegally. Aren't you inviting even more to come to America with such a policy, and wouldn't that add to our already staggering debt? Follow-up: President Trump says we should take care of Americans first. Why

would you use American tax dollars to pay for people who break our laws?

4. Some of you think raising taxes again is a good idea, but with a $22 trillion debt and with record amounts of revenue already coming into Washington, isn't the real problem uncontrolled spending? Follow-up: Are there any government programs you would cut or eliminate?

5. Many of you have criticized this country. Can you say what you love about it?

Immigration should be completely cut off until we can assimilate those already here (and deport those who broke our laws to get here). That happened following the great immigration influx in the early part of the last century. Immigration was almost completely suspended until immigrants could be assimilated, learn English, and become fully American.

America's Founders warned against massive federal debt, but to our detriment, their political descendants have not been paying attention. The Founders spoke to us from the grave to condemn and warn of the consequences now that President Trump and Congress have come to an agreement about lifting the meaningless "debt ceiling" and increasing already massive federal spending and debt, which is at $22 trillion and growing. First to speak was Thomas Jefferson: "We must not let our rulers load us with perpetual debt."

Next was Alexander Hamilton: "Nothing can more affect national prosperity than a constant and systematic attention to extinguish the present debt and to avoid as much as possible the incurring of any new debt." I'm not sure if that line made it into *Hamilton*, the Broadway musical, but if it didn't, it should have to teach a new generation about fiscal responsibility.

Calling someone "racist" became the default position for liberal politicians and certain members of the media who wished to deflect attention from real problems.

President Trump was (again) called a racist for having the temerity to note that House Government Oversight Committee Chairman Elijah Cummings (D-MD) seemed to spend more time criticizing him and the border patrol than he did fixing problems in his home district, which included about half of Baltimore.

When the president noted that parts of Cummings's district was infested with rats, the racist smears began. Why was the president a racist for pointing out what even black leaders in Baltimore said about certain areas of the city?

Jeffrey Epstein was found dead in his New York jail cell. Conspiracy theories abounded. Was it an actual suicide? Why did the guards abandon their posts? His procurer, Ghislaine Maxwell, also went to jail, awaiting trial on charges she recruited underage girls for Epstein. Will Maxwell's book listing prominent men who visited Epstein's island (including Bill Clinton and Prince Andrew) ever be made public?

The *New York Times* announced creation of "The 1619 Project" for public schools. It taught that everything must be viewed through the prism of slavery, 1619 being the year the first slaves were brought to American shores. "The goal of the 1619 Project," said a statement from the newspaper "was to reframe American history." More like rewrite it. This is the stuff of totalitarian regimes where the media serve as a propaganda organ for the state, in this case the surging left wing of the Democratic Party.

They long ago lost their heads in San Francisco. The latest, but surely not the last demonstration of insanity, was San Francisco's Board of Supervisors's adoption of new "person first" language meant to "change the public perception of criminals." The words "convicted felon," "offender," "convict," "addict" and "juvenile delinquent" were out. These individuals would henceforth be referred to as a "justice-involved person." Someone previously called a "criminal" would be referred to as "a returning resident," or "a formerly incarcerated person." Since these changes were made, shoplifting has exploded with some stores forced to close and police not arresting any of the sticky-fingered.

"When would you like to schedule your knee replacement surgery?" asked my American doctor before I left for Ireland. I gave him a date that worked for me (I'm calling it the result of an old basketball injury, not advancing age). His office scheduled it for that date. Contrast this with a headline in the Irish Independent newspaper: "Surgery delays are 'cheating elderly out of precious time.'" While I'm not ready to claim "elderly status," the story was a preview of what could happen in the United States if enough of us buy into the notion that government knows best when it comes to our health and longevity.

Only extreme partisans intent on denying President Trump any credit for success would be critical of the operation he ordered that resulted in the death of Islamic State leader Abu Bakr al-Baghdadi. These extreme partisans included Speaker Nancy Pelosi, who, while praising

the "heroism" of the special unit that conducted the raid in
Northern Syria, could not bring herself to say anything nice
about the president. Instead, she said the House should
have been notified in advance. Why? Does the House command troops?

For conservatives and evangelical Christians, Chick-fil-A
had been a model company that consistently stood against
the "anything goes" spirit of the age. Its founder, the late S.
Truett Cathy, ordered that his restaurants be closed on Sun-
days to allow employees to attend church and spend time
with their families. When LGBT activists learned the company donated to charities that supported the definition of
marriage as between a man and a woman and declared a boycott of the restaurants, others demonstrated their support
by patronizing them. Businesses and individuals can defend
against such attacks if they refuse to bend the knee and stand
firm for their beliefs.

It was Senator Chuck Schumer (D-NY) who said in 1998,
while a member of the House Judiciary Committee, the same
committee that voted articles of impeachment against President Trump: "Impeachment was designed to be used rarely
and only in times of national crisis." Schumer at the time
warned of "profound consequences" for the country and for
the presidency if Clinton were to be impeached. Oops, never
mind. When the shoe is on the other foot, the sock don't
stink as much. Yes, I just made that up.

The departing editor of *Christianity Today* magazine,
Mark Galli, wrote an editorial in which he said President
Trump was an immoral man and his impeachment by the
House was cause for his immediate removal from office. I
wondered what that had to do with his policies. Sure, most

people would prefer someone who had good policies and was upright in character, but these were not the choices presented in the last two elections, and Trump's policies were more in line with evangelical principles than are Biden's policies.

2020

The Year of the Pandemic

The most significant of all is the start of the pandemic. COVID-19 killed millions worldwide. For many, it was a lost year, and 2020 would not be the end of it.

An American drone strike at Baghdad International Airport kills Iranian General Qasem Soleimani and Iraqi paramilitary leader Abu Mahdi al-Muhandis, both terrorist leaders. Hooray!

The impeachment (show?) trial of President Trump begins in the Senate. He is acquitted. A waste of time from the start and diversion from things that really matter.

Chinese authorities publicly confirm human-to-human transmission of SARS-CoV-2 while denying they are its source of the virus. Did we expect them to admit it? Commies lie.

The Chinese city of Wuhan, the epicenter of the initial COVID-19 outbreak, is quarantined with all scheduled public transport services and intercity flights halted.

A conditional peace agreement is signed between the United States and the Taliban. The United States begins gradually withdrawing combat troops from Afghanistan. Who believes the Taliban will live up to anything except their twisted religions/political ideology?

President Trump orders Operation Warp Speed to create a vaccine.

Global stock markets crash due to the pandemic.

President Trump announces the United States will suspend funding for the World Health Organization pending an investigation of its handling of the COVID-19 pandemic and its relationship with China.

NASA officially selects SpaceX, Blue Origin, and Dynetics to build its next-generation lunar lander to carry American astronauts (and possibly civilian billionaires) to the moon by 2024.

Kosovo and Serbia announce they will normalize economic relations with Israel and move their embassies to Jerusalem. Bahrain and Israel agree to normalize relations, making the fourth Israel-Arab peace deal.

Joe Biden "wins" the disputed presidential election. Trump claims fraud in a number of states but has no solid proof. Suspicions arise because of large number of mail-in ballots, which the Trump campaign alleges were tampered with to favor Biden.

The United States formally withdraws from the Paris Climate Accords.

The first successful phase III trial of a COVID-19 vaccine is announced by drug companies Pfizer and BioNTech. They are shown to be 90 percent effective according to interim results. The Moderna vaccine is proven to be 94.5 percent effective against COVID-19 based on interim results, including severe illnesses.

By the end of December, the number of confirmed cases of COVID-19 passes 80 million worldwide.

CAL'S TAKE

"No nation can survive without passing its heritage, language, and, yes, faith to the next generation. A country must be built on something substantial and if the cultural elitists think it can be built on 'diversity,' that is a foundation of shifting sand."

After commenting that impeachment is a serious issue, Pelosi signed the articles with numerous pens, smiling and snickering as she did so. She passed them to other House members as if she was the president signing bills into law.

The Irish and British know how to conduct elections. Their campaigns last a matter of weeks, not months—or even years—as ours do. As a result, people pay more attention and the costs of campaigning are greatly reduced. Why can't we be more like them?

Trump was acquitted by the Senate of having committed "high crimes and misdemeanors," but that won't stop Democrats from continuing to pile on. Why? Because his policies were succeeding and the last thing the Left wanted was for the public to realize what Democrats have been selling us is snake oil.

During President Trump's State of the Union address, Nancy Pelosi distinguished herself (assuming she was ever distinguished) by her facial expressions. After Trump was finished, Pelosi tore up her copy. It was a low moment in a body that has very low favorability ratings among the public.

An Australian TV network pieced together a series of gaffes by presidential candidate Joe Biden that made Porky

Pig sound articulate. I wondered if he was mentally fit to be president?

The pandemic revealed America's overreliance on China. Interviewed by NBC News, retired Brigadier General John Adams said: "Basically, we've outsourced our entire industry to China. That is a strategic vulnerability." Whatever happened to "Made in America," which was as much about quality as patriotism?

President Trump announced he had been taking the anti-malaria drug hydroxychloroquine for "about a week and a half now" to protect himself from COVID-19. The media had a fit, accusing him of selling the equivalent of snake oil. The president later came down with what his doctor called a mild case of COVID-19 and quarantined for a few days before being released from Bethesda Naval Hospital.

Joe Biden told a black talk show host: "If you have a problem figuring out whether you're for me or Trump, then you ain't black." It was not a one-off remark. Given the condescension so many Democrats have for black Americans, it is amazing why this demographic continues to vote for members of that party. As Trump said in a campaign speech referring to some black Americans: "You're living in poverty, your schools are no good, you have no jobs, 58 percent of your youth is unemployed—what the hell do you have to lose?" A more than slight exaggeration, but some good points, nonetheless. Liberal critics again threw out the "racist" charge, but what have Democrats done to help poor minorities emerge from poverty?

George Floyd died while in custody of a Minneapolis police officer. Peaceful protests, riots, and looting swept the nation.

The Minneapolis City Council voted to dismantle the city's police department. The vote came back to haunt them when crime increased, especially in minority neighborhoods. The council was forced to approve the hiring of more police officers after a referendum to replace the department was defeated by voters in 2021.

Sometimes it takes a person from another country to best analyze what was happening in America. One such person was Caroline Glick, who wrote from Jerusalem: "Americans are now expected to kneel for the Star-Spangled Banner and disavow American history while swallowing whole a false, malicious new history that claims America has been a force for evil at home and worldwide since it was nothing more than a sparkle in a racist colonialist's eye."

I suggested we change the designation of District of Columbia. Let "DC" stand for "Dysfunctional City." Far more descriptive.

Why are Republicans almost always said by the media and Democrats to be "divisive," but the reverse never applied? I will answer my own question. It is because the Left believed it should set the standard and if anyone disagreed, they are divisive. Now you know.

The top prosecutor in St. Louis charged Mark and Patricia McCloskey with "felony unlawful use of a weapon" for displaying guns during a racial injustice protest outside their mansion. The media identified the couple as "white and in their 60s." They were personal injury attorneys. Circuit Attorney Kim Gardner said their actions risked creating a violent situation during an otherwise "peaceful protest." Gardner had it backward.

The media called those participating in riots, fire bombings, and looting "protesters." I called them seditionists, who should be arrested, prosecuted, and forced to pay reparations to those businesses they have damaged or destroyed—many of them in minority neighborhoods.

The Acton Institute for the Study of Religion and Liberty may have been the only entity to probe the background of the organization Black Lives Matter (BLM). The major media wouldn't. According to Acton, the founding principles of BLM included guaranteed minimum income for all black people, free health care, free schooling, free food, free real estate, free gender reassignment surgery, free abortions (already disproportionately high among black women, but apparently unborn black lives don't matter to BLM). Washington, DC's local BLM chapter had called for "no new jails" (which would likely guarantee an increase in crime, much of it perpetrated in black communities across the nation). BLM also demanded reparations and wanted to create a "global liberation movement" that would "overturn American imperialism (and) capitalism." White virtue signalers, take note.

Biden promised to name not just a woman, but a black woman as his running mate. It was just the latest example of his party's tribalism in which externals, such as race and gender, are preferred over ideas and competence. In the end it will make no difference because the Democratic Party looks to have been taken over by hardcore leftists.

Mail-in ballots are a bad idea and an invitation for fraud. The postal "service" can't deliver regular mail on time. What makes anyone think they can deliver 100 million ballots efficiently and securely?

If you suffer from depression, the last thing you wanted to watch was the Democratic National Convention. If you did, you heard about an America with which you might not be familiar. Speaker after speaker portrayed our nation as failing, full of misery, poverty, and angst that only they can make better. If they could, would they not have by now?

The Republican National Convention, also held virtually, was the polar opposite. There, you saw a convention portraying America coming back from the pandemic economically and spiritually (the names of God and Jesus Christ were mentioned favorably more than once). Our best days were ahead of us, said speaker after speaker, unless Joe Biden—whom Trump had portrayed as a "Trojan Horse" for Bernie Sanders, Alexandria Ocasio-Cortez, and the rest of the far-left extremists—prevailed in the November election. He was right about that.

Justice Ruth Bader Ginsburg died. Democrats wanted to wait until after the election before a replacement was named, but Trump defied them, nominating Amy Coney Barrett. The attacks began!

The first presidential debate between Trump and Biden resembled a mud wrestling match, only dirtier. The interruptions, first by President Trump and then by Biden, were the antithesis of civility. In this, Biden displayed the worst behavior, calling the president a "liar," a "clown" and a "racist." At one point Biden said, "Will you shut up, man?" You stay classy, Joe.

In a rare moment when a reporter was able to ask Biden a substantive question, Bo Erickson of *CBS News* wanted to know the candidate's response to a *New York Post* story (which was ignored by all other media) that alleged a Hunter Biden laptop discovered at a repair shop in Delaware contained damning evidence of the Biden family profiting from Hunter's relationship with the Ukraine gas company

Burisma and sharing some of the money with his father, reportedly referred to in a Hunter Biden email as "the big guy." If the story was false, as Biden supporters claimed (it wasn't), why, according to the *Washington Times,* had the owner of the repair shop confirmed to a Senate committee that it was Hunter Biden himself who dropped off the laptop? Joe Biden didn't deny the story, but said to Erickson, "It's another smear campaign, right up your alley, those are the questions you always ask."

Just before the election I wrote: Were it not for the invasion of the COVID-19 virus, Donald Trump would likely have been on his way to a national sweep with probable gains in the Senate and House. It was the virus, along with his personality, that rubbed people the wrong way. These made the race close.

Biden was declared the winner by the thinnest of margins. Does he know it?

Trump may have lost the election, but the latest jobs report showed that despite the pandemic President Trump's policies of lower taxes and reducing regulations continued to work. His successor would reverse most of those policies, proving that leftist ideology doesn't work.

The United States attorney in Delaware started investigating Hunter Biden's tax affairs. It's a little late. Would the election outcome have been different if this and other information about the Biden connections had been covered by the media?

2021

The Year of Joe Biden

Some supporters of President Trump invade the United States Capitol to pressure Vice President Mike Pence into declaring the election results illegitimate. Five people die, including an unarmed Trump supporter who was shot and killed and another officer who later has a stroke.

Joseph R. Biden is inaugurated as the forty-sixth president of the United States.

The United States officially rejoins the Paris Climate Accord, 107 days after President Trump withdrew from it. It will make no difference because it is all symbolism, like wearing masks.

Russia warns NATO against sending any troops to aid Ukraine, amid reports of a large Russian military buildup on its borders. It appears that Putin is testing Biden, whom he perceives as weak. There will be more tests.

Benjamin Netanyahu, Israel's longest-serving prime minister, loses in a close race to Naftali Bennett.

A portion of the Champlain South Towers condominium building in Surfside, Florida, collapses, leaving ninety-eight people dead.

The Taliban captures Kabul and the Afghan government surrenders. At least 182 people are killed, including thirteen American service members, in a homicide bomb attack at Kabul airport.

President Biden orders the immediate withdrawal of all remaining troops, ending twenty years of operations in Afghanistan. Chaos follows as many Americans and translators who helped the United States are left behind. The Taliban go door to door looking for them to execute.

The number of recorded deaths from COVID-19 surpasses 5 million.

CAL'S TAKE

"Freedom is a lonely battle, but if the United States doesn't lead it—sometimes imperfectly, but mostly with honor—who will?"

The mob violence that occurred at the United States Capitol January 6 was deplorable and disgusting. It was the antithesis of a free society that wishes to remain free. Any supporter of President Trump and his policies must denounce this horror with even more vehemence than they denounced the riots of 2020, but the two are not equivalent. President Trump stoked these fires of resentment, and his weak comments after the breach of the Capitol were insufficient and lacked the power of sincerity. In this, President-elect Joe Biden sounded more presidential in his statement. He called it an "insurrection." FindLaw.com gave a definition of what happened at the Capitol: "Incitement to riot is when a person encourages others to commit a breach of the peace without necessarily acting themselves. This may involve statements, signs, or conduct intended to lead others to riot."

Twitter and Facebook permanently banned President Trump from their social platforms. Former National Security Advisor Michael Flynn and attorney Sidney Powell were also permanently banned as Twitter announced a purge of "accounts dedicated to sharing content related to the far-right QAnon conspiracy theory."

President Biden and his press secretary, Jen Psaki, assured us that he is a "devout Catholic" who "attends church regularly." The question was not new but should be asked again and a credible answer demanded. How can one be devout about one's faith and not comport with Scripture and the teachings of the Catholic Church?

I again endorsed home schooling. The pandemic gave especially parents of young children an opportunity to seize power they already possessed but have never fully exercised. With teachers' unions dictating when, or if, public schools would open again, parents were discovering the power of educating their children at home where they could teach the real history of the country (as opposed to the revisionist version now taught in too many schools), while adding a moral foundation that secular public schools no longer provide. According to admissionlys.com, "a go-to site for students for reliable and unbiased information and statistics about education," in the spring of 2019 (the last period for which figures are available), "grade K-12 students constituted 2.5 million children who opted for homeschooling. If we observe the trend in the last few years, there is an annual homeschooling growth rate by 2 percent to 8 percent."

The problem with free money is that it leads to an addiction much like drugs. In the case of the $1.9 trillion "relief" bill that had no Republican support, Congress was the supplier, while those on the receiving end became increasingly addicted to government and less self-reliant. The spending will only increase as more is added on.

If the second impeachment trial of Donald Trump had been a play, it would have closed after one performance. The plot was known, the outcome was certain, and the drama was contrived. Proof will come later in the year when the "Russian collusion" line promoted by Democrats and the media proves to have been a fiction.

Rush Limbaugh died, and the conservative world mourned. He didn't tell people what or how to think, as his detractors often charged, but he reflected what many conservative Americans already believed. He often used humor and satire to drive home his points, and he was so good at it that he attracted a huge audience. More than six hundred radio stations carried his three-hour program. He was loved by millions who had never met him. When I finally met him, I was surprised by his humility. He was an entertainer, as well as a commentator, and he understood that to hold the attention of an audience one must do both. In person he was not who you heard on the radio. As with former President Trump, Limbaugh spoke for people who felt disparaged by condescending elites.

Responding to critics of his record spending proposal, President Biden asked, "Where would you cut?" I accepted the challenge. Many who received money from the government during the last stimulus go-round banked the checks and spent little or none of it. Even the *Washington Post* noted that money targeted to state and local governments (virtually all run by Democrats) didn't need it. It referenced Moody's Analytics examination of state finances, which "shows that thirty-one states have enough money 'to fully absorb the economic stress of COVID-19' without substantial budget cuts or tax increases." As the *Wall Street Journal* noted, most of the House bill had less to do with the virus and more to do with paying lobbyists and other groups favorable to Democrats. Elections have consequences.

President Biden claimed efforts to reform voting laws making it easier to vote but harder to cheat "makes Jim Crow look like Jim Eagle." Huh? It looked like Biden skipped history class as Jim Crow laws were the work of southern Democrats, as was the Ku Klux Klan. Congressional Democrats also opposed federal voting rights and other civil rights legislation.

George Floyd was killed by a Minneapolis police officer. The incident was used to justify rioting and looting all over the country. At his trial, a jury convicted former Minneapolis police officer Derek Chauvin on all counts. While the conviction was correctly based on the evidence, the theatrics leading up to the trial and after the jurors had made their decision was outrageous. Demonstrations, riots, and looting around the country since the death of Floyd had to have influenced the jury, the media and public opinion.

MLB announced it was moving the All-Star game out of Atlanta because of the state's voter reform legislation. People who had read the legislation said it didn't say what critics alleged. Atlanta baseball fans would get their revenge when the Braves would win the World Series in October. Sports used to be an escape from political correctness. Not anymore.

A positive side benefit from the pandemic? It helped us focus on what the loss of liberties looked like. Such losses do not occur immediately, but erode over time as people become increasingly comfortable with government claiming to know what is best for us.

The CIA, looking to recruit new agents, created a series of recruitment videos that reflected the spirit of the age in which we live, rather than appealing to abilities and patriotism. The latest featured a Latina officer who identified as a "cisgender millennial." Even the word "cisgender" was so new that my spellcheck did not (yet) recognize it. The video was part of a new series called *Humans of CIA* designed to attract a more "diverse pool of candidates." From the script: "I am a woman of color. I am a mom. I am a cisgender millennial who has been diagnosed with generalized anxiety disorder. I am intersectional, but my existence is not a box-checking exercise."

Really? What else could it be? WebMD defines anxiety disorders as "a group of mental illnesses that cause constant and overwhelming anxiety and fear. The excessive anxiety can make you avoid work, school, family get-togethers, and other social situations that might trigger or worsen your symptoms." Forget the other stuff. Why would the CIA be fine with an agent suffering from such a malady?

Rep. Liz Cheney (R-WY) was ousted from her House leadership position because of her criticism of former president Donald Trump. The Republican establishment may hate Trump, but they would be hard-pressed to deny how effective his policies were pre-COVID-19. The 74 million who voted for him constituted a formidable number. Whatever some may think of his personality—and I deplore how he demeans others—no one can credibly deny he was more successful than any modern Republican president.

More than ninety days after being tasked to stem the record flow of migrants into the United States, Vice President Kamala Harris finally went to the southern border and falsely claimed, "We've made progress." She visited El Paso, Texas, while the real problem was in the Rio Grande Valley. Clearly, neither she nor her handlers wanted pictures of people wading, walking, and jumping fences to get into the United States with her there.

The *Wall Street Journal* reported that several states had stopped, or would soon cease, sending out unemployment checks. Leftists screamed people would starve. Instead, it resulted in many of the former recipients of other people's money going out to find jobs or return to work.

Conflicting statements from "experts" caused many to doubt what they were hearing about the pandemic. People, including two American presidents; Dr. Anthony Fauci, chief medical adviser to the president; Dr. Tedros Adhanom Ghebreyesus, the director general of the World Health Organization; and Dr. Rochelle Walensky, head of the Centers for Disease Control and Prevention, all made statements which, at the time, they claimed were accurate and based on science, but turned out to be inaccurate.

Dr. Ghebreyesus initially dismissed allegations the virus originated in a Wuhan, China, laboratory as "extremely unlikely." Later he said he was "premature" to rule out a lab leak.

Dr. Fauci at first called mask wearing ineffective. In an email to Sylvia Burwell, the secretary of health and human services in the Obama administration, Fauci wrote: "Masks are really for infected people to prevent them from spreading infection to people who are not infected rather than protecting uninfected people from acquiring infection." Fauci said the "typical mask" is "not really effective in keeping out the virus, which is small enough to pass through material." Later he said the opposite. No wonder many people were confused and didn't believe what they were hearing.

On a visit to Rapid City, South Dakota, I interviewed Governor Kristi Noem. She believes Republicans can—and should—retake the law-and-order issue in 2022 and 2024: "What we are seeing . . . on our streets (are) the consequences of . . . what's happening in the Democratic leadership and their lack of support for police officers and those who step up and serve. (It's) being played out in the violence citizens are having to live with. It's going to continue if something doesn't change."

She said the street violence and looting in major cities was not only the fault of judges and district attorneys, but "also overcrowding in our prison system. There's less funding for the judicial system so they release individuals instead of putting them through the process of prosecution and sentencing, or through rehab. It's a problem that hasn't been addressed for many, many years (and) has gotten worse as the violence has escalated. When there's no consequence for it, law and order goes away."

To some, climate change proponents are little more than modern-day soothsayers who the media continue to legitimize, even when their dire predictions of global catastrophe turn out to be not so dire. President Biden's climate envoy, John Kerry, whose scientific credentials are nonexistent, predicted we have only "one hundred days" to save the planet from climate disaster. One hundred days later, nothing happened.

Thirteen Americans were killed along with ninety Afghans in the chaos brought on by President Biden's precipitous withdrawal of American forces from Afghanistan.

With America's deepening debt and a Democrat president and Democrat Congress desiring to spend more, can it be denied that Americans are increasingly relying on government to take care of them, rather than the once-universal value of self-reliance with government as a last resort and not a first resource?

The lyricist Oscar Hammerstein II wrote many beautiful songs for Broadway musicals. One that was not beautiful but powerful for what it said about race relations in 1949 when the show *South Pacific* opened was "You've Got to Be Carefully Taught" to hate. You also must be taught to love. In modern America, it looks increasingly like hate is winning.

The southern border is wide open. Reaction was predictable. Some Democrat progressives shouted racism because the flood included Haitians. Signs rapidly appeared. Some said, "Stop deportation now!" Where did the signs come from? Who were the people carrying them? Was someone paying them? The media never asked.

I labeled the Democrat Party "death, debt, and debauched." I like alliteration.

During Medicare open enrollment, I noticed how many of those Medicare supplement ads contained the words "free," "benefits," and "deserve." A sign of our times.

Glenn Youngkin's impressive victory over Democrat retread Terry McAuliffe in the race for Virginia governor ought to be a reminder that kindness wins over name-calling and that issues are more important than personality. The significance of Virginia Lieutenant Governor-elect Winsome Sears's victory cannot be overstated. Her election was significant, not only because she is a black woman and the "first" of her race and gender to hold the office of lieutenant governor in Virginia, but also because she has been described as an anti-racist. Sears did not buy into a victimhood that characterizes the Democratic Party's view of people of color. In her election-night address she said: "I'm telling you that what you are looking at is the American dream. There are some who want to divide us, and we must not let that happen. They would like us to believe we are back in 1963." She then lowered the hammer about the progress made since then: "We can live where we want. We can eat where we want. We own the water fountains. We have had a black president elected, not once, but twice, and here I am living proof." She could have added that Virginia previously elected a black governor, Douglas Wilder, a Democrat.

2022

The Year of Ukraine

The year begins on a hopeful note. COVID-19 cases and deaths are in rapid decline, and people are getting back to living a life they hadn't known in two years, discarding masks inside and outside most establishments (except for public transportation).

The relief many feel—except for those who lost loved ones during the pandemic—is shattered when Russian President Vladimir Putin launches an unprovoked attack on Ukraine.

A Quinnipiac poll shocks many when it finds that only a minority of Americans would stand and fight should the country be invaded by a foreign power.

Newly installed New York City Mayor Eric Adams, who pledged to fight and reduce crime in the city, criticized reporters for what he says was negative coverage of him. Adams claims a lack of "diversity" in newsrooms with too few people who look like him (i.e., he is black) is one reason for the negative coverage.

The investigation into alleged Russian collusion in the 2016 election grinds on.

Ghislaine Maxwell is convicted on five of six charges regarding recruiting and grooming of teenage girls for sexual encounters with disgraced financier Jeffrey Epstein.

CAL'S TAKE

"Evil cannot be accommodated. It must be defeated."

Using bogus reasons for doing so, Putin invaded Ukraine, and more than three million refugees fled to neighboring countries. Untold thousands of civilians, including women and babies, were slaughtered. Ukraine President Volodymyr Zelenskyy delivered a speech to Congress that produced a rare moment—unity between the parties to help this brave man. The dispute was over how much to help to avoid an all-out war with Russia. Republicans accused President Biden of demonstrating weakness (and President Obama before him) in not challenging Putin over his genocide in Syria and his annexation of Crimea. Critics also claimed Putin was emboldened by Biden's chaotic withdrawal from Afghanistan.

I wrote a column called "Failure to Understand Evil: Then and Now." It was about the consequences for nations that think they can negotiate with devils who do not share the morality of other nations. I mentioned one definition of evil: "The force in nature that governs and gives rise to wickedness and sin." Except the force isn't in nature. It can be found in a much deeper realm than nature.

I wrote in response to President Biden's statement that because Russia has nuclear weapons the United States can't confront him. Is that America's new foreign policy? If it was, it would be good news to China, North Korea, India, Pakistan, and Iran, all of whom either have or are rushing to acquire nukes. If these countries think America will do little to stop them, they might believe they can get away with anything, like invading Taiwan (China) or attacking Israel (Iran).

On the issue of defending the homeland, more Democrats than Republicans said they would cut and run, but the responses didn't bode well for America's future security. I mused that this attitude in part was created by woke public schools and universities that have taught for some time that America was a racist and non-exceptional nation, and this was the rotten fruit of their propaganda.

On NYC Mayor Eric Adams's gripe that newsrooms were not diverse, I replied he was right about the lack of diversity, but the greater problem was a lack of ideological diversity in the media. A liberal is a liberal, no matter the color of one's skin or gender.

Adams's news conference followed the deaths of two New York City police officers, Jason Rivera and Wilbert Mora. Compounding the outrage was news that the gunman, identified as forty-seven-year-old Lashawn McNeil, was on probation after a drug conviction. His mother claimed he was mentally ill. Rivera's widow spoke at her husband's funeral and received thunderous applause when she said: "The system continues to fail us. We are not safe anymore, not even members of the service." She specifically singled out Manhattan District Attorney Alvin Bragg, whose lenient approach to criminal suspects had been denounced by police officers, police unions, and Republican politicians, but insufficient numbers of Democrats.

Senate Minority Leader Mitch McConnell (R-KY) took apart President Biden in a Senate floor speech. He said today's

Biden was far different from the man he knew when both were in the Senate. Following a speech by Biden in Atlanta, during which he accused Republicans of trying to suppress black voter turnout, McConnell said Biden had promised to unite the country, but instead "delivered a deliberately divisive speech that was designed to pull our country further apart."

McConnell quoted from a Biden speech in 2021 in which the president said, "'We should not see ourselves as adversaries, but as neighbors.' Now he calls millions of Americans his domestic enemies." McConnell went further, saying, "A year ago the president called for lowering the rhetorical temperature, but now says if you disagree with him, you're George Wallace. If you don't pass the laws he wants, you're Bull Connor. And if you oppose giving Democrats . . . one-party control of the country, well, you're Jefferson Davis."

I said McConnell might have mentioned that these, as well as many other, elected officials who opposed civil rights legislation were southern Democrats, and that it was mostly Republicans, beginning with Abraham Lincoln, who supported racial equality.

Special Counsel John Durham filed an opinion in federal court, alleging that the presidential campaign of Hillary Clinton paid a technology company to "infiltrate" or "spy"— the word Donald Trump used—on Trump's presidential campaign and as president. We await even bigger shoes to drop. As usual, the media either mostly ignored the story or gave credence to the denials by Clinton and Democrats.

Donald Trump went too far when he attacked his loyal vice president, Mike Pence, for not overturning the election results by de-certifying Electoral College votes from some states with what Trump claimed without proof were dodgy ballots. While some ballots were subsequently found to be fraudulent, their numbers were not near enough to change the results of the election. Trump smeared a man of great character, personal integrity, and faith, and I didn't like it.

After the Ghislaine Maxwell trial, I wrote that this should not be the end of the story and that all of the men who violated these girls, thus breaking the law, should be outed, and brought to justice.

My longtime friend and sometimes writing colleague, Bob Beckel, passed away at age seventy-three after a long battle with multiple health issues. For ten years, we wrote the Common Ground column for *USA Today* and a book by the same title. On the lecture circuit, I used to say that Bob was not on the "other side." He was my friend and fellow American. Our dads were in World War II. They weren't fighting for or against Franklin Roosevelt. They were fighting to defeat evil and preserve the American ideal. We had hoped that our friendship might serve as a model for others. Perhaps it did for some. It should have been for far more. His book, *I Should Be Dead: My Life Surviving Politics, TV, and Addiction*, is a powerful memoir. If you haven't read it, you should.

At the end of June, the Supreme Court handed down perhaps its most consequential decision in fifty years. By a 6–3 vote, it repealed *Roe v. Wade*, the 1973 case that ruled state regulation of abortion as unconstitutional and led to an increase in open abortion practices. With the ruling overturned, states were once again allowed to decide whether to allow, restrict, or ban abortions within their jurisdictions.

I wrote that although neither the 60 million babies killed over the last five decades nor the women who had been lied to about the procedure would receive justice, future babies who might not otherwise have lived would be born as a result of the SCOTUS decision.

It was more than ironic to me that the Left, which had used a liberal court to advance positions it could never have hoped to get through Congress, was now lamenting that the court had become illegitimate and either needed to be "packed" or eliminated. Demonstrations, some violent, ensued, but the persistence of pro-lifers prevailed.

While many well-known, lesser-known and unknown people contributed to the SCOTUS decision, one man deserves special mention. That man is Donald Trump, who despite his flaws, lived up to his promise to name originalists to federal benches, including the Supreme Court. Three of his selections were with the majority in this 6–3 ruling. Whatever ultimately happens to him, this decision will be part of his legacy.

As I write this in June 2022, it appears the November election will produce a "red wave" and knock Democrats from their majority positions in the House and the Senate. Traveling is back to nearly normal as face masks are no longer required on domestic and many international flights. Inflation continues to cause concern along with record-high gas and food prices and a declining stock market. A Gallup Poll found 50 percent of those surveyed believe the state of "moral values" in America is "poor." Thirty-seven percent say they are only "fair." The trend is not headed in the right direction as 78 percent think they are getting worse.

What will happen in the near and long-term future? It's anyone's guess.

READ MORE BY CAL THOMAS

I have to stop writing about 2022 now so this can get to the publisher. You can read what I wrote about events through the rest of the year and after that by visiting my website:

calthomas.com

Epilogue

"The measure of a great writer is not how many weeks his books spend on the best seller lists, but how many years his books remain in print after his death."

No one was more surprised than me when I was given the opportunity to write a newspaper column. My background had been in broadcast news, starting on a local radio station in suburban Washington, DC, when I was sixteen. I read newspapers but never thought I would write for one, much less have a column appearing in hundreds of them across the country. Most reporters I knew at NBC News in the 1960s, where I worked as a copy boy (a label carried over from newspapers), came from print. I went the other way.

How much longer I will write depends on at least two things: my health and the health of newspapers. Many have websites, which is good, but I have always preferred to hold one in my hand. Generational, I guess. Many young people no longer read them and that is a shame because reading exercises the mind, just as going to the gym, rather than watching an exercise video, strengthens the body.

In 1984, when the column started, I told God I would seek to honor him with the gift He has given me. I trust He is pleased.

As C. S. Lewis wrote, "Further up and further in," or as Dr. Ed Feulner of The Heritage Foundation likes to say, "Onward!"

Acknowledgments

Most writers who make a living at the profession owe a great deal to their editors. They generally are good fact-checkers and keep us from lawsuits and more-than-predictable ridicule. Over nearly forty years of writing my syndicated column, I could not have asked for two better editors than Connie Pollock and Tracy Clark. Connie was my editor for the sixteen years I was with the Los Angeles Times Syndicate, before it was sold to Tribune in Chicago. Tracy has been my editor ever since. Tracy's "side job" is writing highly readable crime novels.

Thanks to Abigail Ruth Sadler, the librarian at Liberty University, for organizing my columns by years and months. Without her help, I could not have compiled this historical and journalistic retrospective while continuing to write the column.

Thanks also to my longtime speaking—and more recently literary—agent and much appreciated friend, Wes Yoder.

Appreciation also goes to Humanix Books for enthusiastically accepting the idea of this book.

If there were a word greater than "thanks," I would use it to describe the joy my wife CJ has brought to my life.

Photography Credits

- **[WINX]** From Cal Thomas's personal photography collection

- **[Armed Forces Radio]** From Cal Thomas's personal photography collection
- **[Award for radio documentary]** Texas Heart Institute
- **[Cal taking a nap]** From Cal Thomas's personal photography collection

- **[Reporting on prison riot]** Channel 2 KPRC-TV Houston photographer Bob Brandon
- **[Channel 2 crew]** Channel 2 KPRC-TV Houston photographer
- **[Reporting live TV]** From Cal Thomas's personal photography collection
- **[Colleague Ray Miller and anchor Steve Smith]** From Cal Thomas's personal photography collection

- **[President Reagan]** The White House photographer
- **[Ted Kennedy and Cal]** From Cal Thomas's personal photography collection
- **[Elizabeth Dole and Cal]** From Cal Thomas's personal photography collection

- **[Cal in Israel]** From Cal Thomas's personal photography collection
- **[Then Vice President H. W. Bush]** The White House photographer
- **[President George W. Bush]** The White House photographer

- **[President Obama]** From Cal Thomas's personal photography collection
- **[Trump in Trump Tower]** From Cal Thomas's personal photography collection
- **[Pence, wife CJ, and Cal]** The White House photographer
- **[Trump at the White House]** From Cal Thomas's personal photography collection

- **[Press passes]** Emilce Gomez, egozphotography

- **[Barbara Cook]** From Cal Thomas's personal photography collection
- **[Actress Roma Downey]** From Cal Thomas's personal photography collection
- **[Rachel Maddow]** From Cal Thomas's personal photography collection

- **[Louis Zamperini]** From Cal Thomas's personal photography collection
- **[Paul Anka]** From Cal Thomas's personal photography collection
- **[CJ, Lesley, and Kathie Lee Gifford]** From Cal Thomas's personal photography collection

- **[Daughter Caray]** Lynchburg Christian Academy

About Cal Thomas

CAL THOMAS is a journalist, pundit, author, TV & radio commentator, and one of the most widely syndicated columnists in America. His over fifty-year journalism career includes anchoring and reporting for KPRC-TV in Houston, NBC News in Washington, Fox News Channel, and other outlets. For ten years, he co-wrote the "Common Ground" column for *USA Today* with his colleague Bob Beckel. He is the author of *America's Expiration Date, What Works, The Things That Matter Most, Common Ground, Uncommon Sense, Blinded by Might, The Death of Ethics in America, Book Burning, Liberals for Lunch, A Freedom Dream*, and *Public Persons and Private Lives.*

Thomas is a wide-ranging social commentator, not a "beltway insider," who supports traditional conservative values and the American "can-do spirit." For his life's work and values of faith, family and freedom, Thomas is the recipient of the prestigious William L. Armstrong Award, Colorado Christian University's highest award for leaders who have made a difference in America's culture.

A native of Washington, DC, and graduate of American University, Thomas is married to Christie Jean ("CJ"). The couple live in Coral Gables, Florida.

Visit calthomas.com.